SPIELBERG

SPIELBERG

The Man, the Movies, the Mythology

Frank Sanello

Taylor Publishing Company
Dallas, Texas

Published by Taylor Publishing Company
        1550 West Mockingbird Lane
        Dallas, Texas 75235

Library of Congress Cataloging-in-Publication Data

Sanello, Frank.
    Spielberg : the man, the movies, the mythology / Frank Sanello.
      p.   cm.
    Filmography: p. 000.
    Includes index.
    ISBN 0-87833-911-6
    1. Spielberg, Steven, 1947– . 2. Motion picture producers and directors—United States—Biography. I. Title.
PN1998.3.S65S26   1996
791.43'0233'092—dc20
[B]   95-39329
                                           CIP

Printed in the United States of America

10 9 8 7 6 5 4 3 2

This book has been printed on acid-free recycled paper.

CONTENTS

The Reluctant Jew

For a Jew, it's a shame Steven Spielberg is so white bread.
> —megafilm producer Don Simpson
> (*Crimson Tide*)

The conventional has always appealed to Steven.
> —Leah Adler, his mother

There are literally six million stories that could be told about the Holocaust. It speaks volumes about Steven Spielberg that he chose perhaps the only one with a happy ending.
> —an industry source

I F EVER AN ARTIST'S BODY OF WORK WAS A product of his upbringing and background, director Steven Spielberg's films are exactly that.

His mother Leah was an accomplished classical pianist. His father an inventor and electrical engineer who designed computers for RCA, GE, and IBM.

Spielberg and his work can be seen as a fusion of these two very different parents. His father's influence contributed the techno-wizardry which is the hallmark of most Spielberg films, all those sci-fi epics and scare-'em-to-death roller-coaster rides. His mother's artistic bent provided the aesthetic balance which enriched his low-tech, character-driven films like *Schindler's List* and *The Color Purple*.

Spielberg's religious upbringing—or lack thereof—influenced not only his formative years but the flavor and content of his films.

"I wasn't a religious kid, although I was Bar Mitzvahed in a real Orthodox synagogue," he once recalled. His earliest memory was of entering a Cincinnati synagogue for services with Hasidic elders. "The old men were handing me little crackers. My parents said later I must have been about six months old!"

His early works were indeed as Don Simpson said, "white bread." Spielberg's fascination with Waspy suburbia under siege in everything from *Close Encounters of the Third Kind* to *Poltergeist* reflected his own childhood, growing up Jewish in primarily Anglo-Saxon neighborhoods. He was at once the alien and the insider. The local boy who was somehow different by reason of his Jewishness.

In childhood, it's fair to say Steven Spielberg was a reluctant Jew. The theme of longing to belong permeated much of his work until only recently. It was only after fully accepting his Jewishness that Spielberg flowered as a mature artist, capable of producing his Oscar-winning masterpiece, *Schindler's List*.

CHAPTER ONE

Baby Mogul

STEVEN SPIELBERG WAS BORN DECEMBER 18, 1946, in Cincinnati. (For years he asserted that his birthdate was 1947. But in 1995, in response to a long-running legal battle, Spielberg acknowledged that 1946 was the correct year.) His father's work as an electrical engineer led to a change of jobs and home every few years. Young Steven remembered himself as always being the new kid on the block, the new boy at school, never fitting in. Whenever he finally did manage to insinuate himself into the local crowd, the family would up and move to a new city.

After Cincinnati, there was a brief stop in Haddonfield, New Jersey. Then the family settled for its longest period in Scottsdale, Arizona. Steven lived in this Ur-Wasp suburb from the ages of nine to sixteen.

His mother, Leah, an adventurous type, did not want to live in a Jewish neighborhood and always plopped the family down right into the middle of Gentile, U.S.A. Today, his mother regrets this rejection of her roots. "I was raised in an Orthodox home, but I chose to rear my children in non-Jewish neighborhoods. That was my one really big mistake. The kids next door used to stand outside yelling, 'The Spielbergs are dirty Jews.' So one night Steven snuck out of the house and peanut-buttered all their windows."

Spielberg found belonging to the only Jewish family on the block a lonely position, especially at Christmas, when theirs was the sole house in the neighborhood unlit by decorations. In vain, the dying-to-assimilate youth begged his father to at least put a red light in the window. "I was ashamed because I was living on a street where at Christmas we were the only house with nothing but a porch light on," he has said.

His parents refused, but not out of any great sense of Jewish identity or pride. In fact, he remembers that when the family moved from New Jersey to Scottsdale, they stopped keeping kosher for no particular reason.

Spielberg has described his family as "storefront kosher." That's the equivalent of cafeteria Catholics, those who pick and choose what dicta of the Pope to believe or discard, sort of like selecting the broccoli but rejecting the jicama at the salad bar.

The Spielbergs' storefront kosherism had the flavor of an ethnic sitcom. Leah Spielberg (*nee* Posner) loved shellfish, a food strictly verboten by Judaic dietary laws. One day when she and her son, who shared his mother's fondness for crustaceans, were about to pop two giant lobsters into a pot of boiling water, their rabbi pulled into the driveway for an unannounced visit.

You can almost hear the television laughtrack in the background as Leah instructed her son to hide the offending creatures under his bed.

"The rabbi came to my room to see how I was doing," Spielberg wrote in a first person memoir in *Time* magazine. "You could hear the lobsters clicking and clacking at each other with their tails. The rabbi just sort of stared and sniffed the air; he must have wondered what that *tref* (unkosher) scent was, lingering in the kid's bedroom. The minute the rabbi left, my mom and I gleefully threw the lobsters into a pot of boiling water and then ate them."

Years later, Leah, divorced and remarried to Bernie Adler, would atone for such sins by opening a popular kosher deli in west Los Angeles, called the Milky Way in honor of her son's galactic epic, *Close Encounters of the Third Kind*. But back then, she now concedes, her faith was less than integral to her life. "It was a very nothing part of our lives. All we did was light candles on the Sabbath," she recalls.

While these close encounters with strict Judaism had a sit-com whimsy to them, other incidents relating to the Spielbergs' faith ranged from scary to downright ugly.

Growing up, Steven never recalled his parents or relatives referring to the Holocaust or Nazis by name. He did remember hearing, however, terms like "those murdering bastards. My parents referred to the Holocaust as 'those murdering sons of bitches.'" In fact, distant cousins perished in Poland and the Ukraine, victims of the Final Solution.

His grandmother taught English to Holocaust survivors who had emigrated to America. His earliest encounter with the event that would lead to his greatest film involved a survivor of the death camps who studied English in his grandmother's home. The man taught the preschool Steven his numbers by displaying the concentration camp number tattooed on his forearm. Even then, the event involved a touch of magic, which the youngster would later depict on a big screen in 70 mm. The man delighted young Steven with a grisly magic trick. By bending his arm he could make the number six on his arm turn into a nine.

Other Holocaust memories were appropriately more bleak and anticipated the terror component of his masterpiece. A relative told a story of an accomplished classical pianist in Berlin. (Shades of mom.) During the Nazi era, this woman had the temerity to play a work by a forbidden Jewish composer in public. In the middle of her performance, Nazi thugs ran up on stage and broke all her fingers so she would never be able to play again.

"I grew up with stories of Nazis breaking the fingers of Jews," Spielberg has said.

Pop psychologists might say he later tried to domesticate those fears in two Indiana Jones films with cardboard Nazis who weren't nearly as scary as the real thing from his childhood. But ultimately, he would confront these childhood bogeymen in an authentic way in *Schindler's List*.

Another story which could have come from *Schindler's List*, but instead came from a Spielberg relative, dealt with a woman who was wearing a wedding ring which the Nazis demanded she surrender. The woman apparently had put on weight since her marriage, and the ring refused to budge. The Nazis were about to cut off her finger when nervousness caused the ring to miraculously slip off her hand.

These stories no doubt instilled awe and wonder, but they didn't instill a whole lot of pride. All children long to belong, and Steven, growing up in Wasp-ville, was no different. His desire to assimilate, however, was so shameful a memory that it wasn't until years later, when *Schindler's List* had forced him to confront his own ambivalence toward Judaism, that he finally told his mother an embarrassing incident from his youth.

Every night before he went to bed, he would fasten duct tape to his nose, pushing it toward his forehead in the forlorn hope of developing an upturned, Wasp-like snout.

Groaning, he recalled the incident in a magazine interview: "Oh, god, oh my god! It's true! I used to take a big piece of duct tape and put one end on the tip of my nose and the other end as high up on my forehead line as I could. I had this big nose. My face grew into it, but when I was a child, I was very self-conscious about my schnozz. I thought if you kept your nose taped up that it would stay. . . like Silly Putty!"

Years later, Don Simpson and film critics would complain that the director's fascination with Waspy suburbia in films like *E.T.* and *Poltergeist* were the cinematic equivalent of taping his nose to his forehead. In fact, one critic derisively described the director's infatuation with white-bread suburbia on film as a "triumph of assimilation."

Growing up presented big and small problems of assimilation and acceptance. Spielberg once recalled: "We were always leaving schools and relocating. My father assimilated into the gentile world of computers, and that's a very Wasp world. We didn't live in a big Jewish community. We'd move into gentile neighborhoods where there'd be no Jewish community center. There'd be a temple somewhere where we'd go on Friday nights and High Holy Days, but I was pretty much the only Jew I knew for many years outside my family."

He also recalled with classic Jewish guilt his formative years as a reluctant Jew. "It isn't something I enjoy admitting, but when I was seven, eight, nine years old, God forgive me, I was embarrassed because we were Orthodox Jews. I was embarrassed by the outward perception of my parents' Jewish practices. I was embarrassed because I wanted to be like everybody else. I didn't feel comfortable with who I was. I was never really *ashamed* to be Jewish, but I was uneasy at times. My grandfather always wore a long black coat, black hat and long white beard. I was embarrassed to invite my friends over to the house because he might be in a corner *davening* [praying], and I wouldn't know how to explain this to my Wasp friends."

This internalized anti-Semitism didn't become external, he said, until the family moved to Saratoga, California, near San Francisco, when he was sixteen. His father had gotten a job at a nearby Palo Alto computer company, and Steven was once again the new kid in school.

And the only Jewish one.

Here his aesthetic desire to look gentile from the tape duct days turned into a matter of survival, not just cosmetics. During his senior year at Arcadia High, students would cough the word "Jew" as he passed them in the hall. In study hall, other kids would throw pennies at him, hoping he would pick them up and "prove" how miserly Jews were.

"It was six months of personal horror. And to this day I haven't gotten over it, nor have I forgiven any of them," he told an interviewer years later. And he still doesn't suffer anti-Semites gladly. Recently, he purchased a car for a friend from a Santa Monica, California, dealer. The salesman boasted after the sale, "I just got a Jew to pay full price for a car!" Somehow this comment got back to Spielberg, and he cancelled the order. The horrified owner of the dealership apologized profusely, but Spielberg refused to reinstate the order.

The salesman's anti-Semitism obviously opened old wounds that have never and probably will never completely heal. But that slur was mild compared to some of the anti-Semitism he experienced in high school. "I was embarrassed, I was self-conscious, I was always aware that I stood out because of my Jewishness. In high school, I got smacked and kicked to the ground in P.E., in the locker room, in the showers. Two bloody noses. It was horrible. We couldn't stop it. So my mom picked me up in her car every day after school and took me home."

One nemesis left a legacy that still embitters him to this day, although at the time his knack for filmmaking helped him cope and even conquer.

A bully, the biggest boy in class, used to bloody his nose, stick his head in the water fountain, and grind his face into the dirt. Once, the young thug threw a cherry bomb between Steven's legs while he was sitting on the toilet at school. "I got up before it exploded," Spielberg recalled.

Adding insult to injury, his tormentor would shout anti-Semitic slurs at Spielberg. "He had a very limited vocabulary," Spielberg recalled dryly.

"Then I figured, if you can't beat him, try to get him to join you." Spielberg told the delinquent he was making a film about World War II and wanted to cast the bully (against type) as a John Wayne-type hero. "He did look a little like John Wayne. He sure was as big as Wayne," Spielberg recalled with perhaps the exaggerated memory of childhood. At first the bully continued to torment him, but eventually succumbed to the lure of movie stardom.

"I converted him to being my friend, even though I don't think I was ever his friend, because I never quite forgot the taunting and how intimidated I was around him. Even when he was in one of my movies, I was afraid of him. But I was able to bring him over to a place where I felt safer: in front of my camera. I discovered what a tool and a weapon a camera was, what an instrument of self-inspection and self-expression it is." And in the case of the bully-turned-buddy, one of self-preservation.

The film, entitled *Escape to Nowhere*, also introduced him to the world of special effects. It was the beginning of a love affair that continues to this day. He took his adolescent cast to the desert to shoot an "epic" battle between Nazis and British. To create a low-tech shell explosion, he dug two holes in the ground and put a wooden plank with flour between them. He covered the construction with a bush. When the soldiers ran over the board, the flour seesawed and made a perfect geyser in the air.

"Matter of fact," he said later, "it works better than gunpowder used in movies today."

The fifteen-minute film cost fifty dollars and won first prize at a teen film festival.

Steven's three younger sisters also were cast in his films, but he didn't treat them with the fearful respect he extended to the class bully. Instead he specialized in terrorizing his siblings, a feat he would accomplish on a much larger scale with a much larger audience—the whole world—years later.

"I would experiment with terror on my sisters. I killed them all several times," he has said. He loved casting his sisters in his epics "because I could trash them any way I felt like. I killed them over and over again, and it was all in the interest of telling a good story. After my third or fourth little 8 mm epic, I knew this was going to be a career, not just a hobby. I had learned that film was power."

"Steven was not a cuddly child," his mother has recalled. "He was scary. When he woke up from a nap, I shook. He was quite weird as a child and prone to terrorizing his three sisters." She mentions the time he decapitated his sister's favorite doll and served it to her on a bed of lettuce. Another time he bought a plastic skull at a novelty store and hooked it up to a flashlight. Before locking his sister in the closet, he switched on the flashlight, then enjoyed the screams that came pouring out from behind the closed door.

His sister Sue, a mother of two in suburban Washington, D.C., remembers adventures with her older brother baby-sitting that were pure torture. "When he was baby-sitting for us he'd resort to creative torture. One time he came into the bedroom with his face wrapped in toilet paper like a mummy. He peeled off the paper layer by layer and threw it at us. He was a delight, *but a terror*. And we kept coming back for more."

His sister also could be describing her brother's uncanny knack for getting young filmgoers to see his films multiple times, thus ensuring their blockbuster grosses (about the only way a film can make a half billion dollars).

His youngest sister Nancy, now a jewelry designer in New York City, remembers being one of the first actresses ever cast by the fledgling director. Even then, there were creative differences on the set.

When Steven was sixteen, he made a science fiction thriller called *Firelight*, whose theme would eerily foreshadow *Close*

Encounters of the Third Kind. "I played a kid in the backyard," Nancy remembers, "who was supposed to reach up toward the 'firelight' [UFO] in the sky. Steven had me look directly at the sun. 'Quit squinting,'" the pint-sized De Mille would shout. "'Don't blink!' And though I might have gone blind, I did what he said because after all, it was Steven directing."

It wasn't just family members he managed to wrap around his fingers in pursuit of filmmaking. Adults found themselves curiously corralled by his obsessive will. "People ask me if I knew Steven was a genius," his mother says. "I didn't know what Steven was. From twelve on, he was always writing little scripts and enlisting everyone to act in them. I supplied the cold cuts.

"Once he got a hospital to close off a wing for one of his location shots," Leah continues adding that the wing included the emergency rooms. "Another time he got the airport to close a runway. No one ever said no to him, and it's a good thing. Steven doesn't understand no."

A forerunner of bigger things to come, *Firelight* was his first film to turn a profit. He borrowed the $400 it cost to make the film from his father. Later, it premiered at a local movie theater and grossed $500. His first net was a whopping $100.

When they weren't collaborating on films, he still enjoyed tormenting his siblings. "We were sitting with our dolls," Nancy says, "and Steven was singing as if he was on the radio. Then he interrupted himself to bring us an important message. He announced a tornado was coming, then flipped us over his head to 'safety.'

"If we looked at him he once said, we'd turn to stone."

Spielberg doesn't deny his wild child days and has offered up his own anecdotes almost proudly: "I loved terrifying my sisters to the point of cardiac arrest. I remember a movie on TV with a Martian who kept a severed head in a fishbowl. It scared them so much they couldn't watch it. So I locked them in a closet with a fish bowl. I can still hear the terror breaking in their voices."

His mother recounts other deeds committed by her demon seed: "He used to stand outside his sisters' windows at night, howling, 'I am the moon. I am the moon!' I think those poor girls are still scared of the moon."

While he could instill terror, Spielberg wasn't immune from the sensation himself. His childhood, as he tells it, was full of fears of things that go bump in the night. At six, the death of Bambi's mother and just about everything in *Fantasia* scared the hell out of him. But he remembers enjoying the sensation. "There were scenes of utter violence and sheer terror in *Bambi* and *Snow White*. They terrorized me as a child and I'll never forget them," he has said.

These childhood phobias later would be re-created in his films, especially *Poltergeist*, the ultimate child horror film, which he wrote and produced. A clown doll, which Spielberg called his "biggest fear," figured prominently in one of *Poltergeist*'s scariest sequences. "Also the tree I could see outside my room." (Another *Poltergeist* element.) "Also anything that might be under the bed or in the closet. Also 'Dragnet' on TV. Also a crack in the bedroom wall—I thought ghosts might come from it." (They did, again in *Poltergeist*.)

Many of his childhood fears remain with him to this day. Like so many artists, he seems to hold on to the awe and fascination—and fear—that make childhood such a magical and scary time. To this day, he refuses to go into an elevator alone because he fears it will get stuck between floors and his whitened bones will be found two weeks later. Whenever possible, he skips elevators altogether. Amblin, his production office on the backlot at Universal, was built specifically with only two stories so he'd never have to set foot in an elevator at work. In fact, he has been known to hold business meetings in the lobby of a building to avoid using the lift.

He's a hypochondriac, beset by fears both rational and irrational. He has nightmares that his house is being engulfed by waves and dreams about piling sandbags around the foundation, yet he lives on the beach. He refuses to go in the water because "there are sharks out there," although the closest sharks have ever come to southern California is twenty miles off shore. "And they were baby sharks," Captain Bob Buchanan of the Los Angeles County Fire Department/Lifeguard Division says, dramatically easing any fears the phobic director may have about taking a dip in the Pacific Ocean. Unless, of course, Spielberg is a champion marathoner who likes to swim to Catalina as a lark.

He's also afraid of furniture with feet. "I wait for them to walk out of the room," he has said, only half joking. Other phobias includes snakes and insects, both prominently featured in several of his films. "I think we survive on our fears," he has said.

His mother remembers, "Steven always had a highly developed imagination. He was afraid of *everything*. When he was little, he would insist that I lift the top of the baby grand piano so he could see the strings while I played. Then he would fall on the floor, screaming in fear."

But as she also remembers, it was more common for her son to be the terrorist rather than the terrorized. She tells anecdotes that sound like fodder for an episode of the *Addams Family*, not a nice assimilated Jewish family in Scottsdale, Arizona. "He terrified everybody," she says. "Baby-sitters would come into the house. They'd say, 'We'll take care of the girls if you take *him* with you.'"

His sister Anne remembers, "Every Saturday morning my parents would escape from the four of us kids. The minute they were out of the house I would run to my room and blockade the door. Steven would push it all away and then punch me out. My arms would be all black and blue. Sue and Nancy would get it next, if they had done some misdeed. Then when he was through doling out punishment, we would all get down to making his movies."

His sister Anne, who later would earn an Oscar nomination for her screenplay for *Big*, remembers her brother's earliest days as the director from hell: "He'd always have us in crazy costumes doing outrageous things. At the preview of *Jaws*, I remember thinking, 'For years he just scared *us*. Now he gets to scare the masses.'"

Spielberg has never disagreed with his mother's assessment of his formative years. Like her, he seems to feel a certain warped pride. "I often think depravity is the inspiration for my entire career," he said recently. "My parents were rigid about not letting me see horror films, so I staged my own, faking the chopping off of arms and legs and using buckets of fake blood."

Leah Adler had grown up in a poor family in Cincinnati. But despite the lack of material wealth, her childhood was like a fairy tale. Her father adored her. Her mother adored her. "She'd look at me and just grin," Adler said of her mother. Adler in turn raised her four children that way, adoring and encouraging every one of them.

Mom Spielberg had to be the ultimate permissive parent, but she was also a good child psychologist. She would break up fights among the children by having each side tell his or her story. Then she'd say, "Go back to arguing." The kids were so shocked by her reaction they'd stop fighting.

She was also a stage mother, film division. Basically, the word "no" was the only thing forbidden in the Spielberg household, at least as far as his mother was concerned.

"His room was such a mess, you could grow mushrooms," she says with a mixture of pride and horror. "Once his lizard got out of its cage, and we found it—living—three years later! He had a parakeet he refused to keep in a cage at all. There would be birds flying around and birdseed all over the floor. It was disgusting. Once a week, I would stick my head in his room, grab his dirty laundry and slam the door. If I had known better, I would have taken him to a psychiatrist, and there never would have been an *E.T.* His badness was so original that there weren't even books to tell you what to do.

"My mother used to say, 'The world is gonna hear of this boy.' I think she said that so I wouldn't kill him."

Actually, Mrs. Spielberg encouraged her son in his film endeavors.

"I was a very delinquent parent," she says without any discernible guilt. "I became a member of my kids' gang. If they wanted to stay home from school, they did. I'd say, 'Let's go out in the desert, guys,' and then I'd write lying notes to their teachers about gastrointestinal diseases."

Once, when he needed to shoot a scene that called for gore, he persuaded Mom to boil thirty cans of cherries in a pressure cooker until they exploded and covered the kitchen cabinets with ersatz blood. She remembers that for years after, "Every morning, I'd come downstairs, and while I made coffee I'd clean the cherries off the cabinets."

On another occasion, when he was shooting a mini war epic on 8 mm, he persuaded his mother to participate. "She'd drop everything, climb into the Jeep, race out behind Camelback

Mountain and helter-skelter barrel through the shot, hitting the potholes, her blond hair sticking out from under the pith helmet," he told *Time* magazine. Even back then, Spielberg was learning how to stretch a movie budget, making less look like more. With his mother impersonating a male GI, he recalled, "I would have my 'production value.' My $7 film suddenly looked like a $24 film."

Although he may have gotten all his artistic inheritance from his piano-playing mother, Spielberg got his first break as a moviemaker from his father. When the youngster was twelve, his mother gave his father an 8 mm Kodak camera to memorialize their camping trips.

Spielberg describes his father's home movies and how the young would-be director soon was hogging his dad's Father's Day gift. "The events of the trips were pretty El Snoro, so I tended to sort of tweak reality and try to get a little more drama into, say, catching trout.

"He'd take the camera out on family camping trips, and then we'd have to endure his photography. So one day I said, 'Dad, can I be the family photographer?' And he gave me the camera. My dad had to wait for me to say 'Action!' before he could put the knife into the fish to clean it.

"That was my first PG-13 moment."

Soon, the avid filmmaker had graduated to more spectacular subjects than fish gutting. "My first real movie was of my Lionel trains crashing into each other. I used to love to stage little wrecks. I'd put my eye right to the tracks and watch the trains crashing," he recalled.

Spielberg became obsessed with his new hobby. He would spend hours alone in his room writing scripts and storyboarding shots on paper, a practice he continues to this day during preproduction on a film.

"Movies took the place of crayons and charcoal, and I was able to represent my life at twenty-four frames a second," he later said, describing the beginning of a lifelong love affair with celluloid.

Although his father launched him on his film career, the two were never close. At least that's how the younger Spielberg remembers the relationship. Once, an interviewer asked him point-blank if he ever felt affection from his father. Spielberg said, "No, and I think that was a mistake on his part. I don't want to repeat that error. I know that I always felt my father put his work before me. I always thought he loved me less than his work, and I suffered as a result.

"I remember being bored to tears when my father had businessmen over to the house and they would always talk computers. My own technical proficiency is knowing how to use the Yellow Pages when something breaks." Years later, he would finally come to appreciate his father's high-tech world when he was forced to comprehend the arcana of computerization that made the dinosaurs in *Jurassic Park* come to life. The Yellow Pages apparently didn't have a listing for computer-operated tyrannosaurs.

His father's recollections, perhaps in self-excusatory hindsight, suggest he was more hands-on than his son has asserted. "It was creative and chaotic at our house," Arnold Spielberg said in 1985. "I'd help Steven construct sets for his 8 mm movies, with toy trucks and papier mache mountains. At night, I'd tell the kids cliffhanger tales about characters like Joanie Frothy Flakes and Lenny Ludehead. I see pieces of me in Steven. I see the storyteller."

And it is indisputable that his father gave him his first movie prop, a Lionel train set which his son happily crashed on film over and over again. "I would stage these very complex accidents on the rails," Spielberg said, "and somehow, intuitively, I would film these perfect crashes. When I got the film back, I would be amazed at how my little trains looked like multi-ton locomotives."

He was also a natural cinematographer who managed to make the toys look like gigantic locomotives by unconsciously realizing that by shooting the trains from a low angle, they would appear life-sized on screen.

Arnold Spielberg had mixed feelings about his son's burgeoning interest in filmmaking, even though he was the originator and willing participant in his son's budding career. Arnold came from a poor family, and he pushed a practical, scientific career on his son in reaction to his own childhood poverty. During an amazingly successful career, Arnold worked for IBM,

RCA, and GE. He holds a whopping twelve patents in his name. Today, retired, he makes industrial sales films, which he shows to his son for input.

Dad was pure left-brained, analytical, scientific. Young Steven was his mother's son, creative, free-spirited and undisciplined about everything but making movies.

Still, Steven undeniably got half his chromosomes from his father. "Steven's love and mastery of technology definitely comes for our father," his sister Sue says.

There's a telling incident from Spielberg's youth which sounds like myth but actually happened, or so the director insists. The scene also encapsulates the subtle tension between father and son.

One day, the elder Spielberg came home and showed his son a small object in his hand. "This is a transistor. This is the future." Steven immediately put the tiny gizmo in his mouth and swallowed it. "My parents called the police to get it out," he said.

Years later, Spielberg would claim with some guilt that he was dismissing or denying his father's world by so quickly disposing of the man's prize. Film historians and psychologists might posit another theory: Spielberg at an early age had intuitively grasped that technology later would dominate his filmmaking and swallowed it whole, embracing it as he later would embrace optical effects or interactive video. If Steven had been born ten years later, he might have swallowed a silicon chip instead.

There was no real enmity between father and son, however—just a totally different mindset. Without bitterness, the director later would describe his father's yin and his own ill-fitting yang: "My dad was of that World War II ethic. He brought home the bacon, and my mom cooked it, and we ate it. I went to my dad with things, but he was always analytical. I was more passionate in my approach to any question, and so we always clashed. I was yearning for drama."

There was happily no tension between his artistic mother and her talented son. Sister Sue recalls, "Mom was artistic and whimsical. She led the way for Steven to be as creative as he wanted to be. We were Bohemians growing up in suburbia."

In fact, her permissiveness practically bordered on negligence when she allowed him to stay home from school at least once a week so he could edit the footage he had shot over the weekend. Spielberg recalled, "I would fake being sick. I'd put the thermometer up to the light bulb," just as young Elliot does in *E.T.* so he can stay home and play with his extraterrestrial pal. But unlike the mother in *E.T.*, Mrs. Spielberg knew her son was faking it and let him stay home anyway. "I'd call her in and moan and groan. She'd play along and say, 'My god, you're burning up. You're staying home today.'"

Today, his mother defends her outlandish permissiveness. "I was never a typical parent," she says with understatement. "I think if a kid wants something, he ought to have it." Once Steven wanted a job to finance a "big budget" opus, so she suggested he paint the bathroom. "He did the toilet and the mirror, then he quit," she recalls.

It wasn't only a love of filmmaking that turned him into a frequent truant. Steven hated school. "From age twelve or thirteen I knew I wanted to be a movie director, and I didn't think that science or math or foreign languages were going to help me turn out the little 8 mm sagas I was making to avoid homework."

To instill a love of literature in his son, his father gave him a copy of *The Scarlet Letter*. Steven hated to read so he drew stick figures of a bowler knocking down pins on the edge of each page. When he flicked the pages, the pins went tumbling down. Today, he calls *The Scarlet Letter* his "first film adapted from another medium."

He also has praised his father for forcing him to study "just enough math" so he wouldn't actually flunk a grade. He did flunk gym class three years in a row. "I couldn't do a chin-up or a fraction. I can do a chin-up now, but I still can't do a fraction." In fact, the king of computer-guided special effects has confessed that he still counts on his fingers. "When my dad sees me counting on my fingers, he looks away."

His father used to wake him up early and tutor him in math every morning. These tutorials would have been comical if they hadn't been so frustrating for his well-meaning father. "I hated math. I didn't like when they'd stack the numbers on top of one another. My father used to say things like, '3 into 4 won't go,' and I'd say, 'Of course it won't! You can't put that 3 into the little hole on top of the 4. It won't fit.'"

To this day, Spielberg remains a techno-peasant when it comes to anything more sophisticated than a touch-tone phone.

Based on his lifelong dislike of reading, it seems possible that Spielberg's academic difficulties may have been caused by a learning disorder, perhaps dyslexia. "I was not a reader, and I'm still not a reader. I just don't like reading. I'm a very slow reader. And because I'm so slow, it makes me feel guilty that it might take me three hours to read a 110-page screenplay that I even wrote the story for. So I don't read a lot. I have not read for pleasure in many years. And that's sort of a shame. I think I am really part of the Eisenhower generation of TV."

For all his mother's permissiveness, both she and her husband tried to thwart television's pernicious influence on their children. The television set in the Spielberg household usually had a blanket over it.

In school, Steven was nicknamed "the retard," and once lost a race to a boy in the class who actually was retarded.

As painful as the incident was, the details reveal a young man with a precociously big heart and a capacity for empathy unusual in a preadolescent.

"The height of my wimpery came when we had to run a mile for a grade in elementary school," he has said. "The whole class of fifty finished, except for two people left on the track—me and a mentally retarded boy. Of course *he* ran awkwardly, but I was just never able to run. I was maybe 40 yards ahead of him, and I was only 100 yards away from the finish line. The whole class turned and began rooting for the young retarded boy—cheering him, saying, 'C'mon, c'mon, beat Spielberg! Run, run!'

"It was like he came to life for the first time, and he began to pour it on but still not fast enough to beat me. And I remember thinking, 'OK, now how am I gonna fall and make it look like I really fell?' And I remember actually stepping on my toe and going face hard into the red clay of the track and actually scraping my nose. Everybody cheered when I fell, and then they began to really scream for this guy: 'C'mon, John, c'mon, run, run!' I got up just as John came up behind me, and I began running as if to beat him but not really to win, running to let *him* win. We were nose to nose, and suddenly I laid back a step, then a half-step. Suddenly he was ahead, then he was a chest ahead, then a length, and then he crossed the finish line ahead of me. Everybody grabbed this guy, and they threw him up on their shoulders and carried him into the locker room, and into the showers, and I stood there on the track field and cried my eyes out for five minutes.

"I'd never felt better and I'd never felt worse in my life."

Spielberg's athletic humiliations were not confined to track and field. He was always the last boy to be chosen for the basketball or baseball team. In high school, sickened by having to dissect a frog in biology class, he ran outside to vomit along with other weak-stomached students. "The others were all girls," he wryly recalled.

A photo published by *People* magazine taken circa 1954 shows Spielberg wasn't exaggerating his ungainly appearance. He is shirtless and as emaciated as an extra in *Schindler's List*. He hasn't yet grown into his nose, which is Cyrano-sized. He's wearing only underpants.

"I was skinny and unpopular. I was the weird, skinny kid with acne. I hate to use the word wimp, but I wasn't in the inner loop. I never felt comfortable with myself, because I was never part of the majority. I always felt awkward and shy and on the outside of the momentum of my friends' lives. I was never on the inside of that. I was always on the outside. I felt like an alien [shades of E.T.!]. I always felt like I never belonged to anything. I never belonged to any group that I wanted to belong to.

"Unlike Woody Allen, you know, I *wanted* to become a member of the country club," he said.

At least he wasn't the only one outside the loop. "I had plenty of friends who were just like me in Scottsdale. Skinny wrists and glasses. We were all just trying to make it through the year without getting our faces pushed into the drinking fountain."

High school wasn't a total wash, socially. He found friends in the theater arts programs, which he called "My leper colony.

That's when I realized there were options besides being a jock or a wimp."

Like most childhood memories, Spielberg's were more dramatic than the reality. His sister Anne insists he wasn't quite the pariah he claims to have been. In fact, in a nerdy way, he was attractive to girls.

"A lot of the girls had crushes on him," she recalls. "He really had an incredible personality," says the sister who used to get brushes from her brother's ribbing. "He could make people do things. He made everything he was going to do sound like you wished you were a part of it."

The Boy Scouts finally allowed him to blossom socially, but even in that arena, he now admits, "I was pretty inept."

"Inept" is like saying the shark in *Jaws* has a terrific overbite. While demonstrating ax sharpening in front of 500 scouts one summer, "on the second stroke, I put the blade through my knuckle." Thirty years later he showed the scar to an interviewer to prove it.

His adventures in scouting, like his forays into nonkosher lobstering, sound like the stuff of sitcoms. Once, after building a camp fire, he was so tired he forgot to open a can before putting it into a pot of boiling water. The can exploded, sending shrapnel in all directions. "No one was hurt," he says, "but everyone within 20 yards of the fire needed new uniforms."

To get the canoeing merit badge, he had to capsize a canoe, swim under it, then flip it over his head. Everything went well until it came time for the flip. "It came down on my head. I had to be pulled out of the water."

Somehow he managed to earn the swimming merit badge, even though it required him to swim a mile. "I really couldn't swim a mile, but it was a case of mind over muscle once I determined I was going to do it. I remember pulling myself out of the water after that in a complete sort of wet haze."

He shone brilliantly, however, when it came time to earn the photography badge. The rules required still photographs, but Spielberg convinced the Scout master to allow him to shoot an 8 mm film instead. "If he hadn't," he says now, "I would have ended up becoming the finest still photographer in Scottsdale, Arizona."

The Scout film was a three-minute epic, archly titled, *Gunsmore*, after the popular Western television series of the day, *Gunsmoke*. The extravaganza cost $8.50, which he earned by painting trees with insecticide. The film included a stagecoach holdup, a macho sheriff, and a bad guy who went over a cliff. After the holdup, the bad guy is seen counting his money, a nifty metaphor for the director's sharklike negotiating abilities as an adult. For the special effect of the bad guying going over the cliff, Spielberg stuffed some clothes and shoes with pillows and newspapers, then threw them down a hill.

"The Boy Scouts put me in the center of the loop. It sort of brought out things I did well and forgave me for things I didn't," he said.

Besides scouting, Spielberg also succeeded in fitting in school by joining the school band and the orchestras in the fourth grade. He played the clarinet. "I've marched in more rodeo parades and stepped in more horse pies than anybody I know," he recalled, laughing. "But I chose film instead."

Steven was showing himself to be not just a precocious filmmaker but a savvy exhibitor as well. From the age of twelve on, he rented 8 mm movies which he screened for all the kids in the neighborhood. His three sisters would distribute flyers he had painstakingly printed. On hot Saturday mornings all summer long, the Spielbergs' living room resonated with the screams of more than thirty youngsters. Admission was thirty-five cents, and popcorn cost ten cents a bag.

By now having given up on his son ever becoming an electrical engineer, dad would gamely set up the screen and the Bell and Howell projector for his son's home movie premieres. The movie fare included *Davy Crockett*, which he rented from an 8 mm movie catalog.   "I began wanting to make people happy from the beginning of my life. As a kid, I had puppet shows. I wanted people to like my puppet shows when I was eight years old," he said.

"We all worked for Steve," his mother says. "From the minute he was born I was his employee."

When he was sixteen, the family business collapsed when his parents divorced.

For years before his parents split, he remembers the house being filled with tension between mom and dad, but the tension never erupted into full-scale fights. It was there, palpable, just underneath the surface, like the shark you sense coming in *Jaws* whenever John Williams's *thump-thump-thump* score begins to resonate on the soundtrack.

In a first person account in *Time* magazine, Spielberg remembered how traumatic his parents' split was for him and his three sisters:

"I was about 16. . . when our parents separated. They hung in there to protect us until we were old enough. But I don't think they were aware of how acutely *we* were aware of their unhappiness—not violence, just a pervading unhappiness you could cut with a fork or a spoon at dinner every night.

"For years, I thought the word 'divorce' was the ugliest in the English language." In the *Time* magazine account, Spielberg remembered the word "divorce" and many other painful sounds traveling from his parents' bedroom to his own via the heating ducts. He and his sisters would be kept up all night by the sound of his parents' heated quarrels. The director vividly recalls having a virtual panic attack whenever he heard his parents say the *d* word. While his sisters wept, he held on to them, the big brother comforting female siblings. It took his parents six years of bitter fighting before they finally called it quits. He later admitted that he wished they had split sooner, to save the kids years of anguished eavesdropping at the heating ducts.

Still, he made it clear in his *Time* memoir that the divorce didn't embitter him toward either parent. He concluded the painful recollection saying, "I have two wonderful parents; they raised me really well."

This theme of separation from parents or loved ones would echo again and again in his adult films, whether it was the tot who was sucked out of the doggie door by extraterrestrials in *Close Encounters* or the British schoolboy literally yanked from his parents' arms amid a rampaging mob in *Empire of the Sun*.

After graduating from Arcadia High in Scottsdale, the budding film director applied to UCLA, which has the best film school in the country. The state-supported school was a bargain, charging tuition that was only a fraction of private schools like USC, to which Spielberg didn't even bother to apply because of the prohibitive cost.

Unfortunately, UCLA only accepts students who have graduated from the top 10 percent of their high school classes, and Spielberg, a C-student, didn't even come close.

He ended up at the less prestigious Cal State University at Long Beach, where he majored in English literature. This from a man who still hates to read!

Steve Hubbert, a teaching assistant at Cal State Long Beach, explains why the future filmmaker majored in English. "Back in those days, we didn't have a film program per se. We did have one basic film production course. I think it was a basic video production course. Steven was not too happy with Long Beach. He made films on his own." Hubbert adds that the university didn't institute its film program until the early eighties, by which time the director had already established himself as the most successful filmmaker in history.

In film school, his taste was an avant-garde style of filmmaking he would never return to professionally. His 8 mm opuses sound more like something from the youth-gains-wisdom genre of a Godard or Antonioni, not the auteur of *Indiana Jones and the Temple of Doom*. These film school efforts seem to combine existentialism and surrealism—conjured up by a teenager!

"I once made a film about a man being chased by someone trying to kill him. But running becomes such a spiritual pleasure for him that he forgets who is after him. I did another picture about dreams—how disjointed they are. I made one about what happens to rain when it hits dirt. They were personal little films that represented who I was.

"And then I made a slick, very professional looking film [*Amblin'*], although it had as much soul and content as a piece of driftwood," he said.

This slick film begins with a career-making connection. A fellow student and lab technician named Dennis Hoffman wanted to become a producer and put up the money so in 1969 Spielberg could make a student film called *Amblin'*.

"I crashed into somebody who wanted to be a producer. I

wanted to be a director. Dennis Hoffman gave me $15,000 to make the picture and we made it in ten days. That's what I consider my big break. It was all based on five pages that Dennis believed in," he recalled later.

The twenty-two-minute film had no dialogue. It told the story of a boy and his girlfriend hitchhiking to the Pacific Ocean from the Mojave desert. The film won awards at the Venice and Atlanta film festivals. These prestigious accolades didn't impress Spielberg. In fact, years later, he would dismiss his first professional project as a "Pepsi commercial" he made in "an attack of crass commercialism." Proving he may be his harshest critic, he added, "When I look back at the film, I can easily say, 'No wonder I didn't go to [protest at] Kent State,' or 'No wonder I didn't go to Vietnam or I wasn't protesting when all my friends were carrying signs and getting clubbed in Century City.' I was off making movies, and *Amblin'* is the slick byproduct of a kid immersed up to his nose in film."

There's more than a hint of regret when he discusses his precocious success. A feeling of opportunities lost because other opportunities—commercial ones—presented themselves so early.

"I never counted on getting started as early as I did. It just happened that I started getting jobs before I was ready to say yes," he said.

Then he mentions a colleague, one of a group of artistic directors, whom he still feels a touch of envy toward. "I might have made underground movies first: I might have been like Brian De Palma and made nine films before breaking into the establishment."

In fact, he would later say the only reason he made *Amblin'* was to get the attention of studio executives.

It did. In spades.

CHAPTER TWO

Amblin' Along

I N 1966, THE SAME YEAR HIS PARENTS divorced, Spielberg took the hokey Universal Studios Tour, which purported to be an inside look at the movie business. But the tour had as much to do with the nuts and bolts of moviemaking as a cigar store Indian had with Wounded Knee.

The teenager sneaked off the tram, which was a feat in itself, since the tour-goers on the backlot at Universal are as closely guarded as the presidential motorcade.

"I remember taking a bus tour through Universal Studios. I remember getting off the bus. We were all let off to go to the bathroom.

"Instead I hid between two soundstages until the bus left, and then I wandered around for three hours! I went back there every day for three months. I walked past the guard every day, waved at him, and he waved back. I always wore a suit and carried a briefcase, and he assumed I was some kid related to some mogul. It was my father's briefcase, and there was nothing in it but a sandwich and two candy bars. So every day that summer I went in in my suit and hung out with directors and writers and editors and dubbers. I found an office that wasn't being used and became a squatter! I went to the camera store and bought some plastic name titles and put my name in the building directory: 'Steven Spielberg, Room 23C.'

"I found an empty bungalow and set up an office. I then went to the main switchboard and introduced myself and gave them my extension so I could get calls.

"It took Universal two years to discover I was on the lot. Those two years I was there I never made any deals, but I used the phone a lot and learned how to play the game. I got fed up with the joint, though, and left and went to Long Beach College and made a short called *Amblin'*."

Universal was his off-campus campus. He crammed fifteen course units into two days of classes each week, then spent the other three days sneaking onto the backlot.

The first time he managed to break into the studio, the intruder felt as though he had found his long-lost home. "I was on the outside of a wonderful hallucination that everyone was sharing. And I wanted to do more than be part of the hallucination. I wanted to control it. I wanted to be a director," he said.

Lower echelon executives remembered being embarrassed when Spielberg asked them to remove the pictures from their walls so he could project his little 8 mm epics.

One executive advised him, "If you make your films in 16 mm—or even better—in 35 mm, then they'll get seen."

Spielberg took the man's advice. "I immediately went to work in the college cafeteria to earn money to buy 16 mm stock and rent a camera. I *had* to get those films seen."

One of the studio personnel willing to see his films was Chuck Silver, Universal's film librarian.

Spielberg had met Silver on the day he sneaked off the tram during the bathroom break. Silver spotted him and asked what he was doing. Spielberg somehow managed to communicate his enthusiasm to Silver, because instead of throwing the youth off the lot, he chatted with him for thirty minutes. Silver even asked to see some of Spielberg's 8 mm efforts and gave him a pass so he could come back the next day without having to sneak off the tram.

"He was very impressed with my films. Then he said, 'I don't have the authority to write you any more passes, but good luck to you,'" Spielberg recalled.

But Silver hadn't forgotten his young protege. Part of Silver's job was screening upcoming films for the studio brass. After one such screening for Sid Sheinberg, then head of production for the studio's television production arm, Silver continued to run the projector and showed the executive *Amblin'*. Sheinberg remembered Silver telling him, "There's this guy who's been hanging around the place who's made a short film. So I watched it and thought it was terrific."

Sheinberg told Silver to have the young director come see him. Sheinberg was impressed with the film, but not with the filmmaker.

"I liked the way he selected the performers, the relationships, the maturity and the warmth that was in that short. I told Chuck to have the guy come see me," Sheinberg recalled. He also remembered Spielberg as "this nerdlike, scrawny character."

Sheinberg offered to put the young man under contract with the studio "for the princely sum of $275 a week," the executive recalled with a chuckle. He has good reason to laugh at his early foresight in spotting a future talent, since that initial investment would earn the studio billions later on.

Unemployed, still a student at Cal State Long Beach, Spielberg was not so overawed by this attention from a major studio bigwig that he didn't immediately demand—politely—a concession for signing the measly contract. "I just have one request," he had the temerity to tell Sheinberg, "and I'd like you to give me not so much a commitment but a promise. I want to direct something before I'm twenty-one. That would be very important to me."

Impressed and amused by this young man who still looked like a teenager, Sheinberg promised adding, "you *should* be a director." Spielberg shot back. "I think so too."

Still, the cheeky young man had misgivings. He told Sheinberg he wanted to graduate from college. "I was still several months shy of my twenty-first birthday, and I hadn't graduated from college. But Sheinberg said, 'Do you want to graduate college or do you want to be a film director?'

"I signed the papers a week later."

Spielberg's middle-class obsession with being a college graduate vanished faster than E.T.'s spaceship. "I quit college so fast," he later recalled, "I didn't even clean out my locker."

A brief blurb in the *Hollywood Reporter* at the time announced the beginning of one spectacular and one stillborn career.

The December 12, 1968, issue said: "Steven Spielberg and Pamela McMyler, writer-director and star, respectively, of *Amblin'*, have been signed to exclusive contracts by Universal, per Sid Sheinberg, television production vice president. Spielberg, 21, is believed to be the youngest filmmaker ever pacted by a major studio. Miss McMyler, a graduate of the Pasadena Playhouse, is currently featured in *The Boston Strangler*."

Two years after *Amblin'*, McMyler had a whole gossip column devoted to her in the defunct Los Angeles *Herald-Examiner*, announcing her appearance on a two-part episode of the NBC series, *The Bold Ones*. Buried in the story as a throwaway line was the fact that her part in a "short experimental film, *Amblin'* (no director mentioned) had caught the eye of John Wayne, who cast her as his niece in the 1970 feature *Chisum*." Today McMyler is not listed with the Screen Actors Guild Directory, which means that even if Spielberg or some other filmmaker wanted to hire her, they would be hard pressed to locate the vanished actress.

One wonders if the now long-forgotten actress had any inkling how monumentally significant the little student film she had starred in would be for its director, and how little impact it would have on her own acting career.

Sid Sheinberg was true to his word: his protege was allowed to direct before he turned twenty-one.

Daily Variety, which doesn't seem to miss any show-biz news, no matter how apparently trivial, announced in 1969: "Nine years ago Steven Spielberg borrowed his dad's birthday present, an 8 mm camera, and made his first movie, a Western, and won a Boy Scout Merit Badge. Today, at 21, he is directing Joan Crawford and Barry Sullivan in a Universal World Premiere Movie for TV."

His first assignment was indeed a plum one: one of three segments for a pilot called *Night Gallery*, created and written by the master of television fantasy, Rod Serling.

For all his bravado in sneaking on backlots and demanding concessions from Sheinberg, Spielberg felt panic when he first met one of his idols, the creator of a favorite television show from his youth, Rod Serling of *The Twilight Zone.*

The chain-smoking writer-producer immediately put the twenty-one-year-old novice at ease. "Rod was the most positive guy in the entire production company," Spielberg later recalled. "He was a great, energetic slaphappy guy who gave me a fantastic pep talk about how he predicted that the entire movie industry was about to change because of young people like myself getting the breaks."

The crew was just as encouraging as the creator of the series. No one seemed to mind being ordered about by a pubescent looking director. "I expected hostility when I started on this," Spielberg said at the time. "But no one seemed to think it was unusual. Nobody called me, 'Hey, kid.' As a matter of fact, the older people on the set were the first to accept me. I guess they figured that if someone up there thought I was good enough for the job, then that was enough for them."

Not all his elders were so encouraging. In fact, probably the oldest person on the set didn't like being directed by an adolescent.

In 1969, the year the *Night Gallery* pilot was shot, its star, Joan Crawford, was in her sixty-fifth year and, according to her daughter Christina's memoir, *Mommie Dearest,* in the latter stages of alcoholism, quaffing water glasses filled with 100 proof Stolichnaya vodka.

Her film career all but over, the workaholic actress still needed to get in front of the camera, and like so many movie stars of yesteryear, TV became her living graveyard, the place where she breathed her last, professionally speaking.

For his first directing assignment, Spielberg found himself stuck with one of the most obstreperous stars in Hollywood. Crawford was cast in the middle segment, "Eyes," of the *Night Gallery* trilogy pilot. She played a wealthy blind woman who is given a chance to regain her sight for twelve hours. All she has to do is find a donor. She bribes a down-on-his-luck drunk (Tom Bosley) to surrender his corneas in return for $12,000.

The operation is a success, but just as Crawford regains her sight, everything goes black. The onset of her vision is also the beginning of a citywide electrical blackout. Her expensive operation, which only grants her half a day's worth of sight, is a total waste. Stumbling in the dark, she crashes through the glass door of her penthouse and falls to her death.

Spielberg has only fond memories of the first star he ever directed. "I never saw her drunk on the set," he told me years later, contrary to *Mommie Dearest*'s claim that the star was a full-blown alcoholic by that time.

The book by her daughter, Christina, also claims Crawford was grossly insulted by being assigned a twenty-one-year-old director who looked like a teenager. She apparently managed to hide her distaste from her director, however. Spielberg fondly recalled, "Directing Joan Crawford was like pitching to Hank Aaron your first time in the game. [She] treated me like I had been directing fifty years. She was great. But I did an awful job."

Crawford didn't share his enthusiasm for their collaboration. Confirming the *Mommie Dearest* account, other sources say Crawford campaigned to get him fired, but Rod Serling went to bat for his young protege. Failing to get him fired, Crawford threw herself into the project with the professionalism that had kept her working for more than half a century.

A method actress, she invited the director to come to her penthouse apartment in New York and greeted him at the door blindfolded; she was getting in character.

"She was going to be playing a blind person, and she went lurching around the apartment. I was terrified. When I suggested we go to lunch, she took off her blindfold and said, 'I'm not going to be seen in public with you. People will think you're my child.'"

Despite such put-downs, Spielberg insists, "She was very good to me, very firm, but very kind. I called her Miss Crawford, and she insisted on calling me Mr. Spielberg. I asked her to call me Steven, but she wouldn't. She knew I was just a scared kid, and she was setting an example—of courtesy, and yes, of respect—for the rest of the cast and crew to follow. Once she knew I had done my homework—I had my storyboards right there with me every minute—she treated me as if I was The Director. Which, of course, I was, but at that time she knew a helluva lot more about directing than I did."

They even had creative differences, although not violent enough to cause either the temperamental star or the neophyte director to stomp off the set. "Miss Crawford and I had our first argument," he told *TV Guide* at the time. "It wasn't really much of a disagreement, a little thing over punching up a scene. It's a pleasure discussing such a thing with a woman like that."

Ultimately, Crawford did more than overcome her aversion to being directed by somebody who looked as though he were still going through puberty.

She may even have felt gratitude when he helped her with Serling's complicated dialogue. The creator of the show believed his dialogue was written in stone, and woe to anyone, even a star of Crawford's magnitude, who dared digress from the script.

Whether it was age or alcoholism, Crawford kept forgetting her lines. Finally, Spielberg agreed to have strategically placed cue cards scattered all over the set within her eyesight but out of camera range.

By the time their collaboration was over, it seems Crawford was Spielberg's biggest fan. Or so an eyewitness to the production insists.

The reporter, the venerable Shirley Eder of the *Detroit Free Press*, remembered her visit to the backlot at Universal: "Joan grabbed me and said, 'Go interview that *kid* because he's going to be the biggest director of all time.'"

Years later, at a press junket to promote his film *Hook*, an elderly Eder reminded Spielberg of her visit to the set of *Night Gallery*.

Underneath the rabbinical beard that now covers most of his face, Spielberg looked as though he might be blushing. Grimacing, he said to Eder, "You already told me that story . . . and I thought you were crazy."

Despite his star's enthusiasm, Spielberg wasn't bullish on his first professional directing effort. And for once he wasn't being self-deprecating when he claimed he did an "awful job" on *Night Gallery*.

The producer of his segment had to reshoot part of the director's work. "I was so traumatized. The pressure of that show was too much for me. I decided to take some time off, and Sid [Sheinberg] had the guts to give me a leave of absence," he said.

For all its problems, the segment of *Night Gallery* he directed remains a treasure trove for film historians and movie buffs because it contains the signature style of filmmaking he would later perfect in his blockbusters and masterpiece: the use of wide-angle lenses, lots of dolly and crane shots, and dramatic lighting to maximize the overall visual impact.

The zoom lens had been invented only a few years before, and it was still all the rage, especially on television, where a zoom was cheaper than expensive dolly shots and the tracks that had to be laid down to accommodate them. Spielberg bucked the trend and avoided zoom shots, however, using instead complex tracking shots in which the camera moved toward the actor rather than zooming in. Spielberg also employed some fancy cutting, and one scene was a homage to a similar quick-cut sequence in the film *2001: A Space Odyssey*.

Actually, it wasn't just the *Night Gallery* experience that temporarily soured the young filmmaker on filmmaking. After directing the pilot, he had spent several months writing three screenplays, all of which were rejected by his mentor, Sheinberg.

"I was in a despondent, comatose state and told Sid I wanted a leave of absence," he said.

During a yearlong sabbatical from Universal, he wrote his first feature, which was to become *The Sugarland Express*, and two other screenplays, one of which he sold to the superhot producing team of Richard Zanuck and David Brown. The film, called *Ace Eli and Roger of the Skies*, never made it to the screen, but the importance of the Zanuck-Brown connection can't be underestimated. A few years later the two powerful men would drop, at Spielberg's request, a director assigned to one of their films and give the job to Spielberg. The title of this story: *Jaws*.

But that triumph was six years away. In the meantime, after a year away from Universal, he found himself chomping at the bit, anxious to get away from the typewriter and in front of a camera, any camera, any medium, even television, even though *Night Gallery* had been such a traumatic and unsatisfying experience.

"I suffocated in the freedom," he said about his year off. "I needed to work, and I came back to Universal and said, 'I'll do anything.' But no one would hire me."

Universal did take him back, and he landed an episode of *Marcus Welby, M.D.*, which would be the first of seven shows he directed for the studio's television arm.

The *Welby* episode was titled "The Daredevil Gesture." It focused on a teenager suffering from hemophilia who was determined to prove he was just as fit as his friends by attempting a dangerous rescue on a class field trip. (Shades of Spielberg's Boy Scout misadventures!) Dr. Welby (Robert Young) as usual saved the day—and the hemophiliac's life. The episode is noteworthy because it championed the rights of the disabled long before such causes became politically fashionable.

A year after his unpleasant encounter with *Night Gallery*, Spielberg apparently had forgotten the experience enough to take a stab at another segment of the anthology show. He directed the first half of a two-part episode, a comedy-drama called "Make Me Laugh."

Godfrey Cambridge played a failed stand-up comic desperate to find an appreciative audience. He meets a sad-sack genie, played by comedian Jackie Vernon, who grants him his wish. Cambridge becomes irresistible to audiences. Every word out of his mouth makes people burst into giggles. As in the case of many genie-in-a-bottle stories, the wish becomes a curse. No matter what Cambridge says, no matter how serious, people crack up.

Suicidal, Cambridge throws himself in front of a car and dies. The segment ends, grotesquely, with onlookers laughing their heads off at the corpse!

Due to studio politics, a supporting actor was replaced by another actor, and some original scenes had to be reshot. Spielberg was not asked to do the reshooting, however. He was replaced by Jeannot Szwarc. Ironically, in a case of history repeating itself, seven years later Szwarc would direct the sequel to *Jaws*.

Just as he had championed the rights of the handicapped on *Marcus Welby* years before it was fashionable, Spielberg would tackle the environment on his next assignment, a ninety-minute episode of *The Name of the Game*. Entitled "LA: 2017," the show was a dramatic departure from its usual reality-based flavor. On his way to an ecological conference, Gene Barry, who played a magazine publisher, crashes his car and wakes up in the year 2017 where pollution has all but destroyed the planet and people are forced to live underground.

Barry teams up with a radical group intent on overthrowing the megalomaniac mayor of Los Angeles. Perhaps in a nod to the basic conservatism of Universal, which produced the show, Barry eventually decides the radicals are as distasteful as the noxious mayor. He flees the group and goes above ground. Spielberg very inventively—and inexpensively—filmed the above-ground shots using a red filter to suggest the suffocating pollution.

Barry emerges from his coma in the present day. His magazine's commitment to cleaning up the environment has been reinforced by his coma-induced nightmare.

Marc Wielage, who supplied these synopses in an issue of *Video Review* magazine, wrote of this episode of *The Name of the Game*, "It's all a bit heavy-handed, but still a step up from most of the series' pretentious treatment of issues."

The Spielberg touch already was evident, even in these television assignments.

Two months after his innovative work on *The Name of the Game*, Spielberg came to the attention of the powerhouse producer-writer team of Richard Levinson and William Link. They hired him to direct two episodes of their show, *The Psychiatrist*, part of the NBC anthology series, *Four in One*.

Spielberg later would say that these two episodes were his most rewarding work in television.

The director, who was barely out of his teens, was pulling down an adult-sized salary. Director's Guild minimum for 1969–1970 was $1,000 a week or $4,400 a month. Such a handsome salary for young man in his early twenties, however, didn't seem to confer any social confidence on the director. As he said of his social graces at the time, "I'm usually the guy in the corner at the party eating all the dip."

The first episode of *The Psychiatrist*, filmed in early 1971, was called, "Par for the Course." It dramatized the life of a dying golf pro, played by Clu Galager. Roy Thinnes, who played the title's shrink, helps the golfer cope with terminal cancer. While filming, Spielberg decided to improvise a poignant scene in which the golfer's friends dig up the 18th hole, including the flag and cup, and present it to their friend in his hospital bed.

Spielberg recalled the scene: "It was wonderful. Clu began to cry—as a person and as an actor. He tore the grass out of the hole, and he squeezed the dirt all over himself, and he thanked them for bringing this gift . . . the greatest gift he'd ever received. It was a very moving moment that came out of being loose with an idea."

The second episode of *The Psychiatrist* Spielberg directed, entitled, "The Private World of Martin Dalton," allowed him to tap into his own feelings about his parents' divorce. The title character is a twelve-year-old boy who has slipped away from reality and inhabits his own bizarre fantasy world.

Psychiatrist Thinnes eventually discovers that the boy's problems are caused by his adoption and treatment by foster parents. Spielberg's gentle direction of the twelve-year-old (played by Stephen Hudis) anticipated his later rapport with children in *E.T.* and *Empire of the Sun*.

Both episodes of *The Psychiatrist* stand out because of their Dali-esque fantasy dream sequences. The surrealist painter Salvador Dali usually didn't make "guest appearances" on episodic television, but Spielberg showed early on the classy twist he could give even the most pedestrian of material.

The director never pooh-poohed television, however. After the success of *Jaws* and *Close Encounters*, when he was criticized for neglecting character in his films, he would point to the two episodes of *The Psychiatrist* he had directed as proof that he could serve a master other than plot or special effects.

"I am as proud of 'Par for the Course,' a *Psychiatrist* I did, as any of my film work," he said after *Close Encounters* was released.

Levinson and Link were so impressed with his imaginative direction of the two *Psychiatrist* episodes that they tapped him to direct the season premiere of their immensely popular series, *Columbo*. Entitled "Murder by the Book," the episode starred Jack Cassidy as a duplicitous mystery writer who plots the murder of his partner, played by Martin Milner. Cassidy's crime unravels when he is blackmailed by a store owner (Barbara Colby), whose love for Cassidy is unrequited. For this episode, Spielberg enjoyed the services of Oscar-winning cinematographer Russell Metty.

Perhaps his least successful venture in episodic television, if you don't count the currently dismal *seaQuest DSV*, was his next job on *Owen Marshall, Counselor at Law*, an episode called "Eulogy for a Wide Receiver." Anson Williams, who later would go on to greater fame as Potsy on *Happy Days*, played a football player who is given amphetamines by his hard-driving coach (Stephen Young). When the athlete dies, the coach is charged with murder, and Owen Marshall (Arthur Hill) and Jess Brandon (Lee Majors) are hired to defend him. Wielage in *Video Review* magazine called this episode, "Spielberg's most mundane TV effort, with a pre-dictable script by Richard Bluel and a leaden performance from Lee Majors."

After toiling in episodic television for more than two years, Spielberg finally was rewarded with a step up to the world of tele-vision movies. A friend in the Universal mailroom showed him a copy of a television movie written by *Twilight Zone* veteran Richard Matheson.

The script was called *Duel*, and it would go on to win prizes at film festivals throughout Europe, where the American television movie was released as a feature.

Spielberg fell in love with the script, especially after the constrictive nature of episodic television. As soon as he read the script, he laid siege to the film's producer, George Eckstien, who gave in to the persistent young director.

Despite its supernatural flavor, *Duel* was based on an inci-dent that had actually happened to the writer when an irate truck driver tried to drive him off the road. In the film, we never see the identity of the truck driver who chases the car's driver, played by Dennis Weaver, through a western canyon.

Duel had a shooting schedule of only nine days, and for the first time in his career—although certainly not the last—Spielberg went over schedule, but only by three days. He did stay within his budget of $300,000. The film turned out to be a bonanza for both Universal, which earned a whopping $9 million from its European theatrical release, and for Spielberg, who earned the right to direct his first full-length feature, *The Sugarland Express*.

Duel has many themes which would later be explored in greater detail in the bigger budget *Sugarland Express*, and even in *Jaws* and *Close Encounters*. Weaver, like the characters in *Jaws* and *Close Encounters*, is a middle-class Everyman who encounters a menacing force, a gasoline tanker bent on crushing him for no discernible reason. It's the same mindless menace as the shark that devours Robert Shaw in *Jaws* or the unseen aliens who sweep up Melinda Dillon's four-year-old son in *Close Encounters*.

In addition to breaking box-office records in Europe, the film won numerous prestigious awards, including the Cariddi D'Oro for best directorial debut at the esteemed Taormina Film Festival in Rome and the Grand Prix at the Festival du Cinema Fantastique in France.

In the United States, the film also did not go unhonored. It received Emmy nominations for best cinematography and best sound editing, winning in the latter category.

But perhaps the most appreciated accolade came from his ultimate hero, the man he often credits with making him want to become a filmmaker in the first place. Seeing director David Lean's *Lawrence of Arabia* as a child, Spielberg said years later, convinced him his future lay in the world of cinema. So it must have been especially gratifying when the great Lean himself condescended to watch a television movie and give *Duel* this endorsement:

> Immediately I knew that here was a very bright new director. Steven takes real pleasure in the sensuality of forming action scenes—wonderful flowing movements. He has this extraordinary size of vision, a sweep that illuminates his films. But then Steven is the way the movies used to be. Just loves making films. He is entertaining his teenage self—and what is wrong with that?

Years later, Spielberg, with amazing temerity, asked his idol to direct a half-hour segment of his new television anthology series, *Amazing Stories*. Lean took the offer as a joke but agreed to sign on—if he were allowed six *months* to shoot the thirty-minute episode!

Although it was a love-hate affair at the time, Spielberg today remains grateful for the lessons he learned from the small screen. "Television taught me how to be a professional within a very chaotic business. Making movies is an unnatural act. Really, if God had meant for man to make movies, Thomas Edison would have been born 1,000 years ago!" he said.

Even the drawbacks of television directing had a salutary effect on his evolving talent as a filmmaker. "I remember that when I was first starting out, I used a lot of fancy shots," he recalled a decade later. "Some of the compositions were very nice, but I'd usually be shooting through somebody's armpit or angling past someone's nose. I got a lot of that out of my system and became less preoccupied with mechanics and began to search more for the literary quality in the scripts I was reading."

Grateful as he may have been for the lessons he learned, by the end of 1971 Spielberg was tired of episodic television, taking over characters already created by someone else, having to adapt his style to the established style of the series (except when the unwary producer let him get away with slipping in visual references to Salvador Dali). Toiling in the salt mines of episodic television wasn't all blood, sweat, and tears, but *Duel* had given him a taste of directing an original script, without any baggage from previous episodes. He liked being an auteur, even on the small scale offered by the small screen.

After rejecting several television series in 1971, he learned that the producer of the classic horror fantasy show *One Step Beyond* was planning a television movie called *Something Evil*. The plot of the film intrigued Spielberg immensely, and some of its themes later would show up, considerably enhanced, in *Poltergeist*.

The horror story followed an urban family that moves to the remote Pennsylvania countryside to get away from the evils of the big city, only to find even worse evil, a Satanic presence, lurking in the boondocks. For a television movie, *Something Evil* boasted an A-list star of the time, Sandy Dennis, who had won an Oscar for her work in *Who's Afraid of Virginia Woolf?* only a few years earlier. Veteran character actor Darren McGavin played her husband with Johnny Whittaker and Sandy and Debbie Lempert as their children. If you don't count Joan Crawford, who was all but washed up by the time Spielberg directed her in the *Night Gallery* pilot, Dennis was the first established star he ever worked with. It would be years before he cast anyone but relative unknowns in his films. As Spielberg later would say (and recant), "I don't want to work with anyone who's been on the cover of the *Rolling Stone.*"

Something Evil also was important to Spielberg's career because it was the first time he worked with cinematographer Bill Butler. Four years later he would call on Butler to shoot *Jaws.*

After *Something Evil*, Spielberg spent almost a year in the wilderness, vegetating in development hell as several independent projects he was developing failed to get off the ground. After a year of frustration and underemployment, series television apparently didn't look so bad after all, and he reluctantly agreed to shoot a pilot produced by his old mentors, Levinson and Link. At least with a pilot, he wouldn't be forced to take on some other writer-director's hand-me-down characters and concept. The projected series for which he made the pilot was called *Savage*. It revolved around the world of network news. Its title character, television reporter Paul Savage, was played by Martin Landau, co-starring with his then wife, Barbara Bain. The year before, the couple left the immensely popular show, *Mission: Impossible.*

Savage was designed to be the two stars' comeback series. It wasn't. Despite Spielberg's growing talent as a director, the pilot failed to get picked up as a weekly series.

But the failure of *Savage* soon was forgotten among the exhilaration that ensued when he finally made it to the big time, feature film directing.

The film was called *The Sugarland Express*. At last, Spielberg was free from the artistic limitations of the small screen, which he detested enough not to return to for almost two decades.

CHAPTER THREE

The Big Time, At Last

SPIELBERG TYPICALLY PREFERS FANTASY OVER reality, so it's not a coincidence that only two of his films have been based on real-life incidents. Coincidentally, the two films bookend his feature film career: *The Sugarland Express* and *Schindler's List*.

His feature debut was based on a dramatic incident that intrigued him when he first read about it in newspapers. A woman who had lost custody of her children persuaded her husband to break out of prison and help her get them back from foster parents. The couple lead the cops on a comic chase as they make their way to the kids' new home, Sugarland, Texas.

The film ends in a very un-Spielbergian way—in tragedy.

As the director capsulized the story: "It was about these two young people who had their baby taken from them and were then pursued across Texas by the entire law enforcement division for some very small, petty crimes. It was a media event that just escalated. In Texas there is a posse theory. If a fellow officer is in trouble, everybody, all of his colleagues, jump into their cars and fall in behind to try and help the guy out. In this case ninety police cars were involved in a bumper to bumper pursuit that was strung out 150 miles across Texas.

"And in the end, they actually hired sharpshooters who killed the young man. In the budget of my picture, I could only afford forty or so, but still people could hardly believe it."

After reading Spielberg's script, Zanuck and Brown hired him to direct it, but called in veteran writers Hal Barwood and Matthew Robbins to rewrite the script so thoroughly that the then cloutless director ended up with only a "story by" credit.

In his 1992 monograph, Philip M. Taylor, a film professor at the University of Leeds, England, claimed that the ego-less director was "delighted" by the job Barwood and Robbins did on his script. Taylor used the term "tightened up" to describe the tinkering. Taking the sting out of the situation was perhaps the fact that Barwood and Robbins were old friends of Spielberg's from film school days. Obviously, there were no hard feelings since three years later Spielberg would cast the two writers in bit parts as the missing Air Force pilots who emerge from the mother ship in *Close Encounters*. Remarkably unterritorial at such an age when other Young Turks are sowing their wild oats, Spielberg praised his friends' revisions and said, "I believe I've gotten to the point where I can appreciate a good piece of material and translate it into film without my own ego showing up on the screen." Making up for the slight, Spielberg was awarded the best screenplay award with Robbins and Barwood at he 1974 Cannes Film Festival.

Goldie Hawn, an Oscar winner for *Cactus Flower* and a huge box-office star at the time, agreed to work with a tyro director because the role intrigued her. Despite her commercial success, she was tired of playing dim-witted eccentrics. *The Sugarland Express* offered her her first opportunity to play a more substantive character, but safely within the confines of the eccentric, wacky screen persona she had patented so successfully.

Hawn was both a blessing and a curse. Her participation gave the film instant credibility—not to mention financing. The studio in fact refused to make the film without her, and she agreed to star for only a fraction of her usual acting fee, in this case $300,000 plus 10 percent of the profits. But all the baggage she brought along, going all the way back to her days on *Laugh-In*, drove the director up the wall. Reshooting Hawn's mannered takes made the film go over budget.

"I averaged about four printed takes, and we went over budget in raw stock and printing $50,000 because of that. But the thing of it is, it was so important for Goldie because she never played a consistently dramatic role before this and to get rid of all of Goldie's cutesy-pie crust, I had to print a lot of takes and then in the cutting room select the takes that were the most subtle," he said.

Still, he gave her high marks for her attempts to escape her comedic roots. "I must say that she's totally different than she's ever been before. She really kept all that sugarplum stuff to a minimum."

William Atherton played her husband and reluctant accomplice. After Hawn's character bullies Atherton's into hijacking a highway patrol car to get them to Sugarland, the police trail them for miles in a squad of cop cars. By now, the image has become a cliche in everything from *Die Hard* to police shows, but back in 1974, the image of a dozen squad cars in pursuit was original and indelible.

The critics thought so too. *The New Yorker's* Pauline Kael, usually the Al Capone of film critics, raved, "This film is one of the most phenomenal directorial debut films in the history of movies. It's a debut any director might envy."

Judith Crist of *New York* magazine went even more overboard: "The triumph of *The Sugarland Express* goes beyond its technical accomplishments and substance to Spielberg's own viewpoint. He has held up a mirror and showed us our baser selves clearly and truly, to powerful effect."

Actually, if Crist had been more familiar with the then unknown director's background, she might have commented that he had held up a mirror to his own past. For all the later accusations that he was merely a manufacturer of roller-coaster rides, *The Sugarland Express* was his first, but certainly not his last, film to deal with the theme of a child's separation from parents.

He was mining the emotions of his own traumatic reaction to his parents' divorce ten years earlier when he explored the theme of a child being yanked from his parents.

Despite its deeply felt emotion and the critical hosannas, *The Sugarland Express* was a box-office disappointment, grossing only $6.5 million domestically, with a worldwide take of $11 million. The glowing reviews failed to cheer up Spielberg in the wake of public rejection. "It did get good reviews, but I would have given away all those reviews for a bigger audience. The movie just broke even; it didn't make any money," he said.

Ameliorating the pain somewhat was the real affection he felt for his bosses, the film's producers. "Zanuck and Brown were probably the best experience any first-time-out director could hope for. They allowed me to make the picture my way. They allowed me to cut the picture my way, and when I was six days over schedule, they protected me from studio heads," he said.

Fortunately for Spielberg, the film's poor showing at the box office didn't sour the producers on their director. A year later, while loitering around Zanuck-Brown's production office at Universal, he spotted the galleys of a yet to be published novel about a really mean fish. Spielberg, a notorious nonreader, was intrigued enough to pick up the book and actually skim through it. It was a slim volume about a preposterously large shark that terrorizes a New England beach resort. The book was by a first-time novelist, Peter Benchley.

Zanuck and Brown had already paid $175,000 for the film rights to the unpublished book on their desk and had also already assigned a director, Dick Richards.

"I happened to be in their office one day, swiped a copy of *Jaws* in galley form, took it home and read it over the weekend and asked to do it," Spielberg recalled.

Spielberg liked the novel, but with reservations. He would later deride it as "Peyton Place at sea" after rewriting Benchley's film adaptation. Despite the failure of *The Sugarland Express*, Brown was smitten enough with Spielberg to dump Richards, a more established director, and hand over the project to a twenty-six-year-old film school dropout.

CHAPTER FOUR

Bonanza Time

WITHOUT TOO MUCH EXAGGERATION, YOU could say that with *Jaws*, Spielberg won the cinematic equivalent of the lottery, the Kentucky Derby, and the Irish Sweepstakes all rolled into one. Within a month of its release, it had taken in $60 million at the box office, an unheard of amount at the time.

After the film had grossed nearly half a billion dollars, making it the number-one movie of all time, he was asked by a reporter if its success had in any way intimidated him.

Spielberg said, "It's strange, because at first it had a very negative effect on me. I thought it was a fluke. No movie had ever grossed a hundred million dollars in the U.S. and Canada before. It was regarded by everybody as a kind of carnival freak. So I began believing it was some kind of freak and agreeing when people said it could never happen again."

Jaws was having a "negative effect" on its director even before production began. The problems began with the novel. Not surprisingly, Spielberg loved its action plot but hated the romantic subplot, which involved an adulterous love triangle among the town's police chief, his wife, and the marine biologist called in to help snare the shark.

Although he had virtually no clout after the box-office failure of *The Sugarland Express*, Spielberg retained enough self-confidence to make some pretty imperious demands of his two bosses.

"I told Zanuck and Brown that I'd like to do the film, but only on condition that the love story be dropped, that the shark not be revealed until a good sixty-five minutes into the film, and that in the end I could attempt to exorcise as many of the *Moby Dick* parallels as possible. In the book, [the shark hunter] Quint is snarled in a rope and dragged to his drowning death by the shark [*a la* Captain Ahab]. I wanted the ending to be much more personal and decided Quint should be masticated and emulsified," he recalled with grisly determination.

Spielberg felt the shark caused more than enough heavy breathing and didn't need any of the human variety to enliven the main action.

Not mincing words, he told the book's author flat out that the subplot was "soap opera. I told Peter and he balked for ten hours. After that, he was 100 percent cooperative."

Or maybe just distracted since Spielberg added, "Peter wanted to move on and write another book."

Benchley's recollection of their prickly collaboration was less rosy. After Benchley toiled over three rewrites of his screen adaptation, he said, "I give up."

Howard Sackler, the winner of a Pulitzer Prize for *The Great White Hope*, tried a draft and found the shark harder to knock out than Jack Johnson, the hero of his play.

Finally Spielberg collaborated with a buddy from his college days, Carl Gottlieb, on a fifth and sixth draft.

An examination of how the screenplay evolved is revealing. The first three drafts by Benchley were merely literal reworkings of the novel. Benchley obviously cared more for the private lives of his characters than he did for his toothy villain because his drafts incorporated every heavy breath from the book's adulterous love triangle.

Perhaps respecting the original author's intentions, Howard Sackler, in his draft, kept the romantic subplot, but his version showed none of the talent that had won him a Pulitzer. Spielberg collaborated with Sackler on his version, but their partnership was a bust. "When Howard Sackler came on to the job I sat with him for four weeks at the Bel Air Hotel," but still no dice, the director recalled.

Spielberg found his perfect alter ego in Carl Gottlieb.

In their editions, all the hokey soap opera elements were surgically excised. In fact, at the time of the film's release, one critic pointed out that *Jaws* was the first action film in history that did not have a romantic subplot.

But Spielberg's analytical genius went far beyond deep-sixing amorous characters. In his drafts, the shark became a terrifying cipher, rarely seen but always felt. The shark was both the most important and the least seen character in the script. And it was indeed a character.

"My feeling about sharks is that they've had 80 million years to get their act together," he said in an interview shortly after the film came out. "Parts of the book terrorized me. I tried to translate my fear into visual language. It became a picture book of fears, phobias, and anxieties."

He must have felt personally vindicated when the film critic for the *London Observer* essentially agreed with his aesthetic choices regarding the script: "When the story is hurtling the audience along, who cares that Spielberg's successes are peopled with papier mache characterizations? In *Jaws*, the three principals are carefully individualized, but their personalities are quickly submerged in the elemental hunt for a shark. Indeed, the film succeeds as entertainment in large measure because it completely excises the banal, interpersonal angst Peter Benchley layered over his characters in the novel."

Spielberg felt he had struck just the right balance between light character and heavy action. Years later, after one too many critics complained that he sacrificed character for special effects and cheap thrills in his movies, Spielberg would angrily say, "*Jaws* and *Close Encounters* and *Raiders* would not have involved the audience as entertainment were it not for the characters. Otherwise, people would have rooted for the shark."

The problems with the script development were a honeymoon compared to the nightmare that actual shooting became.

The least of his problems was his youthful appearance. "I looked younger than twenty-six," he recalled years later. "I looked seventeen, and I still had acne, and that doesn't help instill confidence in seasoned crews."

After the watery headache of making *Jaws*, he made and kept a promise to himself that he would never, ever again shoot anything on water.

"If they talk about a sequel, I hope they don't talk to me. I've had it," he said, summing up the experience. In fact, three more sequels were made, the third a weird concoction in 3-D. Spielberg's name appeared nowhere in the credits of any of these knockoffs, not even as the honorific "executive consultant."

The whims of the ocean make even the most temperamental movie star seem positively gracious in comparison. Most days, because of the unpredictable tides and storms, the crew couldn't start shooting until 4 P.M. That meant more than just a late start to a long day. The light would start to fade at 6 P.M., so the production had only two hours of shooting time available each day.

Life on the water was full of perils. The multiphobic director had his worst fears about the water confirmed when he almost drowned. And he would have if he hadn't been wearing a life preserver. On another occasion, he was almost crushed to death when two vessels collided.

It could have been worse. The producers, Zanuck and Brown, originally wanted Spielberg to use real sharks. The director laughed: "Sure, yeah. They'd *train* a great white, put it in front of the camera with me in a cage. They tried to convince me that this was the way to go."

Instead, Spielberg found a safer alternative. He hired Bob Mattey, who had built the giant squid for Disney's 1954 film, *20,000 Leagues Under the Sea*, to create a mechanical shark.

Zanuck and Brown, however, continued to push for the real thing. Spielberg didn't have the clout to say drop dead to these far more powerful producers, so he did an end run around them. Spielberg contacted Ron and Valerie Taylor, Australian documentarians who had made the 1971 film *Blue Water, White Death*.

Spielberg recalls, "They're the foremost authorities on the behavior of great whites, where to find them, how to photograph them. I told them what [Zanuck and Brown had demanded], and they said, 'You've got to be kidding!' For one thing a shark will not live in captivity, especially a great white. It would die in a boat. It has to keep moving. We'd have to shoot an awful lot of sea water through their gills and keep them alive on the journey to the States.

"I also knew they wouldn't allow us to have a great white shark in the waters off Martha's Vineyard! After a few weeks of discussing the practicality of this wonderful concept, Zanuck and Brown agreed with me that we had to build the shark." Spielberg did relent and agree to send a second-unit team to Australia to shoot some long shots of the real thing. These live shots were intercut with close-ups of the mechanical shark.

The mechanical shark, nicknamed Bruce, turned out to be a true enfant terrible. There were actually five rubber sharks, costing a total of $1 million, and every single one of them was more uncooperative than the most egotistical human star. Half the time the sharks' electronics didn't work. It may have been all that salt water messing with the diodes and transistors.

"*Jaws* was physically exhausting because the ocean pummelled us every single day for over eight months. But physical exhaustion and your anger at nature for putting you through so much torment just build up your will to survive. With *Jaws*, I was fighting nature, and I grew stronger," he later said in a calmer, Nietzschean moment. With no exaggeration, he added, "I'm glad I got out of Martha's Vineyard alive. The morale was my responsibility, and it was important to keep people from losing their minds. I watched quiet men on the crew go bonkers in very vocal ways. I saw the vocal type become totally withdrawn to the point where they tore tiny bits of styrofoam off coffee cups and threw them into the tide. It's like giving birth to a baby shark and hoping it has legs."

Perhaps the hardest part to cast was the shark that was caught by the townspeople early in the film and presumed erroneously to be the killer of the beach goers. Local fishermen in Martha's Vineyard promised to catch sharks that could be used in Spielberg's cattle call. But after several days of empty nets, the producers put out an emergency call to Florida; a thirteen-foot tiger shark (dead) was soon flown in, packed in ice. The shark was hung on a hook for five days while it waited for its call to the set. During that time it began to stink in the hot sun. Local people retaliated by dumping dead sharks on the producers' rented digs. (The producers must have wondered, "Where were these people, and their dead fish, when we were casting the role of the dead shark?")

Technical problems and the temperamental sea took their toll on the budget and the shooting schedule. After only three days of shooting, the shark sank, and the production saw its original fifty-five-day shooting schedule balloon disastrously to 155 days! The budget doubled—from $4 million to $8 million. Universal executives threatened to shut down the runaway production and put Bruce on exhibit as part of the Universal Studios Tour.

Mixing metaphors, Spielberg grimly remembered, "It was Mutiny on the Bounty, with me tied to Moby Dick."

"There were so many obstacles in the path on the production of *Jaws*. The experience was so physically exhausting that the only special feeling any of us shared was watching Bruce the shark stay afloat long enough for a shot to be completed," he said.

The dailies saved the production and the director's butt. Even without its terrifying score by John Williams and most of the special effects, the raw daily footage kept the studio from pulling the plug on the project.

Meanwhile, tragedy almost befell Carl Gottlieb, the screenwriter whom Spielberg wisely cast in a small role so the writer would always be available on the set for rewrites. While shooting on the ocean, Gottlieb fell overboard and was almost chewed up by the boat's propeller.

Roy Scheider, on the other hand, wasn't taking any chances. For his scene in which he almost drowns as his cabin fills with water, he brought along his own axes and hammers to free himself if the safety crew failed.

Some days, when the sea was too rough, Spielberg would adhere to the studio's demand that he film every day by shooting close-ups of objects that, unlike the sea, didn't move, such as rope, oxygen tanks, and shark cages.

After five months on location, the crew had become extremely restless—and in Spielberg's opinion, mutinous. Is he joking when he says that he truly believed the tech people were going to drown him? "That's the rumor that went around the set. They were going to hold me underwater as long as they could and still avoid a homicide rap. And I was really afraid of half the guys in the crew. They regarded me as a nice kind of Captain Bligh. They didn't have scurvy or anything, but I wouldn't let them go home [until filming was completed]," Spielberg says.

In fact, after discussing the final shot with cinematographer Bill Butler the night before, Spielberg left without saying good-bye to the cast or crew, taking a ferry from the island to the mainland. From the boat, Spielberg allegedly screamed "I shall *not* return!"—an obvious twist to General MacArthur's famous farewell to the Philippines on the eve of the Japanese surrender.

There was one palliative on the set, and it was a lifesaver. As much as Spielberg hated the mechanical shark, the uncooperative tides, and the nervous studio brass, he loved his star, Richard Dreyfuss.

Ironically, Dreyfuss wasn't the director's first choice for the role of the marine biologist. Spielberg originally went after Jon Voight, who turned him down. Robert Shaw, who played the great white shark hunter, Quint, also was not the director's first choice. He had offered the role to Lee Marvin, who rebuffed him, saying, "I'm going to do some real fishing," before embarking on a fishing trip. It was a big mistake for both Voight and Marvin. Shaw, up to then a character actor, became a major star after appearing in the biggest hit of all time. Another actor, Roy Scheider, who played the police chief, also found himself transformed from supporting actor to handsome leading man after *Jaws* came out.

But it was Dreyfuss who bonded most closely with the director during filming. *Jaws*, in the words of *Casablanca*'s finale, was the beginning of a beautiful friendship, one that would last professionally and personally for two decades.

After the exhausting regimen of sea and studio, Dreyfuss was the director's personal shot of adrenaline. "Richard is a major energy outlet," Spielberg said. "Everyone plugs into Dreyfuss to wake up in the morning. We stretch out umbilicals over to him and join navels. He's like a hydroelectric plant. Ricky and I would get into jam sessions on both *Jaws* and *Close Encounters*. And a lot of good things came out of them."

Dreyfuss didn't share his director's enthusiasm. In fact, he initially turned down the role of the marine biologist called in to offer scientific know-how on how to nail the shark.

Dreyfuss was a serious actor. He had just starred in *The Apprenticeship of Duddy Kravitz*, a low-budget, intensely character-driven study of a Jewish heel in Montreal. Ironically, his fears about *Duddy Kravitz* finally got him to change his mind about taking on Bruce the shark. Before *Kravitz* was released to glowing reviews and predictions that Dreyfuss would become a major star, the actor was sure he had turned in a terrible performance. (He hadn't.) To revive what he thought was a faltering career, he reluctantly agreed to appear in a potential blockbuster like *Jaws*.

As Spielberg wryly described the artsy actor's attitude: "Richard told me he would rather see the film than be in it, and I told him I was interested in making a movie, not a film. Rick said all along he thought the movie would be a turkey."

Once Dreyfuss overcame his artistic qualms, he threw himself into the project with such devotion Spielberg felt himself perpetually charmed during the traumatic shoot.

"I don't have a working philosophy. What I need depends on the story I'm telling and the actor I'm working with. Take Richard Dreyfuss. Working with him is pure joy because we're so close. He's as crazy as I am, and if we aren't fighting like wild men over some electronic computer game or other, we both adore playing board games. Then there are absolutely no problems at all."

Dreyfuss wasn't quite so effusive on his collaborator. "He's a perfectionist," Dreyfuss said of Spielberg. "He shoots scenes again and again until he gets exactly what he wants. But he's good to work with because unlike some directors, he actually knows exactly what he wants."

That character trait—knowing exactly what he wants—was best demonstrated after the film was in the can, edited, and ready to hit the theaters.

Sneak preview audiences were turning in 99 percent approval-rating index cards. Universal executives were ecstatic.

They didn't want the director to touch or tinker with this gold mine waiting to be excavated.

But the perfectionist director discovered what he perceived to be flaws in the final cut during a sneak preview at a Dallas theater.

The scariest moment in *Jaws*, which has people literally jumping up in their seats, has to be the scene where the corpse pokes its head out of a hole in the hull of a submerged boat. As originally shot, the camera first focused on the faces of the actors and the look of horror they expressed before revealing the object of their horror, the corpse's head.

During the Dallas sneak, Spielberg realized the actors' reaction was giving away the surprise.

Spielberg called up the cinematographer and took him over to the pool in the film editor's backyard. There, he re-created the murky waters off Martha's Vineyard by throwing Carnation's powdered milk into the unlucky editor's pool. Then he reshot the corpse scene without showing the actor's reaction first.

The tinkering was a big improvement. People leapt from their seats. The only problem was that Spielberg had violated union rules by not using a union crew. He confessed his crime to the union and voluntarily paid a fine into its retirement fund.

As the film's editor, the late Verna Fields, recalled at the time, "Steven essentially threw himself on the mercy of the union, and they forgave him."

The director, based on the sneak preview reaction, also re-edited the climactic scene when the shark leaps out of the water and on to the boat.

As one studio source says, "Steven is the ultimate tinkerer. On Judgment Day, he'll ask God if he can shoot the Apocalypse from a different angle."

When *Jaws* was released in June 1975, it enjoyed twofold success: it broke box-office records *and* the critics loved it.

There were instant comparisons to Hitchcock and the master's use of relaxation and tension, alternating moments of terror with humor.

"I always thought of *Jaws* as a comedy," Spielberg said.

Gary Arnold of the *Washington Post* took the film much more seriously and compared *Jaws'* montage of swimmers fleeing the water during the shark attack to the classic Odessa Steps sequence of Sergei Eisenstein's *Battleship Potemkin*, one of the greatest films of all time.

"Spielberg's dynamic sense of movement creates a compelling sense of flight, confusion and anxiety. There has never been an adventure-thriller quite as terrifying yet enjoyable as *Jaws*, and it should set the standard in its field for many years to come," Arnold said in his review.

The studio didn't care about esoteric comparisons to fifty-year-old silent film classics. Sid Sheinberg fell all over himself making outrageous predictions in the ecstasy of the moment. "I want to be the first to predict that Steve will win best director Oscar this year," he proclaimed. Sheinberg had an additional reason to be pleased by Spielberg. The director had found work for Sheinberg's wannabe actress wife. With virtually no acting credits to her name, Lorraine Gary, Mrs. Sid Sheinberg, landed the plum role of Scheider's wife. She would find gainful employment in several *Jaws'* sequels.

Sheinberg described his wife's relationship with the director: "Actors love to work with Steve. The one I'm closest to—Lorraine—would keep walking off a building if Steve told her, 'Keep walking off the building.' Steven listens, which is a very important thing. There are a number of important directors around town who are convinced they know it all. Steve sent drafts of *Jaws'* scripts to a lot of people to get their reactions."

Jaws' phenomenal commercial and critical success drew the inevitable backlash, supporting the maxim, the only thing people like more than putting someone on a pedestal is yanking him off it.

Spielberg was no exception. After *Jaws* grossed $60 million in its first month of release, the *New York Times* said, "There are those, of course, who say that no matter what the *wunderkind* does, he will never again have another supercollossal success like *Jaws*. In other words, they think the kid has peaked."

Even Spielberg was wary of his success. The future director of *E.T.* and *Jurassic Park* accurately and inaccurately predicted, "I don't think I'll ever top *Jaws* commercially. But I define my own peak. The peak of my career will come when I make the best film I ever make. I have the right to determine when I have peaked, and when I've slid the other way."

He also refused to take sole credit for the film's box-office performance. Modestly, he insisted, "You know I should write John Williams a check for *Jaws* and George Lucas should write him one for *Star Wars*. If I'd released *Jaws* without John's music, it would still have done 60 million. Because of his score, it did 115."

Despite or perhaps because of its financial success, *Jaws* started an almost lifelong criticism of his works as being commercial drivel. Spielberg, however, liked commercialism. Harking back to the days when he screened 8 mm films like *Davy Crockett* for the neighborhood kids, Spielberg liked putting fannies in theater seats. He had no tolerance for critics who wanted him to make message movies or character-driven "little" films.

"If I had made *Jaws* a vehicle for an actor, and if I made the picture about the effects of one shark attack on the socio-economic decline of a community that is dependent on summer dollars to avoid winter welfare, I think Dick Zanuck, David Brown and I would have been the only three people to have gone to see that movie. I believe there is a way to combine the acting, the personal things inside a director, with a major entertainment experience."

As the director and his work matured concomitantly, he would prove that thesis in spades—even though it would take him twenty years to completely fulfill his desire to combine the personal and the commercial.

The one thing his early success didn't do was turn him into an outrageous egomaniac. For example, even though he was, in the words of the usually restrained *New York Times*, "the most prized and sought after director in the business," he generously agreed to speak to a film class at UCLA only a few months after *Jaws* had been released.

His demeanor in the small classroom proved that success doesn't go to everybody's head. He showed up wearing his now trademark baseball cap, a flannel shirt, and jeans. There was no entourage of publicist, manager, or personal assistant. Only his friend and confidant, director Brian De Palma, joined him for the UCLA visit.

Not only did he show up, he arrived before the teacher, who was late. The door to the classroom was locked when the first students showed up for class. They were greeted by Spielberg, who was standing in the hallway, patiently waiting to be let into the locked room.

Spielberg told the class how he directed one of *Jaws*' most powerful scenes. It focused on Robert Shaw's character, Quint. For a film that wasn't character-driven, Quint was a colorful, at least two-dimensional character. Next to being swallowed whole by the shark, Shaw's most memorable scene may be the one that contained no action save his chugalugging whisky while he recounts a World War II experience in which his shipmates were devoured by sharks.

As Quint drains his whisky bottle, the story gets more and more colorful. Spielberg confided in the class, "Normally, I don't let actors drink on the set, but for this scene I actually let him swig from a bottle of whisky. He ended up improvising most of his speech. Unfortunately, after about twenty takes, his monologue became unintelligible, and we ended up not using any of the later stuff."

Spielberg was modest about his success and attributed much of it to luck—not dumb luck, but smart luck.

"I don't think I'm a phenomenon at all," he said after *Jaws* hit the jackpot. "I think part of my success at the age of twenty-seven has to do with lucking out! I think a lot of it has to do with being prepared when the man with the money comes to you and says, 'What have you got?' And you fast draw two scripts and three ideas. To go back to the Boy Scouts, the motto was, 'Be prepared.' And when the time came, I had *fifteen* films under my right arm. I had three scripts under my left arm, and I was knocking down doors. It was something I wanted to happen, not when I was thirty or thirty-five years old, when most directors start working, but now. By the age of eighteen I was determined to become a professional movie director."

For all his professed modesty, the young director did have occasional brushes with self-importance. In her memoir, producer Julia Phillips claims that Spielberg and a friend, actor-director

Albert Brooks, roamed New York City in a cab, shooting home movies of the people lined up outside theaters showing *Jaws*.

Phillips, who would have a love-hate relationship with the director when she produced *Close Encounters of the Third Kind*, acidly summed up his self-absorption at the time. "He is so blatant in his excitement for himself that he is adorable. I did not notice for at least a year that this kind of behavior bespeaks a childish self-preoccupation that tends to remove all hope."

Who could really blame him, however, for indulging himself on occasion; after all, he was the hottest property in Hollywood. Fame is a powerful aphrodisiac, in the words of Graham Greene, and Spielberg attracted his share of groupies and female admirers. But things never got out of hand. There were no River Phoenix- or Sean Penn-style revels.

"After *Jaws*, I did cut loose a little. I only went a little bit crazy because I was too busy to become a real hedonist," he said of this heady time.

He did find the time to date a few gorgeous actresses such as Victoria Principal and Sarah Miles, but he insists, "I didn't stop to notice if women were interested in me, or if there was a party that I might have been invited to. I didn't ever take the time to revel in the glory of a successful or money-making film. I didn't stop to enjoy. I never had a chance to sit down and pat myself on the back or spend my money or date or go on vacation in Europe."

Not surprisingly, *Jaws* did make him independently wealthy. He told *Women's Wear Daily* that he cleared $4 million after taxes. But this sudden avalanche of wealth didn't transport him to the ranks of the nouveaux riches. "I live as I did before," he said in the wake of *Jaws'* release. "I have the same house I bought for $49,000 five years ago. And I drive a black and white police car with 10 bullet holes in it that I used in *Sugarland Express*."

Instead of partying with starlets, he immersed himself in the business of making movies, since he had clearly already mastered the technical side of it. "I pretty much hung out with the Brooks Brothers realists," including the late Steve Ross, then chairman of Warner Brothers; Terry Semel, the studio's current chairman; and ICM chief Guy McElwaine, Spielberg's agent for years. "I don't think it made me a Brooks Brothers or a realist, but it gave me a real good primer on the film industry," he said of this early mentoring.

"I remember Guy McElwaine taking me over to Terry Semel's house simply so Terry could sit me down and explain distribution, which I knew nothing about."

(Years later, Spielberg would outshark the movie studios by discarding the standard distribution deal in favor of a new deal that would enrich him and pal George Lucas by hundreds of millions. He was a very good student of Ross and Semel.)

"Terry must have talked for four hours straight. And I was taking notes. At the end of the day I knew more about distribution and exhibition than I ever wanted to," he recalled.

His wooing of McElwaine paid off as well. Shortly before *Jaws'* release, when no one knew for certain what a monster hit it would be, McElwaine renegotiated Spielberg's contract and got him an additional 5 percent of the profits. That little negotiating trick earned Spielberg tens of millions of dollars in excess of the paltry $4 million he claimed in the *Women's Wear Daily* interview. Maybe he feared the IRS might read the fashion-industry trade paper. McElwaine's splendid performance was forgotten years later, however, when Spielberg unceremoniously dumped his longtime agent in favor of the number-one agent in Hollywood, Mike Ovitz, who reportedly wooed Spielberg by offering to take less than the usual 10 percent agent's cut.

A year after *Jaws* made him the man of the moment, he apparently grew tired of dating starlets. He had speculated that he dated actresses because he knew he could never become serious about one. Years after the fact, Spielberg was still smarting from his parents' divorce, and he feared a commitment that would lead to the same painful parting.

By 1976, however, it seemed he wanted to settle down with one actress.

At least that's what happened when Brian De Palma introduced Spielberg to Amy Irving, a frizzy-haired actress who played the high school student with a heart of gold in De Palma's sleeper hit, *Carrie*. They met at a dinner party where De Palma played matchmaker.

De Palma recalled, "I think they're very well suited to one another. I had a feeling Amy and Steven would like each other when I got them together. One night, while we were shooting *Carrie*, a group of us had dinner. Martin Scorsese and his then wife Julia Cameron, Steven, Amy and me. All evening they talked."

Irving had a prestigious pedigree. She was the daughter of actress Priscilla Pointer and actor-director Jules Irving, one of the founding directors of the Lincoln Center Repertory Theater in New York City.

Spielberg compared favorably with her much-loved father. "Like Steven," she said in 1985, "Dad was a wonderful, boyish man, a real hard worker—gifted with a silly sense of humor. And, they both loved me, so they always had that in common."

Both Irving's parents were classy and appreciated the arts. So was their daughter. Spielberg was reportedly "immediately smitten" when De Palma introduced them.

But Spielberg didn't let his heart overwhelm his professional sense. A year after they met, she read for the role of the young mother in *Close Encounters of the Third Kind*. He told her forthrightly that she was too young for the role. (George Lucas had similarly nixed her when she read for the part of Princess Leia in *Star Wars*; Carrie Fisher got the job instead.)

Irving said approvingly of her disappointment, "He doesn't come on to young actresses in his office." And later when they became romantically involved, she added, "And I'm glad."

A year after meeting, they were cohabiting in a modest house in rustic Laurel Canyon, just north of Hollywood.

Irving remembered those early, heady days when she was the consort of the king of Hollywood. "I was living with Steven when he was very successful, and I was just starting out. I was insecure in that situation and wanted to go out and find my career by myself. Also, the L.A. life-style didn't come naturally to me. It wasn't a place that nurtured truth and growth for me."

Their relationship was not made in heaven. The tempestuous pairing broke up in 1980 (in the middle of a prehoneymoon flight to Japan), got back together in 1983, wed two years later, only to divorce four years after that.

The biggest problem in the relationship seems to have been Irving's fiercely competitive spirit. She had grown up being the daughter of "famed director Jules Irving," she once said, and now, her biggest claim to fame was being the girlfriend, then wife, of the most successful director of all time.

"I started my career as the daughter of theater director Jules Irving. I don't want to finish it as the wife of Steven Spielberg," she said ominously while they were still together.

Irving wanted her time in the spotlight, even if it meant taking some of her husband's lighting away.

Spielberg's friend, producer-writer Matthew Robbins, put his finger exactly on what was wrong with the relationship from the start.

"I like Amy a lot," he said, covering his flanks. "But when Steven decided to marry her, I was very worried. It was no fun to go over there because there was an electric tension in the air. It was competitive as to whose dining table this is, whose career we're going to talk about or whether he even approved of what she was interested in, her friends and her life as an actress. He really was uncomfortable. The child in Spielberg believes so thoroughly in the possibility of a perfect marriage, the Norman Rockwell turkey on the table.

"And Amy was sort of a glittering prize, smart as hell, gifted and beautiful, but definitely edgy and provocative and competitive. She would not provide him any ease. There was nothing to go home to that was cozy."

Robbins's insight was hardly a closely held secret. One of the infamous quotes attributed to Irving was a sharp put-down of her husband's entire body of work. "Steven makes terrific films, but they're not *my* kind of films," she once said when asked why she had never starred in any of his movies.

This author personally encountered the jealousy she felt toward her husband when he interviewed her in 1987. At one point during the interview at their Coldwater Canyon home, he asked her what her husband was doing.

"He's in China," she said, offering what seemed like the least bit of information she possibly could. In fact, that's all she offered. When asked what he was doing there, she said, "Why don't you ask him? I don't do PR for Steven."

Ouch!

A magazine story at the time had hailed her and her husband as Hollywood royalty. Sounding jaded, Irving replied, "It doesn't surprise me. I *feel* like Hollywood royalty. Steven is such a power in this town," she said, adding with bitterness, "But I didn't get here on my own. I married into it."

"I've never talked to the press about my personal life with Amy," Spielberg once said, inaccurately. "She talks about it."

But only at gunpoint, apparently.

Indirectly, Spielberg hinted that it wasn't just his future wife's competitiveness that soured the relationship. He suggested that maybe it was his tendency to "direct" the relationship rather than share it that contributed to its problems.

"It's a lot easier for me to commit to a movie than a personal relationship. I often want to direct reality, to direct the scene, to say, 'Stay in your frame. I'll deal with it, but stay there.'"

Ultimately, Irving would be unable to take "direction" from her husband, but that climactic epiphany was years away.

CHAPTER FIVE

Close Encounters of the Fabulous Kind

Spielberg's next film would show that *Jaws* was no fluke. *Close Encounters of the Third Kind* only made half of *Jaws'* take, about $270 million, but it was, well, light years ahead of the earlier film in sophistication and maturity. In fact, *Close Encounters* showed Spielberg could inspire awe, not just terror and thrills.

Jaws had made him rich and famous, but more importantly for the self-effacing, nonmaterialistic director, the box-office success of the film had given him Hollywood's ultimate prize, power. Spielberg suddenly was "bankable." He had the clout to film the Yellow Pages in Esperanto if he wanted.

"The minute that *Jaws* hit, I seized the chance to make a movie I'd wanted to do for years—*Close Encounters*. At the time, my script of it was stalled at Columbia, but I marched in and shook those *Jaws* box-office receipts at them and they gave in. I said, 'I want 12 million to do this picture.' They agreed."

Before *Jaws* turned him into Mr. Bankable, every studio in town had turned down his script for *Close Encounters of the Third Kind*. On the surface, the project had a lot of things going against it. Typical visitors-from-outer-space movies, beginning in the fifties, featured extraterrestrials who were malevolent, bent on enslaving or destroying the planet they were visiting. At the turn of the century, H. G. Welles started the ball rolling with *War of the Worlds*, the ultimate visitors-from-hell/outer-space novel. It's a theme that continues to this day, whether on *Star Trek*'s many reincarnations or other popular television series like *Babylon 5*. Extraterrestrial equals evil is the inevitable equation.

Spielberg begged to differ and offered some impressive statistics: "In thirty years of UFO reportings, the encounters have been very benevolent," he said. "No sci-fi death rays, no radiation poisoning… That's the attitude I take in the picture. I have tried to take interspace relationships out of the science fiction closet and give them an aura of respectability."

As for all that extraterrestrial benevolence, Spielberg must have been unaware of other accounts that detailed invasive surgery and anal probes performed on unwitting humans who claimed to have been spirited aboard UFOs. And if Whitley Streiber's alleged real-life account, *Communion*, about close encounters of the grisly kind, had ever crossed his desk, he might have rethought his script and turned it into a sophisticated version of all those campy death-ray extravaganzas.

But Spielberg had only good feelings for any potential extraterrestrial guests touring Earth. The idea for *Close Encounters* came from one of the few good memories of his relationship with his father. His fascination with the sky began one night when his father woke the six-year-old and drove him to a large meadow to witness a meteor shower. He was hooked.

The studios were also negatively influenced by market research that said UFOs were a big snooze as far as the public was concerned. "They tested the concept of *Close Encounters*," Spielberg remembered. "I couldn't believe it. The response was negative. They said I'd better have a lot of sex and sensationalism in it or I'd be in real trouble. But a picture's never succeeded on market research yet. It's still the picture-maker's passion."

The studio executives, however, had ignored an important statistic that showed the film's concept had a built-in audience of millions. According to a Gallup Poll at the time, fifteen million Americans, including the then President of the United States,

Jimmy Carter, claimed to have had some kind of UFO experience. The same poll indicated that 52 percent of the American public believed in UFOs and that they came from outer space.

Spielberg himself was a believer, although to his great regret he wasn't one of the fifteen million who had had a close encounter of any kind with a UFO. "I believe in the UFO phenomenon, yes. Whether I believe that UFOs are of extraterrestrial origin, well, the jury's still out. I would like to believe the hundreds of thousands of people from all over the world have not been hallucinating for three thousand years."

The first draft of the script, which never got made, was written by Paul Schrader, the theology-obsessed writer-director of such ham-handed morality tales as *Hardcore* and *American Gigolo*.

Raised in a strict Protestant sect, Schrader wanted to graft the story of Saint Paul onto a visitors-from-outer-space story. In Schrader's version, his hero Paul Van Owen (after Saint Paul) is an Air Force officer assigned the task of disproving the existence of UFOs. Eventually, this doubting Thomas not only sees a UFO but is abducted by one and whisked away from the earth. The climactic scene re-creates the famous Biblical passage where Paul is knocked off his horse by God and only then becomes a believer. In Schrader's script, God is replaced by extraterrestrials.

The Schrader script was so off-putting, *Close Encounters'* producer Julia Phillips wrote in her acerbic memoir that she didn't even show it to David Begelman, then head of production at Columbia. She wrote that Begelman "has agreed not to read Schrader's first draft, called *Kingdom Come*, because I told him it would make him not want to make the movie. Certainly it was not a screenplay that Steven wanted to direct."

Julia Phillips had only herself—and her husband Michael— to blame for the gobbledygook that Schrader made of the *Close Encounters* script. The husband and wife team had had such a good relationship with Schrader on *The Taxi Driver*, which Schrader wrote and they produced for Martin Scorsese, that Phillips felt he would be perfect for *Close Encounters*. Schrader explained their reasoning, which turned out to be way off base: "They felt that my sensibility, being extremely Germanic and moralistic, was the proper counterpoint to Steve's sensibility," Schrader said.

In fact, Spielberg hated the script, finding Schrader's injection of Calvinist theology laughable in what the director basically envisioned as an A-budget B-movie. The usually diplomatic director even was quoted as describing Schrader's effort as "one of the most embarrassing screenplays ever professionally turned into a major studio or director. Actually, it was fortunate that Paul went so far away on his own tangent, a terribly guilt-ridden story, not about UFOs at all, it was more about the Church and the State and it was. . . horrendous. Absolutely horrendous."

The departure point for Schrader's script was a short story called "Experiences," written in 1970 by Spielberg when he was still a television director. Spielberg's concept was to combine a UFO encounter and a massive Watergate-style cover-up of the sighting. Schrader must have found some comfort in the fact that he did convince Spielberg to junk the Watergate cover-up plot and focus more on the mystical encounter with the spaceship. "The only thing I deserve a credit for is changing Steve's mind about doing the film as a UFO Watergate. I thought it ought to be about a spiritual encounter. That idea stayed and germinated," Schrader told author Tony Crowley in 1983.

Phillips also credited Schrader with creating the Dreyfuss character. However, Spielberg had otherwise so thoroughly rejected Schrader's script that the writer didn't even protest to the Writers Guild's arbitration panel when his name was left off the "screenplay by" or "story by" credits.

Spielberg received solo writing credit on the film, and his version bore no resemblance to Schrader's theological gobbledygook. Hard work must have made it so. Spielberg had been obsessed with writing his own version of an encounter with extraterrestrials. Over a two-year period, he churned out six different versions of the story until he finally was satisfied enough to shout "Action."

Besides dumping Schrader, Spielberg also made quick work of another collaborator, Verna Fields, who had provided *Jaws*' Oscar-winning editing. In a rare snit of jealousy, Spielberg reportedly was angry that the maternal Fields had taken so much credit for the success of *his* film. Fields was supposed to be promoted on *Close Encounters*, with the title of associate producer. Julia Phillips later claimed the director told her "to get rid of her." Phillips did.

Spielberg wasn't that bullish on Richard Dreyfuss, either. The director was angry that the actor was demanding 5 percent of the film's gross. Spielberg was intent on limiting gross participation to himself and the film's two producers, Phillips and her husband Michael.

Spielberg was "pissed about Richard allowing [his agent] to do this to us. Livid in fact. He said he was pissed about the injustice, but it was really the money," Phillips recalled.

So Spielberg offered the role that Dreyfuss eventually made his own to Jack Nicholson, Gene Hackman, and Al Pacino—and they all turned him down. Nicholson complained that the special effects were the star of the film. The imperious actor even refused to meet with Spielberg to discuss the role. Hackman didn't want to work on a film that would take him away from home for four months. Pacino passed, it was rumored, because his manager had a personal vendetta against the head of Columbia.

The head of Columbia, David Begelman, suggested James Caan, who agreed to take on the job, but demanded a million dollars up front and 10 percent of the gross, more than twice the profit participation Dreyfuss was demanding. By now, Dreyfuss was beginning to sound like a bargain. Eventually, Phillips sweet-talked the actor into taking less money.

"We don't mind you making a lot of money, but you ain't making more money than us," Phillips told Dreyfuss, who eventually agreed to forgo *all* gross participation.

An interesting bit of trivia: Meryl Streep, not yet the major talent, actually *auditioned* for the role of Dreyfuss's wife. Although she wasn't a big star yet, her presence was so intimidating that when she sat down to read for the part, both Spielberg and Dreyfuss unconsciously moved their chairs away from hers. Teri Garr ultimately landed the role.

Richard Dreyfuss played an electrical worker who has a close encounter of the third kind with an extraterrestrial spaceship. (The first kind is seeing a UFO. The second kind is finding evidence left behind after a sighting. The movie's third category is actually making physical contact.) The experience literally marks Dreyfuss's Roy Neary, giving him a radiation burn on his face and turning him into a man obsessed with traveling to a spot in the Rockies where the mother ship will eventually land.

Along the way, the extraterrestrials, who aren't completely benevolent, snatch an adorable four-year-old boy, played by Cary Guffey, from his mother's arms (Melinda Dillon). By film's end, it's made clear that they simply want to study the child, and the extraterrestrials do return the kid, but not until the poor woman is nearly driven out of her mind searching for him.

Logistically, *Close Encounters* made *Jaws* look like a day at the beach, without the obnoxious fish. After filming finally was completed, Spielberg would say with a sigh, "*Close Encounters* was the most draining ordeal I ever went through. The feedback is like Chinese water torture, one drop on the forehead at a time, evenly spaced five seconds apart."

The king of special effects would have been happy to abdicate. After one too many instances of Chinese water torture, he said, "Right now, I would take 100 child actors, ten canines, fifteen senile actors and four impossible movie stars over another day with special effects. I swear it. The next UFO I want to see is the one that sits down in my backyard and takes me on an all-expense-paid trip to the Virgin Islands."

Spielberg had a right to be exhausted. Although filming only took five months, another year was devoted to editing and wrestling all those optical effects onto celluloid. More than 350 special effects were employed, and Spielberg insisted on an obsessive secrecy to avoid any quick-buck television movie rip-offs of the film's concept.

In retrospect, Spielberg decided that the trauma was worth it. After his special effects' nightmare had been forgotten or at least repressed, he would say, "I could make *Jaws* every year if I really wanted to. I'm interested, however, in testing other facets of myself. *Jaws* is a movie I could have played on a toy xylophone, but *Close Encounters* made me stretch farther. It required all eighty-eight keys. When you take a dipstick and you measure *Close Encounters* against *Jaws* from an artistic standpoint, *Jaws* is half a pint, and *Close Encounters* is two quarts."

In what might be a fitting epigraph to his entire career, he underlined the importance of constantly challenging himself, even if the challenge involved a lot of suffering and pain.

"If one is to grow bigger in any career," he said after *Close Encounters* wrapped, "you should always undertake something which is a bigger challenge than anything you've done before."

Close Encounters was shot on location in Wyoming; on the world's largest soundstage in Mobile, Alabama; and in Bombay! The India sequence takes only a few seconds of the film, but it is one of the most powerful and doesn't involve any special effects. A giant crowd is asked in subtitled Hindi where the UFO sighting originated, and a thousand hands, accompanied by a thunderous shout, all point up to the sky at once.

The Alabama soundstage was located in a hangar that normally housed dirigibles. The set was six times bigger than anything ever built. Spielberg actually had to enlarge the original 450-foot hangar by 150 feet. It took four months to build the set which used ten miles of lumber, three miles of steel scaffolding, 29,000 feet of nylon for a canopy, two miles of steel cable, 885 cubic yards of concrete fill—more than enough to build a duplicate of the Washington Monument—7,000 cubic yards of sand and clay fill, 150 tons of air-conditioning equipment—enough to cool thirty large homes. The air conditioning was installed after the crew complained to Spielberg about the swampy southern heat. Spielberg, the man who had the biggest money-maker in history under his belt, simply had to pick up the phone to get the money men at Columbia to say, go ahead, air-condition the place.

The cost of building what was simulated in the movie would have been $400 million. The electronic equipment alone, if it had been purchased new, would have cost $100 million. To run all the high-tech equipment required 42 million killowatts, enough power to run the electrical appliances in 500 homes. After the film wrapped, the crew spent an entire month just tearing down the set.

Julia Phillips said, "You can see why the budget kept going up and up."

Despite all the hardware, Spielberg, the writer, insisted that character—not high tech—ultimately would sell his movie.

"If the Dreyfuss character doesn't work and the audience is not interested in the last thirty-eight minutes, I could have done four years of special effects, and it wouldn't have meant diddly. Like the human story in *Jaws*. If those people hadn't worked out, the shark could have bitten all their heads off and you wouldn't have given a damn."

Spielberg didn't ignore the technical aspects. In fact, he drove the crew crazy with his constant tinkering. Dreyfuss recalled, "He'd suddenly get an idea. He'd wander casually on to the set and say, 'Hey, why don't we just turn the shot around and do it again?' Something which gave the crew mild heart seizure. They'd say, 'No, please, that side isn't even built yet . . . .' Then they'd say, 'Jesus, he's right. It *is* a better idea.'" Spielberg continued to tinker with the film until only days before it opened.

Casting the film allowed the director to indulge in what might be called groupie behavior. A huge admirer of French film director Francois Truffaut, Spielberg one night on impulse picked up the phone and called the director in Paris. He asked him to play a bit part as the scientist, M. Lacomb, who acts as the intermediary between the UFO sighters and the inhabitants of the UFO. It's a nothing part that could have been played by any character actor. Spielberg offering the role to one of the greatest directors of all time suggests he simply wanted to work with his idol.

They spent all of five minutes on the phone. Truffaut mulled over the offer for a week, then agreed—for a curious reason. "He sent a telegram saying he wanted to work with [producer] Julia Phillips whom he had admired in her black dress when she picked up the Oscar for *The Sting*." It seemed that Truffaut was something of a groupie himself.

Spielberg later would describe their collaboration in reverent tones. "Directing Francois Truffaut was not only a humbling experience, but one of the great highs of my life. His acting is effortless because he prefers to play closer to his own personality, which is why I cast him in the first place."

Actually, Spielberg wrote the role with Truffaut in mind, never thinking the director would agree to do a bit part.

Truffaut, the consummate artist, was impressed with Spielberg's ability as a field commander. The French director told

Newsweek admiringly, "We had 250 people on the crew in Alabama. When I direct a film I have a maximum of 30 people on the set."

Truffaut was not so kind toward the film's producer, Julia Phillips, calling her "incompetent" in a *New York Times* interview. In her autobiography, she returned the compliment by saying, "Of all the dead people I know, Francois Truffaut wins the prick award hands down."

Ever loyal, Spielberg defended Phillips, even though she later said many unkind things about him in her memoir. Even so, Spielberg wrote the *Times* a letter to the editor, insisting: "I've never had such constructive and consistent support from a producer as I have had from Julia Phillips."

Elsewhere, he was even more effusive about her contribution to the project. "Let me be one of the first directors to say that I need a good producer. I need a confessor, a cop, a bank robber, and I need a buddy. I can't get it from myself because I don't have the time. I go full out on the script, directing, cutting, dubbing and now the actual selling [giving interviews] of the film. Both Michael [Phillips] and Julia were like the front four of the Minnesota Vikings. There was none of that, 'Hey, baby! Time's money.'"

Spielberg compared Phillips to a linebacker, but she was also a big cheerleader for her boss. At times, she had more confidence in him than he had in himself. The director remembers one scary meeting where Phillips made all sorts of outlandish claims that would nevertheless come true.

"My worst moment occurred at an early production meeting when my producer, Julia Phillips, announced to the studio chiefs that this movie would earn more than $100 million. I couldn't believe what I was hearing. She actually predicted $100 million in revenues and was putting both our reputations on the line." Phillips' prediction turned out to be conservative: the film made more than a quarter billion dollars.

A deeply caring person, Spielberg felt guilty about the way he treated another actor on the set, four-year-old Cary Guffey, the tow-headed tot who gets sucked out of Melinda Dillon's kitchen by a UFO tractor beam.

"I had to do an awful thing to get that last shot," Spielberg said, referring to the scene where the child sadly waves good-bye to the mother ship. "I told Cary that the movie was finished, and he wasn't going to see any of his new friends anymore."

Just call him "Director Dearest."

Although *Close Encounters* was the ultimate special effects extravaganza, it was also autobiographical to some extent. Spielberg's *Jaws* star, Roy Scheider, explained, "You remember that kid in *Close Encounters*, looking upwards to the spaceship with its light on his face and wonder in his eyes? That kid is really Steven. That kid made *Jaws*. That enthusiasm, that need to do everything on the technical side. Nobody seemed to mind or think of it as interfering. Because that enthusiasm is catching; it's the enthusiasm of a kid."

Scheider wasn't the first—or the last—to compare the director to Peter Pan.

The release of the film was a nail-biter. Columbia had spent a then whopping $18 million on the film, $10 million over its original budget. Rumors in the press and a disastrous sneak preview caused the studio's stock to fluctuate wildly before the film's release.

Based on rumor rather than a screening of the film, *New York* magazine's financial analyst William Flanagan predicted *Close Encounters* would be a "collossal flop."

When the film finally premiered in November 1977, a handful of critics agreed. *Vogue* called the film "preposterous, trivial, simple-minded, shallow and steeped in pretension."

The majority opinion, however, summarized by the *New Republic*'s Stanley Kauffmann, hailed it as "breathtaking, stunning, dazzling, moving and brilliant." Kauffmann, who had hated *Jaws*, confessed that he was so "happily engulfed" by the film's "dazzling epiphany" that he "just didn't want to leave this picture. It was one of the most overpowering, sheerly cinematic experiences I can remember." Other critics gave it what in Spielberg's estimation was the ultimate accolade, calling the film, "Disney-esque." In fact, Spielberg originally planned to end the film with "When You Wish Upon a Star," Jimminy Crickett's signature song, but even he ultimately decided that including the theme song from a fantasy cartoon like *Pinocchio* would undercut *Close Encounters*' realism.

He explained his decision by saying, "The song was the coat hanger on which I designed the movie three years ago, but it didn't work. It seemed to make a comment that the story you had just seen had been a fantasy. It seemed to belie all the effort that went into trying to shed some verisimilitude on the UFO phenomenon. The song was an overstatement of innocence."

Which led Richard Dreyfuss to comment on "When You Wish Upon a Star": If you ever need an insight into Steven, that song is it." Spielberg bristled at a few critics who called *Close Encounters* "*Star Wars* with soul."

He insisted that the two films were "quite dissimilar. *Close Encounters* is an earthbound movie. Its roots are in the familiar routine of suburban life. *Star Wars* is a beautiful, enchanting space opera—a fantasy. . . . I want people to walk out of *Close Encounters* with more questions than they had when they walked in. I want them to consider the possibility that we are not alone in the universe, that the stars are not simply a kind of nocturnal wallpaper to be viewed indifferently. People should enjoy looking up at night, exercising their imagination a little more."

In effect, Spielberg wanted his thoughtful reverie to be taken more seriously than the Saturday-matinee hijinks of *Star Wars*. "UFOs for me represent a cultural phenomenon rather than a fantasy one. Whether they're real or not real, they have certainly affected everybody's life," he said.

On the other hand, he didn't want his audience to feel he was lecturing rather than entertaining. "This movie is not a didactic trip concerning projects involving UFO-ology. It's not a documentary. I didn't want to be smart-assed. I wanted a *drama* about UFOs over American suburbia—UFOs as seen by ordinary people. It's domestic. This is not *Star Trek*, it's not *Flash Gordon*. It's not even *2001*."

Even more encouraging than the critical praise, especially for Columbia's nervous stockholders, was the reaction of the public, which patronized the film to the tune of $269 million.

Again, box-office clout allowed Spielberg to indulge himself. Originally, he had asked the studio for more funds to shoot additional footage. He was summarily turned down. Prerelease, there were just too many rumors that Columbia had a studio-wrecking disaster on its hands. The term most often thrown around was "Cleopatra," which had almost bankrupted another studio.

After *Close Encounters* cleaned up at the box office, the studio virtually handed Spielberg its checkbook and said, "Go have fun."

He did.

In 1979, Spielberg announced his plans to tinker with a film that was already considered an instant classic: "I will shoot some new scenes—from the original script. They were scenes I couldn't afford to shoot. I was unable to convince Columbia to OK them because of budgetary reasons."

Two years later, the studio released *Close Encounters—The Special Edition*, which picked up where the original left off and took the moviegoer inside the UFO.

As the extra footage showed, his conception of extraterrestrial technology was more spiritual than gadget-driven. The interior of the spaceship, many stories high, resembled, in one critic's words, "a cathedral rather than a humming spaceship filled with knobs and electrodes."

That little bit of extra footage earned Columbia an additional $50 million when the film was re-released.

Close Encounters earned rave reviews. A second version earned the studio even more money. Its box-office take even helped the studio's position when it was sold to Coca-Cola the following year. And the film proved that Spielberg was not a one-trick pony, that *Jaws* was not a fluke.

He was a director with staying power.

He would need all of his staying power to help him weather his next film, which would be the biggest disaster of his career, up to that time and afterwards.

CHAPTER SIX

Pearl Harbor

Steve loves the challenge of doing big jumbo-jet pictures. He thrives on the kind of movies that require terrific planning and perfect execution.
—director and pal, John Milius

O N FEBRUARY 23, 1942, A JAPANESE SUBMARINE surfaced off the coast of Santa Barbara and fired twenty-five shells at the Richfield oil refinery. All twenty-five of the missiles missed their intended target, the huge oil storage tanks, and did only minor damage to the surrounding area. The submarine had an airplane hangar on its rear deck, from which was launched a surveillance plane that flew over Los Angeles two nights later.

After the oil refinery bombing, Los Angeles was in a panic. When the harmless surveillance plane appeared, the city went into overdrive. Antiaircraft batteries began strafing the sky. Civil defense air raid wardens shot out porch lights and even neon signs. The local army depot demanded the return of all the weapons it had loaned to Paramount Pictures for a war picture. Eight hours of chaos, including street riots, ensued.

Two USC film students, Bob Zemeckis and Bob Gale, learned about this historical event while looking through old Los Angeles newspaper clips at the university's library. They used the incident from the days just after the hysteria engendered by Pearl Harbor as the springboard for an over-the-top comedy about an imagined Japanese attack on Los Angeles.

It was called *1941*.

A comedy that sounded like a mainland version of the tragic Pearl Harbor attack sounds like a high concept from hell, and the film would prove hellish for its director, Steven Spielberg.

Somehow, this unlikely script found its way into the hands of Spielberg's buddy, writer-director John Milius (*Apocalypse Now*). But Milius decided to direct the surf and turf epic *Big Wednesday* and passed the script of *1941* on to his buddy.

Spielberg recalled the very moment his ill-fated association with the film began. "John got the kids [Gale and Zemeckis, who later would direct *Forrest Gump*] to bring me the script, and they caught me at a weak moment. I was in the middle of editing *Close Encounters* and in a mood to be cheered up. They cheered me up all right. Reading the screenplay was about as tasteful an experience as reading *Mad* magazine. But the immediate spirit of heightened comic fantasy grabbed me. Besides, I always wanted to do a comedy like *Hellzapoppin*, which I must have watched 100 times on television late-night movies when I was a kid."

The director immediately found a historical reference to another incident of American paranoia, a subject that had always intrigued him, whether it was fear of fish in the water or aliens in the sky.

The script for *1941* recaptured a moment, he said, "when we all lost our minds, thought we were being invaded by Japanese commandos, spent every last bullet shooting at clouds for eight hours straight. It's much like the Orson Welles broacast of *The War of the Worlds* in 1938, except it really happened in Los Angeles."

But verisimilitude does not necessarily translate into good film subject matter.

The bottom line was that the script, however tasteless, reduced him to giggles. "Whatever it is, it's the craziest son-of-a-bitch film I've ever been involved with. I just laughed myself sick," he said.

More ominously, he added, "It's a real risk for me because it's not the linear story form that I'm used to working with."

MGM owned the rights to the script, but Spielberg didn't want to work for the studio. So he took the script to Universal where, as part of his *Jaws* deal, he was still obligated to direct one more film for the studio.

Despite the box-office performance of *Jaws*, Universal balked at the cost of making the film, about $20 million. Encouraged by the dailies on *Close Encounters*, which Spielberg was in the process of editing, Columbia agreed to cofinance the production in partnership with Universal.

The film was a go. And it would almost be a goner for the director's career.

Spielberg hadn't become the hottest, savviest director in Hollywood for nothing. From the beginning of *1941*, an inner voice, the same one that had told him to make *Jaws* and *Close Encounters*, was screaming at him, "Don't make this movie!"

Prophetically, he said before filming began, "Comedy is not my forte. I don't know how this movie will come out. And yes, I'm scared! I'm like the cowardly lion, and two successes back to back have not strengthened my belief in my ability to deliver."

The director didn't listen to the inner voice saying beware. He must have been desperate to lighten things up after the heavy lifting of *Close Encounters* and its logistical nightmares.

"I kept saying to myself from the first day, 'This is not a Spielberg movie. What am I doing here?'" he later realized with the benefit of twenty-twenty hindsight.

"Then I'd get hooked on the utter craziness of the characters, like John Belushi's mad aviator who was obsessed with being the first pilot to shoot down a Japanese Zero [plane] over the continental U.S. Compared to what Belushi does in *1941*, his role in *Animal House* makes him look like the dean of students at Harvard.

"Then I'd backtrack and say to myself, 'John Milius should be directing this picture.' John is Hemingwayesque, with a little touch of Genghis Khan, which I am not."

The film was so decidedly over the top that Spielberg jokingly considered changing the title to *Apocalypse Then*.

His suspicion that he should not be directing *1941* is especially signficant because of when he came to this realization. Spielberg already was bad-mouthing his baby *before* it was released. His golden gut, which had reshaped the *Jaws* novel and written *Close Encounters*, hadn't totally deserted him with *1941*. It had just been delayed. He hadn't realized what a deep hole he had stepped into until it was too late to back out.

He was having second thoughts even before the film went into postproduction. He accurately predicted, "This is either going to be another great white shark—or on the other hand it may turn out to be a great white elephant." On another occasion, he predicted that *1941* could be his personal Moby Dick, "my great white whale."

The movie seemed doomed from the start. War hysteria and paranoia were not felicitous inspirations for a comedy. And matters only seemed to get worse. The original budget, which had terrified Universal at a mere $20 million, ballooned to $30 or $40 million, depending on which newspaper account you read. (Spielberg would claim it only went $7 million over budget. He angrily retorted, "It's not enough that you fall from the twenty-seventh floor here. They want to put you up on the fortieth floor before they push you off. I bring in this picture close to budget at $26.5 million, and yet I keep reading that I overspent up to $40 million. Is it that people prefer to see a 747 crash rather than a DC-3?")

Look magazine gleefully reported, "*1941* is fast becoming the most expensive movie of all time. With only three fourths of the film finished, its costs have already reached the $40 million mark—approaching *King Kong* and *Apocalpyse Now*."

Anticipating the furor and indignation that would over-whelm director Michael Cimino and another runaway epic, *Heaven's Gate*, a year later, *Look* enumerated the excesses that were turning *1941* into Spielberg's personal Pearl Harbor.

The magazine claimed that for one scene in which a plane crashed into Hollywood Boulevard, the sequence had to be reshot three times, with each crash costing $1 million, an improbability since miniatures were used. Another scene, in which thousands of Mexican and Japanese extras appeared, erupted into a real-life riot. The damage caused by the riot cost thousands of dollars and sent the film's stars, Dan Aykroyd and John Belushi, "fleeing for cover," per *Look*.

People magazine couldn't resist an additional dig: "In 1979, the prodigy became a prodigal with *1941*."

Spielberg was infuriated by all this Monday-morning quarterbacking. He felt that much of the negative press coverage obsessing over the cost of the film was based on ignorance.

"When I hear criticism about the big budget of *1941*, I want to ask, 'How do you know? You weren't there. Were you the producer? Do you know how many tanks and cars were needed in *1941*? Do you know we actually used fewer than the script required, and the budget still came out to $30 million?'"

Despite the incendiary nature of the film, one critic noticed that *1941* was strangely sympathetic to its Japanese characters.

Typically, Spielberg was willing to take the blame for the film's failure. "It was the most expensive situation comedy ever conceived. The film essentially missed because it was overdone. It went from a small pepper steak to a burned Chateaubriand. I tried hard to season it and wound up killing the taste."

He was philosophical about its failure, adding glumly, "If we don't take chances, we never learn how to fail."

But still, all the barbs hurt. Because *Jaws* and *Close Encounters* had been such runaway hits, he felt the critics and envious colleagues were gleefully waiting for him to fall flat on his face. "They are just waiting in ambush to tear me apart," he said with atypical paranoia. Some of the criticism was so harsh, his paranoia may have been justified. As Henry Kissinger once said, "Even paranoid people have enemies."

"Making a so-called funny movie is a misery," Spielberg lamented. Then, anticipating another ill-received film of his, *The Color Purple*, he added, "What would really hurt is if I made a very personal movie like *Annie Hall* and people stomped on me. Maybe *1941* will bomb, but it would kill me if I made a movie that said to people, 'This is who I am,' and then they hooted and jeered." Spielberg would have to wait six years for this personal nightmare to come true when his intensely personal film, *The Color Purple*, was reviled by the critics.

Although the normally gentle *Los Angeles Times* called *1941* "Spielberg's Pearl Harbor" and the usually kind *Daily Variety* called the film his "first disaster," the commercial failure of *1941* was more perception than reality.

When the film was released, it was estimated that it would

need to earn $70 million, a huge figure in those preinflation, pre-*Jurassic Park* days, just to break even. An examination of *Variety's* box-office totals for 1979 through 1980 shows that *1941* ended up grossing $90 million. That wasn't *Jaws-* or *Close Encounters*-scale business, but at least *1941* didn't lose money for Columbia and Universal.

Spielberg showed himself to be a savvy bean counter. Rather than be overwhelmed by all the criticism of his film's perceived commercial failure, he calmly looked at the bottom line and pronounced himself—and his film—a winner. "We need $60 million to get into the black, and we're about $11 million short," he said after the end of its theatrical run. "But based on TV, cassette, cable and reissue money, Universal is confident the film will make that $11 million.

"Still, the critics bury their heads in the sand and say, 'How could this film do $50 to $60 million when I gave it the worst review I've ever written?'"

As for *1941's* then extravagant budget, he added tersely, "Believe me, Hollywood is not being crippled by $30 million movies."

The real problem of *1941's* perceived failure was one of expectation. The two studios—and the public—had had such high hopes for the film, based on the director's last two tours de force. The combined take of *Jaws* and *Close Encounters*, by the time *1941* premiered, had grown to two-thirds of a billion dollars worldwide, more than the combined film revenues of Universal and Columbia for all its releases in 1979.

Both studios treated its golden boy shabbily. The November 6 charity premiere at the Medallion Theater in Dallas was abruptly cancelled. Studio executives leaked to the press that they were "panicky" and "nervous" about the results of several sneak previews held before the scheduled premiere.

Universal went so far as to publicly bad-mouth the film after one sneak. Spielberg was furious over this betrayal by the studio he had enriched with the biggest money-maker of all times, *Jaws*. He must have been feeling the awful truth of the old adage, you're only as good as your last picture.

Asked what lesson he had learned from the disastrous sneak previews, he tartly replied, "I learned not to invite Universal and Columbia executives and salespeople to previews any more. Let them stay home and watch *Laverne & Shirley* on TV."

Spielberg rejected the whole notion of relying on a small preview audience to predict a film's box-office performance, which was disingenuous, since he has used sneaks for just that purpose to this day. "Who needs them?" he said. "This preview was for me— to analyze and correct my mistakes, as I always do. But they dragged in a computer-selected audience with a lot of staid older people rather than the younger *Saturday Night Live* crowd this film is aimed at."

Spielberg took issue with the composition of the preview audience, but the preview audience was specifically made up of people aged twelve to forty-nine. The director insisted that composition "did not accurately reflect the probable audience for *1941*." Who then? Tots and senior citizens? "I expected the audience to be younger and more cosmopolitan, the same audience that responded to *National Lampoon's Animal House*." Cosmopolitan? *Animal House*?

As much as he hated sneak previews when they were unfavorable, he still found them a necessary evil. He told *Daily Variety*, in another fit of self-delusion, "It was a very good preview. I use a preview as much as I use a movie camera. It's a process of trial and error to make the film work in the best way possible."

Never one to lick his wounds, he used the audience comment cards to fix his film. "I jettisoned, repositioned and tightened scenes from the first forty-five minutes of *1941*, the part of the film most viewers said caused the most consternation. The first forty-five minutes were very expository, and there was some restlessness and lack of laughs. My job right now is to fix those forty-five minutes. Other than that, the film is what it is." (The biggest embarrassment of his career.)

Spielberg was so furious with Universal's public criticism that he did not make another film for the studio for three years, although when he finally did return, he rewarded them with a monster hit that knocked *Jaws* out of first place, *E.T.*

Columbia was more savvy. Frank Price, then head of production for the studio, apparently felt *1941* was a fluke, a bad fluke, and that Spielberg's next film could very well be another huge hit. (Price was right. Unfortunately for Price, Spielberg would make *Raiders of the Lost Ark* for another studio.) With Spielberg's track record in mind, the day after the disastrous sneak preview in Dallas, Price was quoted in the trades saying, "I loved *1941*."

Years later, with a slew of hits under his belt, Spielberg could be less defensive and more philosophical about his one and only genuine screen embarrassment. "*1941* is a film I look at fondly, but when it was released it was like the critics thought I was Adolf Eichmann. They were that tough on me. Until then I thought I was immune to failure. But I couldn't come down from the power high of making big films on large canvases. I threw everything in, and it killed the soup. *1941* was my encounter with economic reality. I'll spend the rest of my life disowning this movie. I definitely feel that the film has now reached the highest level of its incompetence."

The director had come face to face with the Peter Principle.

In hindsight and with the benefit of maturity, Spielberg was even ready to concede that his own ego had propelled *1941*'s excesses: "I should have done *E.T.* right after *Close Encounters*," he admitted years later. "But I had just finished this giant film [*Close Encounters*], and I was in a giant frame of mind. I wanted to do a little film, an intimate film. They said, 'Anyone can make a little film. We want you to make big films.' It was capricious of me, but I agreed. The budget on *1941* went from $15 million to $26 million. We would have been better off with $10 million less, because we went from one plot to seven subplots. But at the time, I wanted it—the bigness, the power, hundreds of people at my beck and call, millions of dollars at my disposal, and everybody saying, 'Yes, yes, yes!' I plunged into *1941* with such wild abandon that I didn't really focus on the story I was telling. On about the 145th day of shooting I realized that the film was directing me. And finally it just outgrew its Calvins and became this great white elephant. *1941* was my 'Little General' period."

Spielberg tried to hide his disappointment with gallows humor, but the pain showed through despite the gags. "I'm like a ballplayer who finally ends his hitting streak. I'm supposed to feel relieved. Anybody have a pistol I can borrow?" he said. He waited an entire year before reading the scathing reviews of *1941*. But even so, "friends" called to tell him what the critics had to say about his flop.

Not everyone felt that Spielberg had committed the cinematic equivalent of a war crime.

David Denby in *New York* magazine wrote glowingly, "He's made a celebration of the gung-ho silliness of old war movies, a celebration of the Betty Grable-Betty Hutton period of American pop culture. In this movie, America is still a very young country—foolish, violent, casually destructive, but not venal. That we joke about a moment of national crisis shows that we are still young—and sane."

The only problem was that very few people seemed in on the joke.

The turn of the decade, from 1979 to 1980, was not a good time for what Spielberg called, with typical self-deprecation, his "mousepack," a reference to Frank Sinatra's more famous ratpack. The Spielberg mousepack consisted of friends and colleagues who would swap scripts with one another and even do free rewrites. It was an off-campus group of film students whose continuing education extended beyond their college years and lasted a lifetime.

Martin Scorsese, John Milius, Brian De Palma, George Lucas, Michael Cimino, Francis Ford Coppola, and John Landis were the most famous members of the pack. Lucas, Coppola, and Spielberg would screen each other's film in rough cut, exchange profit participation points, and trade ideas back and forth. As one critic said at the time, "Not since the German migration to Hollywood in the '30s has there been such a group of filmmakers unified by age, upbringing and taste."

By the end of this decade, pundits were saying the mousepack should crawl back into its rathole.

Cimino had the most embarrassing fiasco, an out-of-control Western called *Heaven's Gate* that was hell for United Artists, which went bankrupt in the film's red ink. Coppola earned good reviews but failed to turn a profit with his expensive *Apocalypse Now*, which cost a million more than *1941*. John Landis, borrowing Spielberg's *1941* star, John Belushi, flopped with his $30 million *Blues Brothers*, despite a platinum-selling soundtrack.

The *Saturday Review* accused them of creating "movies that tarnished their makers' glory and prompted accusations of excess and self-indulgence."

There's an old but inaccurate saying in Hollywood: You're only as good as your last picture. Actually, the studios will give a star or a director several chances to fall flat on his face before consigning him to television movies—or in the case of actresses, supporting roles as nurturing mothers. (See Sally Field's career.)

At this point in Spielberg's career, it was too soon to compose a eulogy. RIP *1941*. He wasn't just as good as his last picture, a certifiable bomb. He was also as good as his previous two megahits, *Close Encounters* and *Jaws*. By Hollywood's loose rules, Spielberg would be allowed to make a few more *1941*-scale bombs before being forced to return to the living graveyard of feature film directors, episodic television.

"There was a sort of watchful waiting as far as Steven's career was concerned at the time," says a former studio executive who was active in the business at the time. "Most people at the studios were willing to consider *1941* an aberration. How could the creator of such transcendent images as the descending mother ship or eye-covering scares of a bulimic shark turn out such dreck as John Belushi belching for laughs?

"He wasn't even down for the count by this time, but another embarrassment would have been a TKO, and if it was followed by another witless comedy he would have been kayoed to Palookaville, which at the time was another name for *The Love Boat* or *The Dukes of Hazzard*. That's a scary thought, isn't it? Steven Spielberg directing Luke and Bo Duke in rough terrain car chases?"

Of all the mouses in the pack, Steven Spielberg would make the quickest recovery. After *1941*, he'd be back on top within a year—and stay there for the next fifteen!

The ultimate fates of the rest of the mousepacketeers are paradoxical. It's not surprising that Spielberg, a master showman, would survive a setback like *1941* and triumph with box-office hits. But the enduring success of another mousepack member was not so easy to predict back in the late seventies. Among serious connoisseurs of filmmaking, Martin Scorsese is considered the greatest artist of the mousepack. Although Spielberg has one undeniable masterpiece under his belt, Scorsese seems to crank one out every other year or so. Just when you think he's stuck in a rut with one too many examinations of Italian-American gangsters, he treats us to a costume drama, *The Age of Innocence*, with nary a Mafioso among its intriguing characters. The same director who elicited grotesque humor from Robert De Niro chopping up an adversary and stowing him in a car trunk in *Goodfellas* was just as adept at dissecting the social eviscerations of New York City's haute monde circa 1870.

The other members of the mousepack didn't have such happy follow-up stories to their once promising careers.

After his art house movie about the Vietnam War, *The Deerhunter*, Michael Cimino tried to go mainstream with middle-brow thrillers like *The Desperate Hours* and *Godfather*-style ripoffs like *The Sicilian*. These days Cimino is more famous for the films he doesn't make than those he does. Blurbs in the trades always seem to be announcing a film to be "helmed" by Michael Cimino that never gets made. A notorious perfectionist, Cimino has virtually perfected his directing career out of existence.

Francis Ford Coppola was most like Spielberg in being able to combine mass entertainment with great art. For a while early in his career, Coppola seemed to combine the individual strengths of both his pals, Spielberg and Scorsese. He could shoot a Mafia rubout as scary as any shark attack but intercut the murder with scenes of a church baptism that elicited favorable comparisons to Eisentein's Odessa Steps montage. Over the last fifteen years, however, he has descended into such self-indulgent experimentalism as *One From the Heart* or embarrassing self-*hommages* as the third *Godfather* film. The gore of *Dracula*, his only commercial hit since *Godfather II*, was a sad reminder of the aesthetic use he once had for blood and guts. In his next venture, Coppola is set to direct Robin Williams in a comedy called *Jack*, about a ten-year-old boy in a forty-year-old body. He also was producing a four-hour miniseries based on *The Odyssey* for HBO.

John Landis was the most unlikely member of the mouse-pack, the closest thing in the gang to a hack. It still surprises film theoreticians that the director of *National Lampoon's Animal House* was ever accepted as an aesthetic buddy by the auteurs of *Raging Bull* and *The Conversation.* Landis finally has found his fitting artistic niche as the producer and director of a cable sitcom, *Dream On,* about an immature, sex-obsessed yuppie. Landis is still awaiting his big-screen comeback in a much-postponed farce starring Tom Arnold, called, no doubt prophetically, *The Stupids.* As one exceptionally cold-hearted Hollywood observer has said, "*The Twilight Zone* movie wasn't the real tragedy in John Landis's life."

Perhaps the reason a man of limited ability like Landis was welcomed into this clique of outsized talent was, as the director's cousin Dr. Bruce Landis told this author, "John is a really nice man."

George Lucas never felt comfortable directing films, as evidenced by the fact that his last directorial effort was in 1977. He has settled into an apparently happy life as a techno-mogul, the producer of other people's high-tech films. Fans who enjoyed the wistful subtlety of a character-driven film like *American Graffiti* may regret Lucas's retirement from the directing field. It's also just a bit sad to compare his best friend's career trajectory to his own. Where Spielberg matured from mechanical sharks to mechanized genocide, Lucas's latest project is said to be *Star Wars 4.*

John Milius, who was basically the mousepack's writer-in-residence, did his best work as a writer rather than director. His most impressive credit is the screenplay of *Apocalpyse Now.* Two years ago, the trades announced Milius was set to direct a Viking epic called *The Northmen,* a project which mercifully never got off the ground.

Milius, who physically resembles a beefier Hemingway, recently adapted Tom Clancy's cold war thriller *Without Remorse,* which he also was supposed to direct. That project also has stalled, despite the fact that Clancy's books invariably become blockbusters (*Patriot Games* and *The Hunt for Red October* for instance).

Milius is perhaps best known for his gun collection and the writers' group he founded, called Armed and Literate. He also must be the only person in the world to count both Steven Spielberg and Gen. Norman Schwarzkopf as close friends. Spielberg admirers can only be grateful he didn't hire Milius to adapt *Schindler's List*.

CHAPTER SEVEN

Raiders of the Box Office

ONE OF SPIELBERG'S HAPPIEST MEMORIES from his childhood was the Saturday afternoons he spent at the Kiva Theater in Scottsdale, Arizona. The standard fare began with a newsreel, a preview of coming attractions, ten cartoons, a Republic Pictures serial like *Tailspin Tommy* or *Spy Smasher*, then two feature films.

After the disaster of *1941*, it may be psychologically accurate to say that the director retreated to the comforting memories of those suburban matinees because his next film would be an affectionate, big-budget re-creation of Saturday afternoon serials. But instead of Tailspin Tommy, Spielberg's hero would be a fellow with an equally resonant monniker, Indiana Jones.

The idea for *Raiders* was hatched on a beach in Maui, where Lucas and his then wife Marcia were taking their first vacation in ten years. *Star Wars* had just come out, and the Lucases were basking in the glow of a box office that was nearly radioactive. Spielberg soon turned up on the tropical island to help his pal celebrate. Together, these two adults constructed an elaborate sandcastle on the beach. While shoveling sand, Spielberg mentioned that he wanted to make a James Bond-style movie with a swaggering playboy character in the lead. Lucas confided he wanted to make a homage to Saturday matinee serials. They decided to combine their concepts and came up with the rough outline of *Raiders*. (The playboy concept would fall by the wayside after the stoic Harrison Ford was cast.)

Another momentous event occurred while the two men were playing in the sand. Spielberg casually suggested they trade profit percentage points in one another's films. Lucas goodnaturedly agreed. Spielberg gave Lucas one point from his take from *Close Encounters*, and Lucas forked over the same from *Star Wars*. Spielberg made out like a bandit from this casual swap, since *Star Wars* did more than double *Close Encounters'* business.

An industry observer doesn't feel, however, that Spielberg was being disingenuous when he suggested the trade. "Both men had been reading each other's scripts over the years, doing free rewrites, making suggestions. No money ever exchanged hands. The trade was a nice way of saying 'thank you' to each other for all their help over the years, although Steven got a lot bigger 'thank you' than George did."

Lucas would really regret his largesse when he made a similar swap with his good friend, director John Milius, who got an even bigger bargain than Spielberg when he traded one point in his flop surfing epic, *Big Wednesday*, for one point in the billion dollar *Star Wars*.

Though George Lucas and Steven Spielberg had been friends for years, aside from reading each other's scripts and doing an occasional rewrite gratis, they had never collaborated on a film before.

Their first project together wouldn't advance the art of cinema, but they would have a great time making it. In fact, years later, Spielberg would say of the experience, "I can't stand to watch *Jaws*. It was such a painful experience. But I can watch *Raiders of the Lost Ark* over and over again."

Raiders of the Lost Ark even sounds like the title of one of those Saturday afternoon serials that had so enthralled Spielberg growing up in Scottsdale.

With *Star Wars*, Lucas already had reinvented the sci-fi genre, which until then was deader than an imploded star.

Spielberg would perform a similar feat on the Saturday afternoon serial, with the help of a big budget and state of the art special effects. His loving recreation also would wink but never smirk at the conventions of the genre.

"I wanted to create that same kind of entertainment with *Raiders*," he said of the serial format. "A film that took itself seriously when we had to be logical, but could be humorous without sending up anything. All the humor in the movie had to come from the characters, not the situation."

Raiders of the Lost Ark was the story of a crusty University of Chicago archaeologist who leaves the quiet safety of academe for the crazy world of rolling boulders, gin-swilling tootsies and cardboard Nazis.

The Spielberg and Lucas team seemed like a sure bet, but it was a bet that every studio in Hollywood except one was unwilling to take. Maybe it was the failure of *1941* that scared them off. Maybe it was the unprecedented financial deal Lucas was demanding.

Both men should have had the clout to pick their studio and name their price. Lucas's *Star Wars* had grossed almost half a billion dollars and its sequel, *The Empire Strikes Back*, another $300 million. *Jaws* was the number-one hit of all time and *Close Encounters* had made more than a quarter billion.

These guys were the McDonald's of the box office.

It was the nature of the deal Lucas was demanding that had scared off the bean counters.

This was his precedent-setting demand: The studio to secure the services of Lucas and Spielberg would have to pay the cost of the film but would not be allowed to charge interest on the cost, a standard feature of studio financing then and now. The studio also would get no distribution fee, typically 30 percent of the film's gross, and it would not be allowed to charge overhead, another 20 percent.

After the studio had earned back the money it had put up for the budget, it would get 60 percent of the gross up to the first $100 million it earned. After that, the studio would split fifty-fifty with Lucas and Spielberg. Plus, just in the case the movie flopped and there were no profits to divvy up, Lucas would get up front a

$4 million producer's fee, and Spielberg $1.5 million for his directorial services.

Spielberg later would admit, "I personally would have never been so audacious. George made me realize what I deserved."

"A lot of studio executives looked at that first scene with the huge rock and thought it would cost $40 million just by itself," Michael Eisner, then head of Paramount, recalled. Eisner was the only studio chief willing to take the risk. When he caved in to Lucas's financing arrangement, Eisner's colleagues at the other studios were furious that he had set such a precedent. Now all the other Young Turk filmmakers with a big hit under their belt would be making similar demands.

The deal may have seemed crazy at the time, but when it came close to release, Eisner's gamble paid off for Paramount stockholders. The week before *Raiders* opened on June 12, 1981, the stock of Paramount's parent company, Gulf and Western, was trading at nineteen. But when advance word of mouth rumored that Paramount had another *Star Wars* on its happy hands, the stock jumped two and one half points. Eisner's gamble enriched stockholders by $187 million in just one week! Suddenly, Lucas and Spielberg didn't seem so greedy, and Eisner seemed crazy like a fox—with an MBA.

The studio chief later admitted that he had been appalled by *1941*, but he was convinced when he agreed to finance *Raiders* that Spielberg wouldn't make the same mistake twice. With an almost palpable sigh of relief, Eisner said after production wrapped, "Steven got in one or two takes what other people take ten to get. Every cent we spent is on the screen," except for all the money that went into Lucas and Spielberg's deep pockets.

The idea for *Raiders* was hatched on vacation in Hawaii. But more than the idea for a hit film was hatched during that epochal walk in the sand. A movie franchise was born.

A franchise (and we're not talking Taco Bell here) is the happiest word in a studio chief's dictionary. Franchises also are called tent poles. Like the tent poles of a circus tent, a movie franchise can support a studio's sagging fortunes. A franchise is a film concept with sequels naturally built in. They're like big-budget television series, but instead of running weekly on the small screen, they come out every couple of years in theaters. A movie like *Die Hard* is a classic franchise. There's always a new entity that can be taken hostage (office building, airport, New York City), then rescued by Bruce Willis. (Conversely, there's no sequel potential for a film like *Braveheart*, where the hero is disembowelled at the end.)

While Lucas has created a financial and production empire with his *Star Wars* franchise, Spielberg has avoided sequel-mania except for *Raiders*. And the reason has to do with that long ago stroll in Hawaii. Without putting anything in writing, the two men agreed over a handshake that if *Raiders* hit big, Spielberg would direct two sequels. As much as he dislikes repeating himself (the proof being that there's no *E.T. 2*), Spielberg lived up to the handshake deal, even though directing one of the *Raiders'* sequels prevented him from making a film that would win its director an Oscar (Barry Levinson for *Rainman*).

"I made George a promise that if the first [*Raiders*] was successful, I would do two more. It wasn't a contract. It was just sort of a friendly handshake. But George is one of my closest friends, and I take that as a promise," he said.

With the exception of losing *Rainman*, keeping his promise wasn't a burden. In fact, although the handshake deal required only two sequels, Spielberg has gone on record saying he'd love to do a fourth installment. Plus he loves working with Lucas so much he has even volunteered to direct *Star Wars 4*: "I'd love to do the fourth *Star Wars*." Spielberg is not a snob. "I'm not interested in developing a single style like Marty [Scorsese] or Brian [De Palma]. I've alwasy been eclectic. I just want to do something that challenges me." Harrison Ford, who has become a classy actor since piffle like *Raiders* movies, isn't a snob either. He also has signed on for Indy 4. But his love of pulp films goes only so far. He won't be joining Spielberg for the fourth *Star Wars*. Ford revealed to this author, "I would never do another *Star Wars*. I think my character in those films has gone about as far as he can go."

After the excesses of *1941*, which weren't all that excessive, Spielberg felt he was on a probation of sorts. He had to prove he wasn't a profligate director. He may have gone over budget on *1941*, but he was no Michael Cimino.

Lucas was his fiscal chaperone on *Raiders*.

"George knows how to put the most on the screen for the cheapest price," the director told *Time* magazine in 1982. "He did more than anyone to help me make a movie on budget. While we were preparing *Raiders*, he would tell me, 'You've got a $50 million imagination with a $10 million budget behind it.'"

Spielberg, under Lucas's watchful eye, would bring *Raiders* in for under $20 million. Lucas told him point-blank, "You've got $20 million. Make it look like $30 million."

"George really is a producer-director. He taught me about creative shortcuts, how to give an audience an eyeful with *illusions* of grandeur," Spielberg said.

One of the ways Lucas forced Spielberg to pare costs was by demanding extensive storyboarding, which is drawing each scene in advance like a comic strip. Storyboards allow the director and the production team to mentally film each scene before the cast, crew, and props are all in (expensive) place. Spielberg actually storyboarded 80 percent of *Raiders* before principal photography began. His preplanning was so well thought out he eventually used 60 percent of his storyboard illustrations.

Raiders came in under budget and ahead of schedule, a tonic change after the excesses of *1941*. Lucas and Spielberg achieved miracles of economy. Paramount had given them eighty-seven days in which to shoot the film, with severe penalties if they went over schedule. Instead, the team wrapped the film after only seventy-three days. The studio also had agreed to a $40 million budget, but the film ended up costing only $20 million. No word on who got to keep the surplus, the studio or the filmmakers.

Other economies may have been apocryphal. And according to author Tony Crawley, shots from the 1975 blimp epic, *The Hindenburg*, made their way into a thirties street scene. Richard Edlund, who was in charge of special effects, said the story was pure myth and insisted that miniatures were used to shoot the street scene in question. However, the submarine in *Raiders* was borrowed from the 1981 German classic, *Das Boot*. Footage from 1972's *Lost Horizon* was purchased and incorporated in scenes where a DC-3 flies over the Himalayas.

Spielberg didn't resent his mentor's penny-pinching. "George is my brother," said Spielberg who was introduced to Lucas in 1967 by their mutual friend, Francis Coppola. "George knows me better than anybody."

Lucas felt equally comfortable working with Spielberg. He never tyrannized the director about the budget, and Lucas's decisions were suggested gently, never dictated. Lucas recalled, "He's a perfect director for me to work with. We just think the same way about everything. He'll go a little overboard one way, and I'll go overboard another way, but there's no conflict. There's nobody ramming ideas down the other person's throat. We have a great time together. He keeps saying it's my movie and I'll get blamed for it, and I keep saying it's his movie and he'll get blamed for it."

Lucas gave Spielberg an analogy to help guide him in making *Raiders*. "George wanted what I'd call an 'automat' film. 'This is a movie I want to see. Here's five bucks. Get it to pop out.'"

Spielberg explained his economies: "I did a lot of cutting in my head, and for the first time I used a second-unit director who added some great things of his own. The crew wanted an A picture, I wanted a B-plus.

"I brought them down to my pulp eye level."

Spielberg had wanted 2,000 extras to excavate the buried temple of Tanis. He settled for 700 and used a wide-angle lens to literally flesh out the crowd. Miniature "extras" also populated the background of the excavation site. The director, however, refused to cut corners when it came to the snakes, even though he had a powerful phobia for those reptilian creatures. Spielberg demanded and received 4,500 snakes from Denmark to torment Karen Allen on a soundstage at London's Elstree Studios.

As much as he may admire, even envy, auteurs like David Lean or his friend Martin Scorsese, sometimes—most of the time—Spielberg just likes to have fun.

"There were two ways I could have made this movie," he said. "I could have done it as a neo-Brechtian film noir with multiple shadows out of Carol Reed or Orson Welles, like *The Third Man* or *Touch of Evil*." Michael Eisner must have had cardiac arrest when he read that.

"But then I realized that what could be a turn-on for me could wreck a gravy-train movie. I just worked to tell the story. But I was happy making this movie, largely because George Lucas and Harrison Ford both were full-time collaborators. Harrison had seven ideas to my five."

Never the most effusive of conversationalists, Ford returned the compliment: "He makes working fun. He's so secure about what he's doing we welcome input from Steven."

Every Spielberg film has one defining image. In *Jaws* it was the giant white swallowing Robert Shaw whole. In *E.T.* it was the creature racing through the sky in a bicycle basket, framed by the moon in the background. In *Raiders of the Lost Ark* it was, indisputably, the rolling boulder that almost flattens Indy in the film's opening sequence. In real life, the rock, which at twelve feet high was life-sized and definitely not a miniature, almost crushed the man who played Jones. Spielberg shot the scene from five different angles, two shots per angle. That meant Ford had to flee the rock ten times. The boulder wasn't as heavy as it seemed (it was made of fiberglass, wood, and plaster), but it still weighed 300 pounds, enough to turn a slower-footed Ford into a doormat.

Spielberg later said, "Harrison had to race the rock ten times. He won ten times and beat the odds. He was lucky. And I was an idiot for letting him try." Despite the implied apology, Spielberg failed to explain why he simply didn't use a stunt double with the trademark fedora pulled down to disguise Ford's identity.

Spielberg welcomed input from his leading man, even when that input had an unusual origin that had nothing really to do with the concept or plot of *Raiders*.

Harrison's lower-intestinal tract problems created one of the funniest scenes in the film. While shooting in Tunisia, the actor contracted a case of the *turistas*. He was in no mood to shoot a complicated scene that required him to confront a sword-wielding bad guy.

Ford asked the director if the scene could be shot in an hour. Spielberg jokingly replied, "Yeah, if you shoot him." And that's exactly what happened. The swordsman, before attacking Indiana, does an elaborate ballet with his weapon, twirling it around like a drum majorette on speed. Rather than fight him on his own terms, using a sword, Ford simply pulls out his gun and shoots his opponent dead. It's unexpected. It's funny. And it allowed the diarrhea-plagued Ford to spend only an hour shooting.

Spielberg didn't have such a happy collaboration with his other star, Karen Allen, who played the gin-swilling heroine. The role originally was intended for the director's then girlfriend, Amy Irving, but by the time he got around to casting it, they had split.

After filming, Allen bad-mouthed the director in an interview, to the virtual end of her career. When it came time to make the *Raiders* sequel, Ford was invited back. Allen was not.

GQ said in an August 1984 interview that her ideas about her character, Marian Ravenwood, didn't make a "dent in the little Los Angeles Dodgers helmet that Steven Spielberg wears on the set. Talking about the experience, and the fact that Kate Capshaw replaced her as the female lead in the *Raiders* sequel, Allen smiles philosophically, 'They told me in the beginning the stories were really about Indiana Jones, that the woman's role would change. Well, I'm not wild about the idea of sequels anyway.'" Spielberg wasn't lying when he said the female roles would change. When it came time to cast the female lead in *Raiders 3*, he didn't even rehire his wife to return from the second installment!

That same month Allen told *Marquee* magazine that she fought "tooth-and-nail" over the character of Marian. Spielberg saw Marian as a "damsel in distress," which was 180 degrees away from Allen's interpretation. "I fought like hell for that character," she said at the time. "In the first bar scene they made her tough and then afterwards made her this frail little creature in a dress—a basket-case."

Although she claimed the director eventually accepted her input, she fearlessly told *Marquee* that she simply found him "difficult. He is the kind of director who plans it all out in his head and the people he works with are just there to fulfill his plan."

Shades of Teri Garr complaining that Spielberg was just a master puppeteer, pulling strings rather than directing flesh and blood.

By 1988, her career having degenerated to Equity waiver productions in Los Angeles, Allen wanted to get the word out that she really never had a problem with the most powerful man in the movie industry. In an interview to promote a production of *The Glass Menagerie* in a hole-in-the-wall theater on a stretch of Santa Monica Boulevard in West Hollywood that is plagued by male prostitutes, Allen said backtracking, "I liked Steven, but we didn't always agree on things. My approach to working was quite different and because of that we came in to conflict from time to time, but it wasn't anything major. I remember reading an article in *Newsweek* or *Time*. It said something about my being bad-mouthed by Steven. If I was ever bad-mouthed by Steven in the press, I missed it."

Casting director Mike Fenton suggested what went wrong between the director and his heroine. "We would never send an actor with a star mentality to Steven. He doesn't have an ego, and he just doesn't have time for that sort of thing. He just loves making movies." Or as Spielberg said, "I never want to make a movie with someone who's been on the cover of *Rolling Stone*."

Spielberg also hinted at what soured the relationship with his leading lady. (He would have a much better relationship with his leading lady in the sequel, Kate Capshaw, the future Mrs. Steven Spielberg!) "Karen Allen told me, 'I'm from the Al Pacino school of acting.' I told her, 'You're going to get introduced to the Sam Peckinpah school of action.' I threw snakes at Karen, I set her on fire. I tossed a tarantula on her leg," he said, sounding just like the young boy who so gleefully tormented his sisters by locking them in the closet with glowing skulls. "But I always kissed Karen gently after every take."

Even at the relatively modest budget of $20 million, *Raiders* was still a gamble for the money men. As the *Saturday Review* pointed out long before the film tore up the box office, "Budgeted at $20 million, *Raiders* may sound like a cut-rate item by Spielberg's standards, but today's advertising and distribution costs require that the film bring in $50 million to finish in the black." The magazine need not have worried. *Raiders* would gross almost $100 million more than Close Encounters, a whopping $363 million.

As Lucas inelegantly described, "We are the pigs," he said shortly after *Raiders* was released. "We are the ones who sniff out the truffles. The man in the executive tower cannot do that.

The power lies with us—the ones who actually know how to make movies."

After Spielberg turned over his cut of *Raiders* to Lucas, the producer screened it in front of an audience. It was the first time Lucas had seen the completed film. The next day, Lucas telephoned Spielberg and said, "I've got to tell you, you're *really* a good director."

Spielberg's longtime producer, Kathleen Kennedy, recalled how happy his mentor's praise made him. "There aren't a lot of people around who can say that to Steven. Who's going to tell the President of the United States that he's doing a good job? But when George tells you, that's it," Kennedy said.

Spielberg's box-office performance proved that he knew how to make movies, but by now he was getting tired of all the carping that his films were big on plot, but short on character.

Actor Klaus Kinski was offered the lead Nazi role in *Raiders*, but found his character and the script lacking, describing the latter as "the same tired old shit."

Spielberg hated this short-on-character analysis. Displaying a rare hint of anger, he retorted, "If a film works, it's usually because of the characters and not the special effects. Empathy with people in a film is important because you sure can't empathize with a shark or ninety police cars or a spaceship. Indiana Jones is not a cardboard hero but rather a human being with ordinary frailties."

Indiana was no Willie Loman, but Spielberg was right to reject the characterization of his character as a papier mache construct. All you have to do is compare all the tics and eccentricities of Indiana Jones to the ultra one-dimensional character of a James Bond or Mel Gibson's cartoonish *Lethal Weapon* cop to accept Spielberg's plea that there's more to his characterizations than whips and spacecraft.

Lawrence Kasdan, the respected director of such classics as *Body Heat* and *The Big Chill*, paid his dues as the writer of *Raiders of the Lost Ark*. Kasdan recalled their story conferences as a "friendly tug of war" in which he tried to add depth and a certain nastiness to the Jones character. Spielberg and Lucas, in contrast, wanted more action and spectacles, Kasdan insists. "I became worried that the thing was becoming a straight action piece," Kasdan said with regret, "which is probably the way it turned out."

Still, although Kasdan, the writer, may not have been impressed with his boss's writing skills, Kasdan, the director, praised Spielberg, the filmmaker. "I don't think anyone in the world moves a camera better than Steven does. I don't think anyone else has that kind of innate talent for what really works in terms of exciting the eye."

Although the villains, even the Nazis, were mostly cardboard heavies, *Raiders* stands out as one of Spielberg's most violent films. He lays the blame for the high body count squarely on his best friend, George Lucas. "My violence is more psychological. George can outviolence me any day. To me, the moments that are exciting are the ones that occur just before the trigger is pulled— the threat is more horrific than the shot. In *Duel*, what's scary is this big truck bearing down on Dennis Weaver's Valiant; the only blood you see is when Dennis bites his lip.

"*Raiders* is more in George's vein. It's the only film of mine in which scores of people are violently eliminated," he said years before making his most violent film, *Schindler's List*.

At this point in his career, he refused to take his work seriously. Echoing the complaints of many critics, Spielberg admitted with perfect equanimity, "*Raiders* is like popcorn. It doesn't fill you up, it's easy to digest, it melts in your mouth, and it's the kind of thing you can just go back and chow down on over and over again."

Despite the eventual box-office bonanza of *Raiders*, preview audiences hated it. Or in industry terms, "It didn't test well."

When Spielberg read the audience preview cards that said "icky insects" and "Karen Allen is too butch," he went into a panic. After a similar disastrous preview of *1941*, it must have seemed to Spielberg, in the words of Yogi Berra, like "déjà vu all over again."

Spielberg later confessed that he fled the theater during one sneak of *Raiders*, fearing the worst.

Now we know he had nothing to fear. In fact, box office wasn't the only success he enjoyed from *Raiders'* popularity. The film began an entirely new ancillary market for Spielberg, one that would enrich him nearly as much as the films themselves.

It's called merchandising.

Toys for tots. All the ancillary stuff that kids demand their parents buy after they've seen the film. You've seen the film, now buy the junk—so the marketing strategy goes.

It was a strategy that the savvy artist-entrepreneur tried to use way back during the release of *Jaws*. Spielberg begged Universal to market toys based on Bruce the shark.

The studio, to its later horror, turned him down flat, reasoning no sane child would want to play with the creepy creature that devours half the cast of the film. Studio executives aren't children, and they didn't realize that creepy sells in the youth market.

By now it was a cliche to describe Spielberg as Peter Pan, the movie mogul who refused to grow up. He knew early on that creepy sells. So would Indiana Jones's whip and even his trademark fedora, although no one was wearing hats in the early '80s.

Not that he needed more money, but Spielberg's savvy insistence on marketing toys based on *Raiders* and his following films would earn him 10 percent of every E.T. doll and dinosaur action figure. It doesn't take a calculator to figure out roughly how much his merchandising has earned him. The rule of thumb is that a kids-oriented film like *Hook* takes home in merchandise an amount equal to its gross. *Jurassic Park* grossed almost $1 billion. Spielberg personally earned 10 percent of a billion dollars selling plastic velociraptors et al.

As his former agent, Guy McElwaine, once said, "Steven is a businessman."

A man who by his own admission still counts on his fingers, Spielberg disagrees that he's some kind of natural MBA. Typically, he defers to his mentor. "George Lucas is much more business-oriented than I am. He is a business genius, as well as a great conceptualizer, and I'm much more of a hard-working drone. I enjoy rolling up my sleeves and getting into it. I think George has fun thinking up ideas and then sitting back and saying, 'OK, go off and make it. It's your movie now.'"

After the sobering debacle of *1941*, *Raiders* and its $363 million take put Steven Spielberg back on top, a position he would occupy with few missteps up to the present day. After *Raiders*, a criticial and box-office success, it seemed almost impossible that the director could ever top himself in either sphere, the affection of the public or the press.

But with his next film, he not only topped himself in spades, he made one of the most beloved movies of all time. And in the process, he also made the most commercially successful film up to date.

Again, comparing himself to his best friend and mentor, Spielberg put his finger exactly on his particular talent. "George is king of outer space. I'm king of outer space when it arrives on earth."

His next film would prove that he deserved his self-ascribed royal title.

CHAPTER EIGHT

The Best of Times, The Worst of Times

IF EVER A YEAR EPITOMIZED THE OPENING LINE of Charles Dickens's *A Tale of Two Cities*, for Steven Spielberg it had to be 1982.

That year was indeed "the best of times and the worst of times." It saw the release of his *E.T.—The Extraterrestrial*, the number-one money-maker and critics' darling. It was also the year in which he became embroiled in the *Twilight Zone* tragedy, which involved the death of two child actors on a film he produced and codirected.

"This has been the most interesting year of my film career," he said with understatement. "It has mixed the best, the success of *E.T.*, with the worst, the *Twilight Zone* tragedy. A mixture of ecstasy and grief. It made me grow up a little more."

The year started out great for the director. Even *before E.T.* came out, the normally cool *Rolling Stone* magazine got all hot and bothered praising the filmmaker: "At 34, Steven Spielberg is in any conventional sense the most successful movie director in Hollywood, America, the Occident, the planet Earth, the solar system and the galaxy."

Perhaps *E.T.* would be his biggest hit up to that time because it was also his most autobiographical. That may seem like a strange description for a film about a reptilian creature from outer space, but the film's themes of loneliness, fear of separation, and longing for friendship came straight from Spielberg's own lonely, peripatetic childhood.

"My films say exactly what I am. When I look at *E.T.*, I say, 'That was what I was like in 1981.' I don't believe people who say that their films have nothing to do with themselves. In a way, every film is an autobiography, since you express your emotions through it and you impart your experiences."

The human hero of *E.T.*, ten-year-old Elliot, is also the young Steven Spielberg, traumatized by his parents' divorce, longing for a friend his own age, wishing the family would stop moving every couple of years. He later would say *E.T.* was borne of longing for an older brother and a father who had slipped away.

"What inspired me to do *E.T.* more than anything else was that my father was a computer expert and he kept getting better jobs. And we would go from town to town. And it would just happen I would find a best friend, and I would finally become an insider at school, and at the moment of my greatest comfort and tranquility . . . we'd move somewhere else. There was always the good-bye scene. *E.T.* reflects a lot of that. When Elliot finds E.T., he hangs on to him. He announces in no uncertain terms, 'I'm keeping him,' and he means it."

The immediate impetus for creating *E.T.*, however, came from Spielberg's loneliness as an adult.

While making *Raiders of the Lost Ark* in Tunisia, an overwhelming sense of loneliness plagued the director. His girlfriend at the time, Kathleen Carey, a music industry executive, was at work in California. His best friend George Lucas was also back home in California. Even the amiable Harrison Ford was unavailable for companionship on the set because he was holed up in his trailer, suffering from the umpteenth bout of diarrhea.

"I remember wishing one night that I had a friend. It was like when you were a kid and had grown out of dolls or teddy bears or Winnie the Pooh, you just wanted a little voice in your mind to talk to. I began concocting this imaginary creature, partially from the guys who stepped out of the Mother Ship for nine-ty seconds in *Close Encounters*. Then I thought, 'What if I were ten years old again, *where I've sort of been for thirty-five years anyway*, and what if he needed me as much as I needed him? Wouldn't that be a great love story?' So I put together this story of boy meets creature, boy loses creature, creature saves boy, boy saves creature, with the hope that they will somehow always be together, that their friendship isn't limited by nautical miles."

It wasn't just the little green men from *Close Encounters* who inspired Spielberg to make *E.T.* One of the human actors in the film urged him to make a movie about one of his favorite subjects, children. "Francois Truffaut helped inspire me to make *E.T.*, sim-ply by saying to me on the *Close Encounters* set, 'I like you with *keeds*. You are wonderful with *keeds*. You must do a movie just with *keeds*.' He kept saying, 'You are the child.'"

And although Spielberg was happy to concede that *Raiders of the Lost Ark* was nothing more than cinematic popcorn, he was longing to make something a bit more nutritious. "Action is won-derful, but while I was doing *Raiders* I felt I was losing touch with the reason I became a movie-maker—to make stories about people and relationships. *E.T.* is the first movie I ever made for myself," he said.

With box-office hits like *Raiders* and *Jaws*, Spielberg had nourished the studio's stockholders, not to mention his own port-folio. But by this time, he was more interested in nourishment for his soul. His films by now had grossed more than half a billion dollars, but as Jack Nicholson asks the billionaire pervert (John Huston) in *Chinatown*, "How many steaks can you eat? How many yachts can you buy?" Spielberg wanted to make a film for the archives, not just the safety deposit box. Something small and per-sonal that would also, hopefully, make a zillion bucks as a by-prod-uct of his personal aesthetic needs.

E.T. was conceptualized as a small, personal film. Low bud-get. Even the original title was unassuming—*A Boy's Life*. And for the first time in his career, Spielberg, the control freak, decided to make a film without storyboarding every scene first. "I was afraid I would kill the naturalness of the kids in the performance if I spent too much time premeditating the picture on paper. All my movies prior to *E.T.* were storyboarded. I designed the picture visually on paper. . .a nd then shot the paper! After I designed *Poltergeist*, I decided I was tired of spending two months with a piece of paper and pencil and a couple of sketch artists interpreting my stick fig- ures. *I decided to wing E.T.* Winging *E.T.* made it a very sponta- neous, vital movie. I realized I didn't need the drawings for a small movie like *E.T.* I would never wing *Raiders II*, but I could impro- vise a more personal picture like *E.T.*"

Spielberg was intrigued with his own creation—the glimpse of the extraterrestrials he allowed us to see in *Close Encounters* after the studio gave him the extra cash and he went inside the ship to give us more.

But he wanted to see even more. And show us more. He started out by shrinking the gigantic spaceship from *Close Encounters* and creating a small, Jules Verne-type craft for little E.T.

Then reality set in. How can you make a film about a human-acting nonhuman creature without getting into the huge expense of all the special effects needed to create such a creature?

E.T., the movie, may have contained cheap sentiment, according to some hard-boiled critics, but E.T., the audioanima- tronic creature, didn't come cheap. The puppet, created by Italy's Carlo Rambaldi, cost $1.5 million.

Spielberg gave Rambaldi specific instructions on conceptu- alizing E.T. "I told Carlo to build a monster who would also be strange, humanoid and comprehensible to youngsters."

Rambaldi's creation employed two control systems, one mechanical, operated by unseen puppeteers, the other electronic, which gave the creature such lifelike mannerisms that some critics seriously suggested the puppet deserved a best actor nomination at Oscar time. The electronics allowed E.T. to wrinkle his nose, inflate his chest, and roll his eyes. The electronics even created independently operated eyebrows for the quizzical look that made him seem more animated than some actors. For broader move- ments, there was another puppet with a midget inside an E.T. suit.

The cost scared off at least one studio. Showing the same lack of foresight that had every studio except Paramount passing on *Raiders*, Columbia passed on *E.T.*, because the studio had decided to make a more personal sci-fi film, a modest success called *Starman*, a similarly themed story about an extraterrestrial who finds tough times on planet Earth. The studio also feared that *E.T.* would only appeal to children, not the best demographic for creating a blockbuster.

Even more important than the technical wizardry that would make a polyurethane puppet seem alive was the casting of his human companion, Elliot, the suburban youth adrift in a fatherless home and friendless school.

The hunt for Elliot took on the proportions of the search for Scarlett O'Hara. Spielberg interviewed more than 300 kids and couldn't find a single one artless enough to create the crucial character.

"Many of them were remarkable, but they weren't real. They thought before they felt. Then just a few weeks before we were to start shooting, Henry Thomas walked in," Spielberg said.

The director had summoned the youth after seeing him turn in a bravura performance as one of Sissy Spacek's children in *Raggedy Man*.

Their first meeting did not bode well for their future collaboration.

"He gave a dreadful reading," the director later recalled. "I could see he was petrified. But when I asked him to improvise a scene with our casting director, he transformed immediately into Elliot.

"You can hear my voice on the the videotape before we could turn the camera off, saying, 'You've got the job, kid.' I was blown away by this nine-year-old. Then I came to realize that he's an adult actor, not a nine-year-old. He's a very controlled, methodical performer who measures what he does and feels what he does and yet broadcasts it in a totally subtle way. He's just a once in a lifetime kid."

Thomas later would prove himself even more adept at the kind of improv that so impressed the director during his audition. During a break in a scene, he ad-libbed one of the movie's funniest lines when he offered his extraterrestrial houseguest a Coca-Cola. It was product placement of the most ingenuous kind. Thomas apologized for the ad lib. Spielberg loved it and told him to do it again, this time with the cameras rolling.

Time magazine underlined the importance of the young actor to the film: "Thomas is largely responsible for making the scenes between a boy and a pile of steel and foam rubber glisten with feeling."

Other critics fell in love with *E.T.* as much as the public. The *New York Times'* Vincent Canby enthused, "*E.T.* may become a children's classic of the space age . . . as contemporary as a laser beam, but full of the timeliness and longings expressed in children's literature of all ages."

Roger Ebert of the *Chicago Sun-Times* gave it "two thumbs up, way up," adding, "*E.T.* is a reminder of what movies are for . . . some are to make us think, some to make us feel, some to take us away from our problems, some to help us examine them. What is enchanting about *E.T.* is that in some measure it does all of those things."

Life magazine called Spielberg "the most fabulous 34-year-old since, say Wolfgang Amadeus Mozart."

Spielberg's number-one fan, Michael Jackson, even weighed in, admitting, "I must have seen *E.T.* around 40 times, and *Jaws* a good hundred or so. You feel *loved* in his films."

Even the vitriolic Pauline Kael, who had compared watching *Raiders of the Lost Ark* to being consumed by a Cuisinart, waxed rhapsodic: "Spielberg has earned the tears that some people in the audience—and not just children—shed. The tears are tokens of gratitude for the spell the picture has put on the audience. Genuinely entrancing movies are almost as rare as extraterrestrial visitors." Even rarer—the image of the macho Kael shedding a tear over anything.

The critical hosannas must have been particularly gratifying after all those years of being called a technocrat and ticket taker at the roller-coaster ride. Especially since he felt *E.T.* was so autobiographical. The critics were praising when they rhapsodized over *E.T.*

E.T. had a curious effect on the bachelor. After working with so many children on the set, he said, "I have this deep yearning now to become a father."

Spielberg generously attributed much of the film's emotional heft to the fact that for the first time in his career he employed a disproportionate number of women on the film. "I had a lot of women working on the set. So many key positions were filled by women it was amzaing. Not because they're women, but because they were good. And it gave a real maternal feeling to the set. And I'm a sucker for that, because I grew up with three younger sisters, and a mother and her female friends, and I just remember feeling more comfortable on the *E.T.* set because of all the women there. It was much easier as a working environment. It was really like a womb to make that movie. It was a very, very warm womb."

Women reached all the way to the top of the moviemaking heap. One of the producers was his longtime collaboartor, Kathleen Kennedy. The screenwriter was Harrison Ford's wife, Melissa Mathison. Mathison, a former reporter for *People* magazine, was critical in helping Spielberg overcome his fears of making such a personal film.

He later said, "Making *E.T.* was like taking off my shirt in public. There are a few things about my body I'm not proud of. One of them is I have very thin arms. The other thing is I have no hair on my chest. And it's terribly freckled. I have the chest of Woody Allen. And I've always been a little embarrassed to bare that. Woody loves to show off his emotional inadequacies, which is what makes him a master at what he does. But I've always been afraid to do that."

Very afraid. In fact, after telling Mathison his concept for *E.T.*, he added, "But you know something, I may not be ready to make this movie now."

Mathison persuaded him. "You *are* ready to make this movie. But if you don't try, nobody will know, including yourself."

Mathison was an invaluable advisor as well as screenwriter. And she had the courage to stand up to her boss. "None of us is afraid to tell Steven he is wrong," she insisted. "He's a softy, as big a sap as anyone. But he rarely lets that show in his movies. He kept fretting that *E.T.* was too soft, until finally he stopped worrying about pleasing the men in the audience."

Box-office records. Effusive reviews. And the whole thing cost only $10.5 million! And that included the cost of all those rubber puppets!

Spielberg's success was acknowledged by one source that must have been especially delicious since the praise from his old mentor, George Lucas, acknowledged that the pupil had surpassed the teacher.

Six months after the release of *E.T.*, Lucas took out a full page ad in *Daily Variety* on January 19, 1983. The ad contained an illustration of Han Solo and Luke Skywalker hoisting E.T. on their shoulders. The caption underneath took the form of a letter from Lucas to Spielberg. It read: "Dear Steven, Congratulations to you and your Extra-Terrestrial buddy. This week *E.T.* moved ahead of *Star Wars* to take first place in domestic film rentals. *E.T.*'s adventure on earth and his gift of intergalactic friendship continues to touch us all. May the Force always be with you. Your Pal, George Lucas."

E.T. was a bonanza for Universal and the director. The film grossed $700 million, making it the biggest hit in the history of the movie industry (until another Spielberg film eleven years later knocked it out of first place). Years later when an angry stockholder would quiz Lew Wasserman, chairman of MCA/Universal, about the $5 million the studio lavished on Spielberg's production headquarters on the backlot, the octagenarian executive dismissed the complaint, explaining, "Don't worry about it; it's the box office on *E.T.* from Venezuela!"

But the theatrical revenue was just the beginning of an avalanche of riches that fell on the studio and the filmmaker. Merchandising from the film, toys, and other items brought in another $1 billion. And Spielberg's deal called for him to earn 10 percent of every toy, action figure, and pillow case featuring E.T.'s reptilian mug. He took merchandising as seriously as filmmaking. He had it written into his contract that he had approval on every single product. He also demanded that manufacturers submit samples so he could assure their quality.

There were two best-selling novelizations of the film's story line. And stuffed dolls. And talking dolls that capitalized on E.T.'s vibrato phrases like "phone home" and "Eeeel-iot." Atari came out with a video game. Hallmark weighed in with greeting cards from outer space. Two record albums were pressed. Sheets, bedspreads, pillow covers, draperies, bathrobes, nightgowns, pajamas (footed and unfooted for E.T.'s littlest fans), T-shirts, lunchboxes, baseball caps, Halloween costumes, Christmas tree ornaments, girls and even women's underwear, chalkboards, posters, bubble gum cards, stationery, pushpins, magnetized stickers, knit caps, scarves, and the director's personal favorite, an E.T. clock whose belly glows and whose head rises when the alarm sounds.

As one toy manufacturer gleefully predicted, "We think E.T. will be the next Mickey Mouse. And we expect him to be around for just as long."

Not for nothing have critics accused Spielberg and even more so, his pal George Lucas, of making films simply to sell lucrative toys et al.

Novelist and screenwriter David Marlow said, "Whenever I watch one of Spielberg's kiddie movies I amuse myself by predicting which one of the actors will be turned into an action figure, which one will be better as a stuffed toy and whose face will end up on the side of a lunch bucket. You have to do *something* while you're watching all that greasy kid stuff."

But greed just isn't a motivating factor for a man who is conservatively estimated to have a personal fortune of $1 billion. The proof is that for years he resisted putting *E.T.* out on video because he felt the film should only be experienced on the big screen.

He only agreed to release the video in 1988 after one too many fans of the film buttonholed him, demanding to know when *E.T.* was coming out on home video. "It got to be a burden of popular demand. All over the world, it was the number one question people would ask me: 'When is *E.T.* coming out on video?' Everybody from my nieces and nephews to people on the street were badgering me. It was not studio pressure." And it wasn't greed, since as one industry analyst soberly noted, "The man is richer than God."

Three years earlier, he had pronounced himself an implacable enemy of the video revolution, a revolution that would literally double his personal fortune after he finally embraced it. "I am not crazy about [video]," he said in 1985. "For one thing, I like to know that it takes two people to carry a film to a movie theater because the cans are so heavy. But when I sit down upstairs and just pull out a cassette of *Close Encounters*—and I know what went into it, tears and blood and four years of my life—and I can hold it in one hand, and hold it for two years without my hand getting tired because it doesn't weigh anything—there's something about that that bothers me. I think what I am trying to say is that I believe in showmanship."

Despite his misgivings about video, the man with the golden gut foresaw its commercial potential even while loathing the medium itself. He had it written into his contract for *E.T.* that he would earn 50 percent of the video take. At the time, there were relatively few VCRs in American homes, and his demand for 50 percent must have seemed to the studio bean counters like half of nothing.

"I saw that video was going to be a very important ancillary market and in many cases the primary market for film," Spielberg said long before anyone else realized that one day video sales would more than equal the revenue from theaters.

Fortunately for Universal's stockholders, Spielberg finally overcame his aversion to video. When *E.T.* was released on video in 1988, it sold eleven million copies in advance orders alone. His prescience paid off in a big way. His take of the video added $70 million to Spielberg Incorporated.

Just as aesthetic considerations made him stall *E.T.*'s video release, Spielberg has refused to make a sequel to his hit. In fact, he has refused to capitalize on any of his successes, except for *Raiders of the Lost Ark*, which simply represented his living up to a handshake deal he made with his best friend, George Lucas.

"I'm not about to join the Wall Street generation," Spielberg said in the middle of the Me decade, when urged to make *E.T. 2*.

Not everyone was bullish on this avatar of Mozart. Like Karen Allen in *Raiders*, the female star of *E.T.* got into a public feud with the director, an unwise move. Dee Wallace Stone, who played the mother in the film, was miffed when the director asked her to forgo star billing, even though she was one of the stars of the film and her modulated performance provided much of *E.T.*'s emotional pull. The actress agreed to do without a credit that said, "Starring . . . ," but asked that she be featured prominently in the movie ads. Her plea was rejected.

Stone also had problems with the director's obsessive secrecy. Cast and crew were forced to sign contracts promising not to discuss the script with anyone. Usually, such stipulations are verbal. Stone asked for an exemption in the case of her husband, which Spielberg, apparently not so obsessive, agreed to. Still, she complained that his Howard Hughes-like obsession with secrecy "almost got to the point of ridiculousness. But if you go through an eighteen-month pregnancy, you don't want somebody naming the baby before you do," she said.

At about this time, Spielberg confessed to a reporter, "I'm suspicious of women." It was a curious confession to make. Certainly, none of the director's work reflected the kind of misogynism that infected his friends' *ouevres*—whether it was the ham-fisted sexism of a Brian De Palma or the kinky sadism of writer-director Walter Hill. (Not to mention Tobe Hooper's proclivity for slicing and dicing his heroines with chain saws.)

A Freudian explanation of Spielberg's misogyny also falls flat. He always has enjoyed a close relationship with a mightily encouraging mother. And anything but a womanizer, Spielberg was no Warren Beatty using his female stars as girlfriends *du jour*.

An acquaintance who's known the director for a quarter century suggests a much more transparent reason for Spielberg's equivocal relationship with the opposite sex, especially with his on-screen employees.

"Of course he's suspicious of women," this source says. "You'd be too if women—wannabe actresses—were always throwing themselves at you. You couldn't help but wonder: Are they interested in me or do they just want to be in *Raiders of the Lost Ark Part 4*?

"I don't want to overstate the case, but both his wives were the aggressors in the relationship. Steven is a shy guy. And while he's far from being a dog, he's not exactly a young Robert Redford. He has to wonder why all these beautiful babes want to get to know him."

Stone's career went downhill after *E.T.*, and she ended up emoting opposite a collie in a syndicated television version of *Lassie*. Asked if she had been blacklisted by the director, she chose the resonant, "No comment."

Spielberg suffered a much bigger snub at Oscar time. *E.T.* received as many nominations as the year's "quality" picture, *Gandhi*, but won in only a few technical categories. Even in losing, Spielberg showed he had more than a touch of class. The winner of the best director Oscar that year, Mark Rydell (for *On Golden Pond*) said, "I was very touched by Steven Spielberg's admission that he voted for me. I wish I had that kind of class. Remarkable."

Spielberg was indeed a gracious loser. The day after the Oscars, he told the *Los Angeles Times*: "If the Academy decides to give me an Oscar some day, I'll be glad to accept it. But I don't think I'll get it for a film that I really care about. *E.T.* is my favorite movie, although it's not my best-directed film. That's *Close Encounters*."

He was also philosophical about the reason for losing. "There's always a backlash against anything that makes more than $50 million in film rentals," he said.

After his good friend was snubbed by the Academy for *E.T.*, the normally reticent George Lucas publicly defended Spielberg. He was even willing to bad-mouth the Academy and Gandhi!

In 1983, he told Gene Siskel of the *Chicago Tribune*, "We all knew, Steve included, that he wasn't going to win. The only question was whether or not he should go and sit through losing. I think he made a wise decision to go. But I'm saddened by his not winning. I think he was the best director there, and *E.T.* was the best film . . . . I wish there was *a more professional* organization voting that tried to reward professional excellence. *Gandhi* [which shut out *E.T.* at the Oscars that year] is good, but there are a lot of flaws in it. It looked to me like [director Richard Attenborough] had a 12-hour story that he cut down to three hours, leaving out everything but the crowd scenes."

If *E.T.* was the zenith of Spielberg's professional life, two months after its release he experienced the nadir of his personal life.

On the last day of shooting one episode of an anthology film based on the classic television series, *The Twilight Zone*, a helicopter crashed into three of the film's actors, Vic Morrow and two small children of Asian descent.

Spielberg was the producer of the film and the director of one of the anthology film's segments. The segment in which the crash occurred was directed by John Landis (*Animal House*).

Landis was ordered to stand trial for involuntary manslaughter. Although he ultimately was acquitted, the tragedy cast a pall on what was the best year of Steven Spielberg's life.

At first, it seemed that he would be implicated in the negligence that allowed two underage actors to be filming in the wee hours of the morning in distinct violation of union roles.

The rumor that Spielberg had been present when the tragedy occurred gained weight when one of the chauffeurs on the set, Carl Pittman, said in a deposition that the director had asked to use his car after the incident: "Mr. Spielberg was on the set. In fact, I didn't want him to have the car. I wanted to keep it there in case anyone else needed the car. At this point, no one knew how many people were injured," Pittman told the Los Angeles County Sheriff's Homicide and National Transportation Safety Board in secret sworn testimony leaked to *Daily Variety*, which printed excerpts from the deposition.

Pittman said he was particularly disturbed by Spielberg's demeanor after the children's death. "I had to walk away from Spielberg. I was mad enough at him that I had to walk away from him. He was too cold about it."

Everyone else on the set thought Pittman was hallucinating. The rest of the cast and crew swore that Spielberg had been nowhere near the Indiana Dunes location outside Los Angeles. Of the thirty-two crew members interviewed by the National Transportation Safety Board, only Pittman claimed a Spielberg sighting.

The studio was quoted as saying, "Warner Bros. categorically denies that Steven Spielberg was on the set the night of the unfortunate accident. Nor was he on the set of the Landis segment at any other time. Any statements to the contrary are simply not true."

The studio, Spielberg, and eight other individuals were slapped with a $100 million lawsuit by the parents of one of the children.

Although Spielberg was exonerated, he still felt some responsibility for the tragedy. And he even took a backhanded swipe at the director of the segment, Landis. "No movie is worth dying for. If something isn't safe, it's the right and responsibility of every actor or crew member to yell, 'Cut!'" he said.

In a sworn deposition to the National Transportation Safety Board, which was also reprinted in *Daily Variety*, Spielberg testified, "I was never at the Indiana Dunes location of *Twilight Zone* on the night of the accident or at any other time. I declare under penalty of perjury that the foregoing it true and correct, executed at Los Angeles, California, this first day of Dec. 1981." The letter was written on Spielberg's personal stationery.

Later, he would admit, "The accident cast a pall on all 150 people who worked on this production. We are still just sick to the center of our souls. I don't know anybody who it hasn't affected."

In counterpoint to the tragedy of *The Twilight Zone* deaths, an amusing example of the movie industry's power politics also took place the eventful summer of 1982.

It's a story about a powerful mega-director, a minor-talent director, and a studio's marketing strategy. It's also an abject lesson in, as the old saying goes, when you're hot, you're hot, when you're not, you're not.

After *E.T.*, Steven Spielberg was hotter than a supernova. The same summer that *E.T.* made box-office history, another film he produced and cowrote, but did not direct, also was released.

It was a finely crafted ghost story, *Poltergeist*, about evil spirits who take over a placid suburban tract home, abduct its four-year-old occupant, and generally wreak hell on earth.

Tobe Hooper was the nominal director. A good-old Texas boy, Hooper's main claim to fame was directing a hideously violent cult film, *The Texas Chain-Saw Massacre*, eight years before *Poltergeist*. The film had achieved cult status primarily because of the protagonist's original way of carving up victims with the help of power tools.

Hooper was a strange choice to direct a mainstream film about suburbia, but Spielberg was a big fan of Hooper's cult film.

Unfortunately for Hooper, the studio was a bigger fan of the hottest director in town. When it came time to release

Poltergeist, the studio spread the rumor that Spielberg actually had directed the film.

Studio publicists dropped hints to the press, and there was even a documentary about the making of the film that showed Spielberg clearly directing a scene, even though his credits were as producer and cowriter. Usually, the producer is the guy standing in the background, and the director is the guy calling the shots.

Spielberg may not have been the auteur of the film, but he was the author of the script. It was his conception. His baby. And much to Hooper's discomfort, Spielberg didn't try to quash rumors that he was the actual director.

In a circuitous way, *Poltergeist* was actually autobiographical. Spielberg remembered childhood reveries when he would lie in bed and stare at a crack in the bedroom wall. The youth's overactive imagination would visualize all sorts of creepy critters from Beyond crawling out of the crack.

"I remember lying there, trying to go to sleep, and I used to always imagine little Hieronymous Bosch-like creatures inside, peeking out and whispering to me to come into the playground of the crack and be drawn into the unknown there, inside the wall of my home in New Jersey," he said at the time of *Poltergeist*'s release.

The concept of *Poltergeist* also was stoked by the making of *Close Encounters*. The movie's theme of alien abduction, a subplot in the earlier film, became the main story line of *Poltergeist*.

"*Poltergeist* was something I conceived while I was doing *Raiders*. I always wanted to make a ghost movie, ever since I was a kid. I loved what happened in *Close Encounters* when the child was kidnapped by the mother ship and taken away by his friends of equal proportion. So I kind of blended a little bit of the kidnapping of the child in *Close Encounters* with the research I had done about poltergeists, and made a movie about a child who's kidnapped by ghosts in her own suburban home in middle America."

Spielberg also made *Poltergeist* as a counterpoint to *E.T.* If the latter expressed all his hope for humanity, *Poltgergeist* encompassed his primordial fears.

"*E.T.* is a whisper. Poltergeist is a scream," he said. "*Poltergeist* is what I fear, and *E.T.* is what I love. One is about suburban evil and the other is about suburban good. I had different motivations in both instances. In *Poltergeist* I wanted to terrify and I also wanted to amuse. I tried to mix laughs and screams together. *Poltergeist* is the darker side of my nature—it's me when I was scaring my younger sisters half to death when were growing up. *E.T.* is my optimism about the future and my optimism about what it was like to grow up in Arizona and New Jersey."

Poltergeist may have owed its verisimilitude to the fact that the producer actually believed in ghosts. When an interviewer asked Spieblerg point-blank if he believed in the "stars" of his movie, he replied seriously, "Yes, I do. I absolutely do. I believe in poltergeists and UFOs. In every movie I've made, I've essentially believed in what the films were about. Even *Jaws*. I did believe there are sharks close to twenty-six feet long in the ocean. The largest ever caught is twenty-one feet.

"If I ever make a film about a fifty-foot woman, I'll believe that too."

Whether or not he directed the film, Spielberg usurped one job traditionally reserved for the director—casting. He discovered the beautiful child who is abducted by ghosts Lana Turner-style, not at Schwab's but at the MGM commissary. Spielberg wanted a "beatific four-year-old, every mother's dream."

Spielberg spotted exactly what he was looking for when he saw four-year-old Heather O'Rourke at a nearby table. The director walked over and asked, "Who's the proud mother *or agent* of this child?" He claimed that two hands went up immediately—the mother's and the agent's. He signed O'Rourke the next day.

Just as he took full credit for casting a crucial role in *Poltergeist*, Spielberg also insisted that he was the hands-on producer, not just the titular producer. "I line produced *Poltergeist*," he said proudly. "That was my production. I was very involved from the beginning."

Poor Tobe Hooper.

The alleged director of *Poltergeist* found himself in a very delicate situation. He didn't want to tick off the most powerful director in Hollywood or the studio which had given him his big break into the big time. On the other hand, he *had* directed the film—at least that's what the credits said.

I interviewed Hooper shortly after *Poltergeist* came out in the summer of 1982 at his modest home in the San Fernando Valley. Amid memorabilia from his films, including the notorious chain saw, he fidgeted nervously when I asked him who had directed Poltergeist.

"That question isn't good for business," he said, neatly summing up his quandary.

Spielberg had already gone on record, saying he had "designed" the film, a nonexistent credit as far as the Directors Guild was concerned.

Spielberg's longtime, faithful collaborator Frank Marshall, who coproduced *Poltergeist*, called him the "creative force" behind the project.

To the casual moviegoer who pays his money and just wants to be entertained in the dark for two hours, all the brouhaha might have seemd to be the stuff of semantics and Directors Guild arbitration.

It was and it wasn't. With *Poltergeist* the number-two film of the summer, the question of who made the film was also the stuff that careers are made of. Hooper wanted the credit, literally and figuratively. But he didn't want to anger Spielberg.

The matter became so volatile that the Directors Guild investigated and ultimately declared Hooper the director.

Hooper did agree with me that the issue had been "manufactured."

"I just don't know who the manufacturer is," he said disingenuously. If an outsider knew the studio was spreading the rumors about Spielberg's input, certainly the nominal director of the film knew as well.

One rumor Hooper was willing to spike was that he was yanked off the film after principal photography had been completed and that he was shut out of the postproduction process. The rumor had a reliable source: Craig T. Nelson, the father in the film and current star of television's *Coach*, publicly stated that Hooper had not been allowed into the editing room.

"I was in the editing room for ten weeks. There's very little difference between my cut and Steven's. I like the final cut very much," Hooper told me, but refused to say how his cut differed from the final one. "The differences were just too minor," he insisted.

Ever the diplomat, Hooper said without much enthusiasm, "I found it a very good experience working with Steven. He wanted input—absolutely. Change that 'absolutely' to a 'yes.'"

On June 9, 1982, Spielberg took out a full-page ad in *Daily Variety*. The letter, on Spielberg's personal stationery, said:

> Dear Tobe,
>
> Some of the press has misunderstood the rather unique, creative relationship which you and I shared throughout the making of *Poltergeist*.
>
> I enjoyed your openness in allowing me, as a producer and a writer, a wide berth for creative involvement, just as I know you were happy with the freedom you had to direct *Poltergeist* so wonderfully.
>
> Through the screenplay, you accepted a vision of this very intense movie, and as the director, you delivered the goods. You performed responsibly and professionally throughout, and I want to wish you great success on your next project. Let's hope that *Poltergeist* brings as much pleasure to the general public as we experienced in our mutual effort.
>
> Sincerely,
> Steven Spielberg

That letter could be interpreted as an example of Spielberg's good-hearted generosity or his extreme disingenuousness. The latter interpretation gained credibility from the rumor that the letter was part of a secret Directors Guild settlement that allowed Spielberg's name to be featured in movie trailers in letters twice as big as Hooper's. That plus $15,000. Not much compensation if Hooper was indeed hung out to dry by the studio and his producer.

We will never know who actually directed *Poltergeist*, but if the following work of the two men is any indication, *Poltergeist* was either just a lucky fluke for Hooper or Spielberg did indeed direct the film.

Poltergeist was a tour de force, brilliantly crafted, subtly humorous, and scary. Spielberg would continue his string of popcorn classics with *Jurassic Park* and *Indiana Jones and the Last Crusade*.

Whither Tobe Hooper?

On the strength of *Poltergeist*'s performance, Hooper lined up another big-budget, special-effects extravaganza called *Lifeforce*. It was supposed to be a terrifying story about vampires who suck the life force out of their victims. The film was so incompetently made that audiences hooted with laughter at scenes that were supposed to be as frightening as anything in *Poltergeist*.

As one industry source said, "If Hooper actually directed both films, his body must have been possessed by a *poltergeist* when he made one of them because the same man couldn't have made both."

As a high school student in Phoenix, Arizona, Spielberg was already directing films on his father's 8mm camera. He specialized in devising new ways to terrorize the stars of these early films—his three younger sisters.
SETH POPPEL/SHOOTING STAR

Spielberg took on a rather formidable project for his debut—directing Joan Crawford in the 1969 premiere episode of *Night Gallery* when he was only twenty-one. "It was like pitching to Hank Aaron your first time in the game," he said.
PHOTOFEST

After his start in episodic television, Spielberg was given the opportunity to direct a television movie, *Duel*. The film, starring Dennis Weaver, was a great success, both on television and in its European theatrical release where it earned more than $9 million and numerous awards.
PHOTOFEST

Goldie Hawn and William Atherton hijack a highway patrol car to rescue their children in Sugarland, Texas, in Spielberg's first feature-length film, *Sugarland Express*. Although a box office disappointment, the 1974 film was highly praised as a directorial debut.
COURTESY UNIVERSAL PICTURES

Although now considered almost a visual cliché, the image of dozens of squad cars in pursuit was pioneered by Spielberg in *Sugarland Express*.
COURTESY UNIVERSAL PICTURES

Steven, his parents, and future wife Amy Irving revel in the success of *Jaws* at the 1976 Screen Director's Guild Awards. The film catapulted Spielberg into the big time both by shattering box office records and earning high critical acclaim.
ARCHIVE PHOTOS/FOTOS INTERNATIONAL

Beachgoers are attacked by the infamous shark in *Jaws*. The mechanical shark used in shooting, nicknamed Bruce, cost more than $1 million—and a lot of headaches. Aside from constant technical difficulties with Bruce's electronics, the first Bruce sank after only three days of shooting.
COURTESY UNIVERSAL PICTURES

Spielberg relaxes on the deck of the *Orca*, the ship used in the filming of *Jaws*, with great white shark hunters Richard Dreyfuss, Roy Scheider, and Robert Shaw.
COURTESY UNIVERSAL PICTURES

Both *Jaws* star Roy Scheider and Spielberg attended the 1976 Golden Globe Awards. Composer John Williams came away with the film's only award for best musical score.
ARCHIVE PHOTOS/FOTOS INTERNATIONAL

Close friends and Hollywood megamoguls Spielberg and *Star Wars* director George Lucas appear together at the 1978 Director's Guild awards dinner. The pair conceived of the Indiana Jones trilogy on a beach in Hawaii.
ARCHIVE PHOTOS/FOTOS

After appearing in Spielberg's first blockbuster hit, Richard Dreyfuss returned to work with Spielberg on *Close Encounters of the Third Kind*. The two had become friends on the set of *Jaws*, and despite contract disputes on *Close Encounters* they've maintained their friendship for more than two decades.
COURTESY COLUMBIA PICTURES

By 1978 Spielberg was on a roll after the huge success of *Jaws* and *Close Encounters*. His next film, *1941*, may have registered the performance anxiety brought on by his new reputation.
ARCHIVE PHOTOS/LONDON EXPRESS

Comedian John Belushi starred in Spielberg's first big-budget bomb, *1941*, a black comedy about an imagined Japanese WWII attack on Los Angeles. Although the film "flopped" by Spielberg standards, it still grossed $90 million, turning a $20 million profit.
COURTESY UNIVERSAL STUDIOS

Steven and his first wife, actress Amy Irving, met in 1976. The tempestuous relationship would lead to a 1980 breakup, a reunion in 1983, a wedding two years later, and a divorce four years after that.
FRANK EDWARDS/ARCHIVE PHOTOS

Spielberg conceived of the Indiana Jones films as a tribute to the Saturday afternoon serial movies from his childhood. The character has provided one of Harrison Ford's most popular and enduring roles. In fact, the actor has already signed on for *Indy 4*.

Although the production of *Raiders of the Lost Ark*, starring Harrison Ford and Karen Allen, came in under budget at only $20 million—a cut-rate item by Spielberg standards—studio executives still worried about whether it would bring in the $50 million necessary to finish in the black. They needn't have worried: *Raiders* would gross more than $360 million!

Spielberg with his most enduringly popular character, E.T. The audioanimatronic creature, designed by Italy's Carlo Rambaldi, cost $1.5 million. The puppet's lifelike mannerisms had some critics suggesting it deserved a Best Actor nomination.

Nine-year-old actor Henry Thomas stepped into the crucial role of E.T.'s earthling pal, Elliot, after Spielberg had already auditioned more than 300 kids.

The image of E.T. and Elliot pedalling across the moon was perhaps the most spectacular and memorable of Spielberg's 1982 blockbuster. The movie remained the highest-grossing of all time until it was toppled from first place by another Spielberg hit, *Jurassic Park*.

Spielberg and then-girlfriend Amy Irving take young Drew Barrymore, co-star of *E.T.*, on a shopping trip in 1984. After working with so many children on the set of *E.T.*, Spielberg said, "I have this deep yearning now to become a father."

BOB SCOTT/FOTOS INTERNATIONAL

Steven Spielberg—the quintessential Hollywood director. The King of Hollywood has repeatedly broken box office records with films like *Jaws*, *E.T.*, and *Jurassic Park*. He may be poised to break another: rumors place Spielberg as the potential director for both *Star Wars 4* and *Jurassic Park 2*.

Scatman Crothers (right) appears in the Spielberg-produced *Twilight Zone: The Movie*. The moderate success of the film was overshadowed by the tragic deaths of two child actors in a helicopter crash on the set.
COURTESY WARNER BROS. PICTURES

Executive Producer George Lucas and director Spielberg on the set of *Raiders* sequel *Temple of Doom*. Spielberg was disappointed with his performance on the film. Later, he said he made the third Indiana Jones film "to apologize to fans for making the second one."
PHOTOFEST

A year after working with Spielberg on the set of *Indiana Jones and the Temple of Doom*, Kate Capshaw, here with Harrison Ford, became the director's second wife.

Actor Danny Glover stars as Celie's (Whoopi Goldberg) abusive husband in Spielberg's screen adaptation of Alice Walker's Pulitzer Prize-winning novel, *The Color Purple*. Despite critical misgivings about the white-bread director's ability to tackle a project about black lesbians, Spielberg successfully cast off the label of action director and delivered a mature and sophisticated film.
COURTESY WARNER BROS. PICTURES

Actors Sean Connery, John Rhys-Davies, and Harrison Ford
quest for the Holy Grail in *Indiana Jones and the Last Crusade*.
Spielberg had to pass up a chance to direct Oscar champ
Rainman to honor his handshake deal with George Lucas
to do Indy 3.
COURTESY PARAMOUNT PICTURES

Jaws star Roy Scheider teamed
up with Spielberg again for the
disappointingly low-rated
television series, *seaQuest DSV*.

"The director who wouldn't grow up" takes a break on the set of *Hook* with stars Robin Williams and Julia Roberts. Although the star-studded cast was a box office plus, it inevitably created substantial behind-the-scenes ego friction.
PHOTOFEST

A ravenous T-rex eyeballs actor Sam Neill and young co-star Ariana Richards, in the 1993 Spielberg ultra-hit, *Jurassic Park*. The film knocked another reptilian Spielberg creation—*E.T.*—out of the number one slot for highest-grossing film, earning at last count more than $850 million.

Jurassic Park stars Laura Dern and Jeff Goldblum rehearse their lines under Spielberg's direction on the set in Kauai.
PHOTOFEST

After recent earthquakes, Spielberg may be unloading his multimillion dollar Los Angeles home overlooking the Pacific Ocean to move permanently to the more stable ground of his Long Island house.
MARIO RUIZ/PEOPLE WEEKLY

Filming *Schindler's List* on location in Poland was an emotionally trying time for Spielberg. Addressing such a subject as the Holocaust was draining. "Twice during production, I called Robin Williams just to say, 'Robin, I haven't laughed in seven weeks. Help me here.' And Robin would do twenty minutes on the telephone," he said.

Spielberg takes a well-deserved break with his wife from the hectic shooting schedule of *Schindler's List*. After twelve-hour workdays on the set in Poland, Spielberg would fly to Paris on the weekends to edit *Jurassic Park*.
MOSHE SHAI/SHOOTING STAR

In the 1994 film *Schindler's List*, Liam Neeson (on platform), plays Oskar Schindler, a German who saved the lives of hundreds of Jews during the Holocaust by enlisting them to work in his factory. The film earned Spielberg his greatest critical acclaim, sweeping the Oscars that year.
COURTESY UNIVERSAL PICTURES

Ben Kingsley, co-star of *Schindler's List*, chats with Spielberg at an American Film Institute event honoring the director for his magnificent work on the movie.
LEE SALEM/SHOOTING STAR

After the release of *Schindler's List*, real Holocaust survivors saved by Oskar Shindler, one of whom appears here with Spielberg, gave the director a replica of a ring they had made for Schindler inscribed, "You save one life, you save the world."
MOSHE SHAI/SHOOTING STAR

Spielberg basks with wife Kate Capshaw and mother Leah in the glow of long-withheld Oscar recognition. Spielberg took home Best Director and Best Picture awards for *Schindler's List* in 1994.
SPIKE NANNARELLO/SHOOTING STAR

CHAPTER NINE

Doomed, Temporarily

E.T. WAS A FILM VIRTUALLY IMPOSSIBLE TO top commercially or critically, and with his next film, Spielberg didn't even come close.

The only reason Spielberg made a sequel to *Raiders of the Lost Ark* in 1984 was his handshake promise to best friend George Lucas that if *Raiders* was a smash, he'd make two sequels.

The second installment, *Indiana Jones and the Temple of Doom*, would test the boundaries of Spielberg's keeping his word. And it would show just what a good friend he was to his mentor, Lucas.

Friendship, however, didn't stop him from some amazingly honest self-criticism. He later would say he made the third Indiana Jones adventure to "apologize to my fans for making the second one.

"I wasn't happy with the second film at all. It was too dark, too subterranean, and much too horrific. I thought it out-poltered *Poltergeist*. There's not an ounce of my own personal feeling in *Temple of Doom*."

The film was indeed very dark for a movie that was supposed to be pure entertainment. There are scenes of human sacrifice, child slave labor, and the murderous Kali cult. Even the humorous elements, like the monkey brains dinner, were more gross than amusing. Spielberg himself admitted, "I think it's too intense for children under twelve."

The ironically titled *Temple of Doom* was even more significant because of the impact it would have on his personal life. Spielberg cast the woman who was to become his second wife, Kate Capshaw, in the female lead. With only one film under her belt, a flop called *A Little Sex*, she beat out 120 actresses for the job of the nightclub chanteuse, Willie Scott.

In a Valentine's Day issue of *Entertainment Weekly*, Capshaw recalled their first meeting when she was a struggling actress driving a no-status car and he was the king of Hollywood:

"I met Steven 12 years ago when he was casting *Indiana Jones and the Temple of Doom*. It was raining and my hair was soaked. I wore jeans, a work shirt and cowboy boots.

"He was sitting with his back to me. When I came into view, he looked at me and said, 'Oh, you're not who I thought you were.' I thought, 'Great!' Then I found myself thinking, 'Well, maybe I can make this work for me.'

"Instead of an interview or audition, we started talking. I couldn't get relaxed and kept trying to move closer. I moved from the couch to the fireplace, from there to a chair. I asked him to remove his sunglasses so I could see his eyes. It was like some sort of mating dance. Sparks were flying. When I got into my Volkswagen bug, my heart was racing, and it was five minutes before I could turn the key in the ignition. I thought, 'I'm in big trouble.'"

Sparks flew, but Spielberg had married his on-again, off-again girlfriend, Amy Irving, only the year before. They were still in love. That would change, and Capshaw would get her chance to get into "big trouble" sooner than she thought.

Although Capshaw was smitten by the director the first time they met, she wasn't overly impressed by his reputation. In fact, when he called to let her know she had landed the starring role in *Temple of Doom*, she almost hung up on him because she was busy moving into her new home in Los Angeles.

"Boxes were everywhere. There was a Czechoslovakian paperhanger upstairs, the baby-sitter was here with [her daughter] Jessica for the first time, and a girlfriend had stopped over to look at the house. It was Grand Central Station and I was late for work on *Dreamscape* when Steven called. I said, 'Steven, you've caught me at a bad time. I really can't talk.' And he said, 'But I'm calling from New York, and I just wanted to let you know . . . ' I said, 'Steven, can you please call me tomorrow? I can hardly hear you now.' This went on for a few minutes, and finally he said, 'Would you sit down? I want you to play Willie Scott in *Indiana Jones*.' I went, 'Steven, I do not have time to talk about this . . . *what*?!!!'

"I got off the phone and started crying. I had such mixed feelings. Jessica was only six years old and had already been to six schools, but I wasn't going to leave her in L.A. I had a lot of other reservations, like would Meryl Streep do the sequel to *Raiders*? I was very ambivalent."

But at this point in her career, Capshaw was no Meryl Streep, and she couldn't afford to be choosy with only one flop under her belt. So putting aside her reservations and packing her daughter along with her things, she flew off to the jungles of Sri Lanka to shoot the film.

It was a momentous decision. As she would admit later, "*Indy* was a milestone. It changed my life in every way."

Filming *Temple of Doom* took an exhausting five months on three continents. Further problems were caused by a three-week halt in filming due to problems the star, Harrison Ford, was having with his back. Ford's recovery was speeded by special papaya enzyme treatments.

The film also allowed Spielberg to confront one of his phobias—insects. Even more than he enjoys scaring everyone from his sisters to the moviegoing public at large, the director apparently loves to terrorize himself. *Temple of Doom* literally employed a "cast of thousands," 20,000 bugs. "Bugs absolutely terrify me, but it was my idea to put them in. I didn't want to bring snakes back from *Raiders*—I was snaked out. I thought I could stand on a ladder and direct the bug scenes, but Kate [Capshaw] said she wouldn't put up with the bugs crawling on her unless I stood right next to her. So I did, and they crawled all over me too. I could feel them walking on me with their sticky little feet," Spielberg said.

Capshaw rarely used a stunt double, and all her creepy co-stars were real. She insisted, "Let me say this: all creatures, great and small, were real. I think this movie came out of a contest. You know what pajama parties were like when you were young—how you'd get together and tell awful stories? Well, I think Steven and George must have done that one night and then put all of it into the movie!"

Although he was attached to Amy Irving while filming *Temple of Doom*, he couldn't resist praising his leading lady's professional accomplishments. The personal stuff would come later, when he was available for other things besides film directing and coaching.

"Kate's a natural comedian," he said. "A cross between Lucille Ball and Ann Sothern."

For her part, Capshaw was otherwise engaged—involved with her live-in lover, Armyan Bernstein, who wrote and directed Capshaw in *Windy City*.

Despite the bugs, Capshaw was a good sport about the hard shoot. They worked twelve-hour days in jungle temperatures that zoomed to 130 degrees. Capshaw wasn't made of steel all the time, however. At one point during filming, she burst into tears and refused to embrace a fourteen-foot boa constrictor.

"The animal trainer assured me I had nothing to worry about, and a lot of people came up and told me such snakes were harmless, but it didn't help," she recalled. "And I was terrified that my fear would somehow communicate itself to the snake, which would then turn dangerous."

Spielberg turned into her knight in shining armor. "Seeing me in tears, Steven came up and said, 'I won't make you do it!' He scrapped the scene, and on the plane back to London he wrote that other scene where we're in a clearing and all those animals keep scaring me. I'm afraid my fear of snakes must have cost Steven a couple of hundred thousand dollars shooting that new scene."

For Capshaw, making *Temple of Doom* was a scream—literally. "I felt that some days all I did was shriek, and it was exhausting. It wasn't hard to play Willie Scott, who is always bitching about things, because it *was* hot, the bugs were disgusting and the elephant was a pain in the butt."

After filming *E.T.*, Spielberg felt an emotional letdown because he missed working so closely with children. When it came time to make *Temple of Doom*, he decided to throw in a lot of kids because he had enjoyed the *E.T.* experience so much. However, most of the kids were depicted in the movie as slave laborers. It was also the director's decision to write in a child sidekick for Harrison Ford. After an open casting call in Chinatown and looking at thousands of Asian children from around the country, he settled on a Vietnamese child named Ke Huy Quan, a product of the open casting call.

"I wanted a kid in this movie," he explained. "I thought Harrison would be great bouncing off a pint-size kid. I've seen Harrison with his own kids, and he's a fabulous father."

Spielberg finds communicating with pint-size thespians much more sympatico than with their older counterparts. "I'm not as articulate with adult actors. Kids are the best when they're ad-libbing, and I work extremely well with that kind of improvisation."

(Teri Garr, who played Richard Dreyfuss's much put upon wife in *Close Encounters*, would agree about Spielberg's problems with adult actors. She told me, "He treats his actors like marionettes. When you want to discuss motivation with him, he just says, 'Stand there and do this.'")

The critics were incensed by the film's violence. One critic for a local Los Angeles station, the curmudgeonly Gary Franklin, took special pleasure bad-mouthing both *Raiders* and its sequel. He complained that the first made light of Nazis, turning them into cartoons instead of mass murderers. The sequel was just too violent. In May 1984, when Lucas and Spielberg were imprinting their hands and feet in wet cement outside Mann's Chinese Theater in Hollywood, the director used the occasion to toss a barb back at his critic.

A reporter asked Spielberg who he thought should see his film. Spielberg responded, "I think everybody can see this film except Gary Franklin."

Franklin happened to be at the publicity stunt, covering it for his station. When Lucas defended the film's violent content by saying there was a disclaimer in the ads that the film "might be too intense for younger children," Franklin shouted over the heads of his fellow reporters, "Like tearing the heart out of a person's chest?"

Violence wasn't the only thing the critics disliked. Capshaw's Willie Scott, many complained, was a gross, misogynistic stereotype, the female sidekick as disposable bimbo. Even the normally gentle *Los Angeles Times* film critic Sheila Benson harumphed, "She seems to have been hired for her shriek."

It's probably inaccurate to call Spielberg's depiction of Willie Scott misogynistic. If anything, he was guilty of displaying his trademark, one-dimensional characters. You didn't have to be a female to be less than multidimensional in a Spielberg film. Indiana Jones was no Willie Loman or even Oscar Madison. First and foremost, Spielberg was a *technical* director. You need split-second timing where a boulder intersects with the hero? You got it. But at this time, with the exception of *E.T.*, which was seeming more and more like an artistic fluke after the adolescent *Poltergeist* and *Temple of Doom*, when it came to shading characters, Spielberg had only two colors in his palette: black and white. In the future he would delicately dissect black lesbians and nice-guy Nazis, but at present, women were for screaming and men were for cracking whips.

Capshaw at first was inclined to agree with the critics. "When I first read the script, I didn't like Willie Scott. I thought she was snotty and pretentious. I didn't know how I was going to play her. Usually, I love the woman I'm playing, and I find all the things in myself that I can fill her up with. I didn't know where to go to find Willie Scott, because I didn't experience myself as being anything like her," the actress said.

Eventually she reconciled herself to playing Harrison Ford's shrieking arm ornament. "Willie is a fun companion for Indiana," she decided. "Had she been a classy broad who embraced the adventure, you would have had no conflict."

Spielberg also took umbrage when others accused him of crass exploitation for making an unfelt sequel to *Raiders*.

"Everything is exploitative," he insisted. "Everything is trying to glean a buck from the weekend consumer. Movies are big business. In that sense, every movie is exploitative, even *Bridge on the River Kwai*, if it's out to make money, if it's out to be successful as well as make a statement and share an emotion with the audience. But there are certain pictures that are blatantly exploitative, that are terribly cast and executed, like poorly made sequels or bizarre remakes."

Ironically, he might have been talking about *The Temple of Doom* and his unsuccessful remake a few years later, *Always*.

"They get a big following because they are very much like our TV series today. They are continuing stories, with the same cast and characters, the same ingredients, and you know what you're going to get before you sit down in your seat."

Making *Temple of Doom* wasn't an entire loss, personally or directorially. He had always wanted to film a lavish Busby Berkeley dance sequence, but his kind of filmmaking and thematic interests seemed unlikely to ever give him the opportunity.

Indiana Jones and the Temple of Doom finally would allow him to indulge himself. The opening number features the female lead singing Cole Porter's "Anything Goes"—in Mandarin Chinese! Spielberg originally had wanted to choreograph the title song from *Forty-Second Street* for the opening sequence, but ultimately decided on "Anything Goes" to let the audience know it should expect anything to happen in the rest of the movie.

It's arguably even more energetic—and definitely more frenetic—than anything Busby Berkeley ever concocted for his 1930s confections. The sequence also allowed him to continue the trend he began in the first Jones adventure by showing the climax of an imaginary previous episode, which reinforced the serial flavor of the genre he was so lovingly re-creating.

CHAPTER TEN

Turning Points

A WATERSHED YEAR FOR STEVEN SPIELBERG, personally and aesthetically, was 1985. It was the year he became a father, a husband (in that order), and made his most adult, personal film to date.

His relationship with Amy Irving, which began in 1976, had been as big a roller-coaster ride as any of his films. They broke up in 1979 amid mutual career disasters, got back together again in 1983, had a child in 1985, and married six months later.

The year 1979 had been awful for both the director and his girlfriend. There was the public humiliation of *1941*. And Irving's career took a nose dive when her romantic film and first starring vehicle, *Honeysuckle Rose*, with Willie Nelson as her unlikely love interest, failed at the box office. (The film did earn her some of the best reviews of her career, however, with the *Los Angeles Times* inaccurately predicting it would be the hit of the summer.)

Licking their wounds, the couple decided to escape to Japan where, they told friends, they planned to marry to avoid the United States paparazzi. "I'll be pregnant by April," Irving told friends. "We can't wait to start a family." Within three weeks, they were back in the United States, separated. One unconfirmed story claimed they fought during the flight to Japan and broke up over the Pacific!

Irving hated their high-profile life together in the movie industry. "We lived together for four years and were engaged for three months. It didn't work out. We weren't ready. We've both grown into different people now. But I love him still.

"Our social life was going out to dinner with studio heads. I wasn't honoring myself there. The values are movie values. They only want to be your friend if your name is above the title of your movie," she said.

Particularly irksome was the general assumption that her career thrived because of her relationship with one of the most powerful men in Hollywood. "I knew it wasn't true but I still resented it," she admitted.

If anything, her alliance with Spielberg on balance hurt more than it helped her career.

"I know I've never gotten work because of Steven. I know I have *not* gotten work because of Steven. Certain directors' egos are such that they don't want somebody from Steven's camp in their territory. I've known of instances when I was supposed to get a part, but they started to worry about Steven Spielberg getting more of a focus than them—that happens. But you know what. It was a great trade-off," she said.

A mutual friend explained the split: "There was an awakening of sorts, and they may have realized they weren't meant for each other."

Spielberg was devastated by the breakup. He said, "Life has finally caught up with me. I've spent so many years hiding from the pain and fear behind a camera. I avoided all the growing up pains by being too busy making movies. I lost myself to the world of film. So right now, in my early thirties, I'm experiencing delayed adolescence. I suffer like I'm sixteen. It's a miracle I haven't sprouted acne again. The point is, I didn't escape suffering. I only delayed it."

Irving felt adrift as well, even though their friendship survived the end of the romance. "We did what we both had to do, and we remain great friends. In fact, we're talking of doing a project. But I am alone—and I don't like that situation too much."

Spielberg remained philosophical about the double whammy of the Irving split and the fiasco of *1941*. "It's almost a good thing that everything happened at once, and I got it over with."

The director spent about a year as an unattached bachelor and played it safe—emotionally—by dating a series of nearly underage girls. His most famous liaison was television's Valerie Bertinelli, but it was in his mind no liaison at all. He described the relationship as "south of casual. We never got past the hand-shaking stage."

In fact, all his relationships were uninvolving. "They were all nice girls, but I was playing big brother," the emotionally wounded man said.

There was a two-year affair with a Warner Records executive, Kathleen Carey. But still hurting, Spielberg took the relationship slowly. Comparing his previous relationship to his current one, he said, "Amy and I must have been together for a year and a half before we got to be friends, but Kathleen and I were friends before we were lovers. That makes a real difference."

Carey, whom one magazine described as a "pretty, slight blonde woman," provided an emotional counterbalance to a life that up to that time had been all work, work, work. She said, "Steven inspired me in my career, and I help him to be a more rounded person. He was always so busy working before he never had time for real relationships. He needs friends, not people telling him how wonderful he is."

Spielberg agreed. "She has taught me that there's a life after movies."

It's hard to determine how serious their relationship was since they never lived together. Anyway, it was over within two years, just in time for Spielberg to bump into Irving in India.

Irving was on the subcontinent shooting an HBO movie, *The Far Pavilions*. "One night, in front of three friends I made a wish," she recalled. "I said, 'I wish I'd have a visitor and I want it to be Steven.'" A few hours later, her assistant told her, "Steven Spielberg arrives in the morning."

Irving surprised him at the airport. He was in the country to scout locations for *Indiana Jones and the Temple of Doom*. At least the movie wasn't a total loss, since it reunited him with his first love.

Their first meeting after the breakup was touchy. He recalled that there was "love in her eyes, and anger in mine. But we fell in love again."

Irving's recollections were more upbeat. "From that moment, I knew. Now we're really in love. And here I am with the Prince of Hollywood. I guess that makes me the Princess."

It was only a few years since they had first split, but both had matured. Irving was less competitive with her mate. Spielberg was more emotionally open. The couple moved in to Spielberg's comfortable, but not palatial, home in the Coldwater Canyon section of Beverly Hills—the house that *Jaws* built, as he put it. Irving promptly redecorated the place in Southwestern style, which she had fallen in love with when she'd lived in Santa Fe.

A year after they reunited, rumors in the press percolated that Spielberg had dumped Irving for actress Debra Winger. Spielberg dramatically scotched those rumors during a 1984 interview with *Rolling Stone*. In the middle of the interview, Winger telephoned, and Spielberg refused to take the call. When Irving called a while later, he interrupted the interview to chat with her.

A year after that, the relationship climaxed in the most romantic of settings. They were walking hand in hand in the garden of Claude Monet's house, now a museum, in a Paris suburb. Irving remembered the romantic incident for a very specific, unromantic reason. "Just as we arrived, the rain stopped, so we were able to walk around the garden. When we walked inside it started pouring again. Then, during lunch, a double rainbow appeared outside our window. It was very magical . . . and then I threw up. That was the first time I realized I was with child."

In honor of the event, Spielberg bought a painting by Monet, which he hung on their living-room wall. The double rainbow, the Monet garden—Irving was right when she said, "Fall in love with Spielberg and you fall into a Spielberg movie."

The marriage proposal was the antithesis of romantic, however. Film critic Roger Ebert quotes Spielberg as saying, "I was sitting in a bubble bath . . . Amy had stuff on her face. It wasn't very romantic. More like the Marx Brothers." Then a nasty note enters the recollection, which doesn't sound at all like the director. After he proposed, according to Ebert, Spielberg realized, "I knew Amy would say yes because she'd already asked me to marry her seven or eight times!"

One of the reasons this anecdote doesn't ring true is that in so many other interviews Spielberg pronounced himself gaga over Amy. In the September 1984 issue of *Cosmopolitan*, which named them couple of the month, he thrilled, "I'm intolerably happy! I've been dedicated to films before. Now for the first time in my life, I'm committed to another person."

Spielberg wanted to direct the wedding the way he directed a film—with lots of visuals and drama. "When I asked Amy to marry me, we began to plan a wedding in France, in Monet's garden." It would be a Monet painting come to life, just like the one hanging on the living room wall. "But then we found out you had to live in France for thirty days before you could get married there, so we went from the very romantic to the very unromantic." Although still cinematic. "We got married like the characters in a Frank Capra film, before a wise old judge in Santa Fe."

They were married on November 27, 1985. The birth of their first child, Max, preceded the wedding by six months. Even before the baby was born, Spielberg was feeling paternal, predicting the child would have a major impact on him. "I have a baby on the way, and the child is going to change my life."

After his son was born, he explained how becoming a father had changed his priorities. "For one thing I don't think I'll make any films with kids for a while. Because I'm so satisfied having Max, I don't want to substitute surrogate children in my pictures to be a surrogate daddy. Before I had Max, I made films about kids; now that I have one, I'll probably start making films about adults." Spielberg was wrong about that. His next film would star a twelve-year-old as the sole lead. But that was two years away.

In the meantime, Spielberg wasn't just a hands-on dad, he was a hands-on mate even during the pregnancy. Irving remembered his behavior while she was expecting. "He doesn't want to miss a thing. He was in Los Angeles when I bought my first maternity dress, and he was furious when I told him. He said, 'I wanted to be there.' When I heard the fetal heartbeat for the first time, he said, 'We've got to go back to the doctor so I can hear the heartbeat, too.' When the baby comes, Steven will have somebody to share his toys with. And he's got a lot of them. He's going to be a great father!"

Pregnancy made Irving less career driven, which bode well for her relationship with Spielberg.

"I love to work, but I know having children will be a better project than any movie or play could ever be. I have a feeling that after I have children, it won't be the last you've heard of me, but you'll hear of me less."

Motherhood confirmed her prediction. After her son was born, she stayed home longer than she originally planned, eight months. "It's just that considerations for accepting a job changed: Is it good enough to disrupt my family for?"

Still, the siren song of her acting career continued to play during her pregnancy, but Spielberg was always there to puncture her insecurities.

"When Steven and I would be with a group of friends, all of them talking about their rather intriguing next projects, I could get a little insecure. But when I voiced any of these feelings, my husband always confirmed that mine was the most important 'project' of all."

In the full flush of his wife's pregnancy, Spielberg waxed ecstatic about the relationship. "Amy has managed to hold my attention for almost eight years now," he said somewhat presumptuously. "What's truly amazing about her is that I have not yet managed to figure her out. Mystery can be very romantic."

After being so involved with the minutiae like maternity dresses, it wasn't surprising that when it came time to have the baby, Spielberg continued to exercise his hands-on approach. He in effect directed the birth of his son. He participated in the natural childbirth—by snapping photos during the delivery!

He immediately became an indulgent parent. "My mom spoiled me. I'll spoil the baby. Amy will be strong with Max, and I'll be the pushover."

She was indeed. Irving laid down the law. There would be only two television sets in the Spielberg household. Shades of his own childhood, when mom and dad put a blanket over the television. The two-television rule was "hard for me," Spielberg complained, "because I'm used to a TV in every room."

Irving didn't disagree with that assessment, calling her husband, "the fun parent." But he was always a hands-on parent. "Steven is great," Irving said. "I hear other mothers talk about how their husbands won't do anything to help out. Steven will stay up all night with Max." Still, Spielberg confessed that he rarely changed diapers. That's what nannies are for.

As far as he was concerned, Max couldn't have timed his arrival any better. "I had Max when I was thirty-seven and had already reached the top of my career," he said, inaccurately, since *Schindler's List* and *Jurassic Park* were nearly a decade away. "I was ready to be a full-time father. If I'd been twenty-four, for example, I wouldn't have been quite so batty about him as most of my energy would have been concentrated on my career."

Years later he would impishly admit that while his second wife was trying to get the kids to bed, he'd be thinking up ways to let the kids stay up late.

Fatherhood, however, didn't make him any less romantic. While Irving was filming the television-movie *Anastasia* in Austria a year after Max's birth, he showed up unannounced—and unexpected—on the set with a fabulously extravagant gift—a Fabergé egg, circa 1914, with the initial "A" on it. The egg hadn't been personalized for Irving. The "A" stood for its original owner, the same Russian archduchess, Anastasia, she was playing in the television production.

<hr />

The year 1985 was very fertile for the director, professionally and personally.

As he would put it, "1985—It was the best year of my life: my marriage to Amy, the birth of our son, Max, *The Color Purple* and the other movies, *Amazing Stories*."

During his favorite, fertile year, he also produced *Goonies*, *Young Sherlock Holmes*, and the monster hit, *Back to the Future*, which would be another lucrative sequel franchise for a studio.

Less successfully, he produced the television anthology series, *Amazing Stories*, his first failure since *1941*.

Amazing Stories would be the beginning of a dreadful relationship with a medium he adored. But before *Amazing Stories* got
a chance to die a two-year death on national television, the director would enjoy a personal triumph, his most sophisticated and
adult film to date, about two black lesbians and all the awful men
in their lives!

CHAPTER ELEVEN

The Color Versatile

WAY BACK IN 1974, BEFORE *Jaws* HAD EVEN been released, Spielberg already was worrying about being labeled an action director. He said at an American Film Institute seminar shortly before *Jaws* made him the premier action director, "I'm already boxed into [action]. And I'm trying to get myself out. I'm interested in movement, I love movement, but when you're known, they put you in a box and they say, 'You're this kind of film director, so we're only going to offer you action pictures that involve machines and movement.' I would not like to do this for the rest of my life. I'd like to do a personal story."

In 1985, Spielberg would dramatically break out of the box he had been placed in. Whether it was "personal" was another matter, and one of acrimonious debate.

When it was announced that Steven Spielberg would make a film with a predominantly black cast, a joke made the rounds in Hollywood: "Yeah, it's called *Close Encounters of the Third World*."

Even after the transcendent subtlety of *E.T.*, no one except Warner Brothers thought Spielberg, the ultimate white-bread director, could bring Alice Walker's Pulitzer Prize-winning novel about black lesbians, *The Color Purple*, to the big screen.

Least of all the would-be director. He asked the man who would coproduce it, record mogul Quincy Jones, "Don't you want to find a black director or a woman?" The color-blind Jones sagely responded, "You didn't have to come from Mars to do *E.T.*, did you?"

Even the author of the source material was bullish on his participation. He remembered discussing his inappropriateness for the project with Alice Walker, who reassured him just as powerfully as Jones had.

"She gave me some background," Spielberg recalled. "'You know it's a black story. But that shouldn't bother you, because you're Jewish and essentially you share similarities in your upbringing and your heritage,'" Walker told him.

With understatement, he added, "I had some anti-Semitic experiences when I was growing, including prejudice and everything else that I had to go through at one particular high school. So I read the book and I loved it, but I didn't want to direct it. Then I picked it up again about a month and a half later, and I read it a second time. And I couldn't get away from certain images."

It was his in-house producer Kathleen Kennedy who brought the project to his attention. Kennedy recalled, "I always believed he would feel confident at some point to do other things. That's why I brought him *The Color Purple*. After he read it, he said, 'I love this because I'm scared to do it.'"

Indeed, *The Color Purple* seemed like a project he wouldn't touch with a ten-foot wand, which is exactly why he went for it. "*The Color Purple* is the biggest challenge of my career. When I read it, I loved it. I cried and cried at the end. But I didn't think I would ever develop it as a project. Finally, I said, 'I've got to do this for me. I want to make something that might not be everybody's favorite, but this year at least it's my favorite.' *The Color Purple* is the kind of character piece that a director like Sidney Lumet could do brilliantly with one hand tied behind his back. But I'm going into it with both eyes wide open and my heart beating at Mach 2."

Spanning the first forty years of this century and set in rural Georgia, *The Color Purple* focused on an oppressed black woman named Celie. During her teens, Celie is raped by her father and has two children by him. He sells the children at birth and then sells his daughter to a vicious farmer (Danny Glover, in a career-making role), who treats her more like a slave than a wife.

During her ordeal, Celie draws strength from two other black women: her sister, a missionary in Africa, and her husband's girlfriend, with whom she has a lesbian affair. Celie eventually triumphs over her tyrannical husband and becomes her own woman.

The story sounds more appropriate for public television, off-Broadway or a black repertory group. Instead, a director whose name was synonymous with special effects decided to make an extremely low-tech movie: no flying saucers, cuddly extraterrestrials, or obnoxious gremlins. Just raw emotions like pain, anger, and love.

Warner Brothers already owned the rights to the novel when Spielberg expressed interest it. The studio feared that the movie was uncommercial, so Spielberg, who some have claimed can be awfully greedy during contract negotiations, agreed to work for scale—only $40,000 in 1985. And when the film ran overbudget, he even kicked back his forty grand to Warner Brothers. The studio had expressed concern that the film wouldn't make any money, so Spielberg went out of his way to shoot it as cost effectively as possible. Warners needn't have worried. The film, budgeted at a minuscule $15 million, went on to earn $142 million in the United States and Canada alone!

Although Spielberg admitted he was "scared" to make the film, he didn't think *The Color Purple* was all that much of a stretch. "The human element has been present in all my films, especially *E.T.*," he said. But he conceded that the film was "a departure for me in that it deals with emotional crisis and tremendous growth. It's as if I've been swimming in water up to my waist all my life—and I'm great at it—but now I'm going into the deep section of the pool."

Spielberg's movie characters normally didn't experience growth. Teri Garr already had gone on record complaining that he treated his actors like puppets, telling them by way of direction, "Just do it."

But Spielberg retired his puppet strings and became an actor's director to make this character-driven project. "I want the audience to feel every color of Celie's rainbow," he said.

It also helped that he had made a personal effort to understand the actor's craft by studying it firsthand.

"I spent two years in acting classes," he said when asked at an AFI seminar how he managed to achieve such rapport with his cast. "I wasn't studying to become an actor. It was—if anything—a vent for psychological frustrations. I studied dutifully for a while. I grew to be concerned with the actor's understanding of the movie the director wants to make. Usually the actor entertains a totally different concept of the movie, and that's where many of the battles begin. And I think that the director's first accomplishment, if he ever accomplishes this, is to get the actor to understand the director's vision of the piece. If the actor can't understand it that way, then you shouldn't hire the actor. Unfortunately, the way the business is structured, all the idealism is taken out of it."

By the time he came to direct *The Color Purple*, the megadirector could afford all the "idealism" he wanted to cast the film exactly the way he wanted to—even if it meant hiring a first-time film actress and the host of a local talk show for the lead and a pivotal supporting role.

The Color Purple was a relief for Spielberg's more sophisticated fans, who felt guilty enjoying his previously high-tech, lowbrow films. All along, the director's potential had been tantalizing by what it promised, but until *E.T.*, it had failed to deliver literate, sophisticated filmmaking. He had managed to coax an incredible performance out of a polyurethane dummy from outer space. Just think what he could do with a flesh-and-blood creature if the actor were the main character instead of backup for a rubber puppet.

Spielberg fell in love with Whoopi Goldberg, who would play Celie, when he saw her perform her stand-up comedy act on Broadway. She later auditioned for the role, strangely, by performing part of her act in his office.

"Whoopi is more than special. It's kind of scary. She has a gift. I cast her after she performed her one-woman show for me in my office. I'm sitting there watching this person who is going to arrive, who is going to be a major movie star," he said, accurately predicting her later superstar success when for a brief while she would be the highest paid actress in an industry notorious for underemploying African Americans of either sex.

Spielberg found her face so expressive that after casting her he cut her dialogue by 25 percent. Her face, he found, could communicate just as eloquently as the written word.

The Spielberg-Goldberg collaboration was a match made in movie-trivia heaven. Both the filmmaker and the actress were movie buffs. Spielberg, who had had trouble communicating with actors in the past, found he could use a directing shorthand with fellow movie buff Goldberg.

Goldberg recalled, "He could say, 'I want Ray Milland in *The Lost Weekend*,' and I would know exactly what he meant. We didn't have to spend hours discussing it."

Steven Spielberg may have had prickly relationships with most of his other female leads, but he and Goldberg could cover the Paul McCartney-Michael Jackson duet, "Ebony and Ivory."

On the set of *The Color Purple*, Goldberg raved, "Steven is the best at that, bringing out humanity. He's just the greatest, most wonderful director an actor could want. We taught him a lot as actors, because we weren't walking on with special effects. We were *there*, he had to deal with us—he couldn't cut to a boulder or something."

Spielberg, in Golberg's account, is even kind to animals, even reptiles. While driving back to their hotel after a day on the set in North Carolina, he abruptly stopped their car. Spielberg had spotted a tortoise in the middle of the road, right in front of their car. He got out and moved the creature to the shoulder of the road. An observer noted that a motorcade of production's cars then passed over the spot and would have crushed the turtle had it not been for Spielberg's quick eye.

Spielberg also discovered another crucial cast member, Oprah Winfrey, before she became a national phenomenon. He was struck by her animation while watching tapes of her local Chicago talk show.

"Oprah is the secret weapon of this movie," he said of the television personality he cast as Goldberg's independent daughter-in-law, Sophie. "I found her on videotape. Quincy Jones [the film's coproducer] and I were watching tapes of her TV show, saying, 'That can't be real, all that hurrying around, so full of life and energy and love.'"

Spielberg in fact cast Winfrey solely on the basis of her talk show performance. He didn't ask her to audition. Years later, Spielberg recalled, "I saw this fearlessness in those tapes. I certainly wouldn't cast her today because she is svelte and picturesque, which is not the physical image of Sophie. Oprah convinced me that she was this character in our very first meeting. She has remained a good friend over the years, which is nice."

Another woman who was more famous in another medium, Tina Turner, managed to elude the director's overtures. He asked the pop star three times to play Shug Avery, the singer who liberates Celie emotionally and sexually.

Shug is Celie's husband's girlfriend, and despite her equivocal position in this unloving triangle, she becomes Celie's biggest booster and helps the woman leave her abusive husband. Turner, who later would write a best-seller about her years as an abused wife, found the story line a bit too autobiographical and painfully close to home.

"The third time she turned me down, she said she'd been through too much of this story in her own life to ever want to do it in a movie. We tested fifty to sixty actresses. I think I was always seeing Tina in the role," Spielberg said. True to her word, when Turner was asked to play herself in the film of her autobiography, she also passed on reliving her real-life traumas.

Spielberg may have been the ultimate white-bread director in producer Don Simpson's mind, but he felt comfortable directing an almost all-black cast. He did, however, pay the entire race a compliment that is on a par with praising black people for having rhythm or athletic prowess when he said, "They're the same and different. What's different is that because of years of discrimination, I think they're more quickly responsive and expressive of their feelings." You can almost hear an unsophisticated cracker adding, "And they dance real good, too."

When *The Color Purple* came out, the critics seemed personally offended that the king of techno-popcorn had dared to make such an artistic departure from his patented style. Even rarer in an industry where you never bad-mouth in public someone you may work with one day, several other filmmakers weighed in against Spielberg's audacity.

The normally benign critic for the *Los Angeles Times*, Kenneth Turan, said, "He was too young to make *The Color Purple*. He overemphasized every emotion in sight." Contradicting himself, Turan later said, "After *E.T.*'s Oscar snub, his movies got blander and blander as their popularity increased."

Turan's critique was gentle compared to the barbs of Henry Jaglom, an avant-garde director whose films invariably flop.

Although the Academy of Arts and Picture Sciences gave the film a whopping eleven nominations, it snubbed Spielberg in the best director category. The Directors Guild made amends by giving him its best directing award that year. In some ways, that was a greater compliment than winning an Oscar, since the Guild award represented an accolade bestowed by his peers, not the entire Academy membership, which includes such down-scale crafts as makeup and special effects.

Even so, Jaglom was amazed by the Academy's largesse: "What is astonishing to me is that they would give *The Color Purple* eleven nominations. I think the actors deserved the nominations, but the rest of it was such a cartoon. He took this wonderful material and turned it into a zip-a-dee-doo-dah *Song of the South*."

Another director, who more circumspectly refused to be quoted by name, weighed in with, "It's appalling what he did with Alice Walker's book. He either does not know how to explore relationships or he doesn't want to deal with them. Either way, he turned *The Color Purple* into a two and one half hour episode of *Amazing Stories*."

Spielberg defended taking the hard edges off the novel. "If you're a nightclub entertainer, do you want to perform for three drunks or for a packed house? Any artist wants the largest possible audience."

Jaglom wasn't impressed with that logic and retorted, "An artist by definition isn't facile, pandering to everybody. An artist tries to get people to understand something about the human condition and be true to himself in doing it. He hopes everybody will appreciate it. That's different from trying to calculate what every-body will appreciate."

Not everyone in the industry acted as though Spielberg had betrayed West Point to the British. Gene Siskel of the *Chicago Tribune*, one of the most influential film critics in the country because of his syndicated television show, hailed the film as a "feminist Oliver Twist or Nicholas Nickelby of the South" because of its horrific Dickensian depiction of poverty and abuse.

Warner Brothers issued an outraged press release, saying, "The company is shocked and dismayed that the movie's primary creative force—Steven Spielberg—was not recognized" by the Academy.

To make up for the domestic brickbats, Spielberg, like a prophet who is not honored in his own land, received an honor in Britain—the Fellowship of the Academy Award—that had only been given to Alfred Hitchcock, Charlie Chaplin, and his personal idol, director David Lean.

Barry Diller, the Attila the Hun of movie moguls, made a rare statement actually praising someone. Commenting on the Oscar snub, Diller said, "There are always high prices to pay for success, but to have his peers act this way is an unflattering reflec-tion on themselves. Certainly everyone has the right to vote his own way, but to deny him is an act of meanness."

More understandably, Universal chief Sid Sheinberg expressed indignation over the snub in not one but two lead items in Army Archerd's overly friendly column in *Daily Variety*.

Spielberg remained philosophical about the snub—and hopeful about the future. "The most coveted respect I get is from my peers. I've been honored six times by the Directors Guild, so when I get a DGA nomination, that's recognition enough. Still, I'd love an Oscar. I'd never snub an Academy Award. I'm not Marlon Brando. I'll never send someone to accept an Oscar for me."

What most enraged the critics was the director's soft-ped-alling of the book's lesbian elements. The *New York Times* summed up the critical reaction, labelling the film "shallow." Spielberg admitted, "I downplayed the lesbian scenes. I confined them to just a series of kisses. I wasn't comfortable going beyond that. In the book, which handles the scene beautifully, Shug actually holds up a mirror to Celie's private parts. But a scene like that plays at least 150 times bigger on the screen, and I just couldn't do it. Marty Scorsese could do it; not me. Any woman director would have done that brilliantly. And I was afraid of it. I didn't know how to direct actors to do that."

The novel dealt with such horrific experiences as rape coupled with incest, spousal abuse, and alcoholism. The director did a typical Spielbergian take on these elements and managed to find the positive in an otherwise horrendous situation. "The incest, the rape, the brutality are more the surface than the foundation of the book. What attracted me was the *underlying sweet optimism*. The idea that this sweet girl will grow up to be a strong person with a full sense of her own worth," he said.

Maybe it was simply lack of screen time, but Spielberg also cut down the amount of male-bashing that took place in the original novel. As one pundit said, "It would have been a six-hour movie if he had included all the potshots Alice Walker took at men in the book."

The most disappointed group was Spielberg's hard-core fans who loved the director's mix of sci-fi and fantasy with a heady dollop of chills and thrills. All those elements were sorely missing in *The Color Purple*.

One Spielberg aficionado at a preview screening was said to have kept searching the top corner of the screen until an exasperated companion asked what he was looking for. "I'm waiting for the Mother Ship to descend," the disappointed fan explained.

Spielberg also was criticized for hiring a Dutch-born writer, Menno Meyjes, to adapt this most American of novels. The screenwriter defended his hiring, saying, "The authenticity was handled in the book. Besides, all people are the same underneath."

Meyjes, who would go on to write the third installment of *Indiana Jones*, also defended the PG depiction of sex between the two female stars. "The foremost experience was of love, not sex. Anything more graphic would have been distracting."

One important voice in the debate lined up squarely behind the director: Alice Walker, the author of the book. Spielberg later said that one of the fringe benefits of making *The Color Purple* was that "I get two lovely letters a month from Alice Walker."

Unlike the critics and gay activists, Walker obviously didn't object to the PG treatment of her book's sexuality. In an interview with the *Wall Street Journal*, Walker said she was particularly impressed with Spielberg's special trip to visit her home in a working class neighborhood of Eatonton, Georgia. She wasn't impressed by the block long limo he showed up in but with his intuitive understanding of her work. "He really loved the people in the book. He had internalized the anguish, the struggle, and the liberation of Celie [Whoopi Goldberg's character] and everyone."

The mutual admiration continued when Walker visited the shoot in North Carolina. "When I got to the set and saw him working, he was excruciatingly sensitive to detail. Not just physical things, but also emotional complexity and truth. He was incredibly good with people," Walker said.

The Pulitzer Prize-winning novelist, however, wasn't intimidated by the whole Hollywood megalith that had transplanted itself to rural North Carolina. Before signing away movie rights to the book, she had it written into her contract that at least half the cast and crew had to be either women, black, or other "Third World" people.

To this day, Walker keeps a photograph of Spielberg directing a scene from *The Color Purple* on a shelf in her living room.

Ironically, it was a Jew from white-bread Scottsdale, Arizona, who introduced Walker's work to her own family. Before the film was released, the author claimed none of her relatives ever bothered to read her books. "That's how my family read me in the first place," she said. "They'd never read me. But when they saw the movie, they thought, 'Gee, there must be something to this.'"

The Academy's snub of *The Color Purple* was Walker's fault, not Spielberg's, the novelist generously insisted. It was her vicious portrayal of black men, which the film graphically dramatized with beatings and rape, that turned off Academy voters. "I don't think they could accurately judge *The Color Purple* because I frankly think they were intimidated by the controversy about the film's portrayal of black men . . . . If they had real integrity they would take a stand if they thought it was good. And it *was* good," Walker said.

Spielberg had enjoyed the biggest success of his career with *E.T.*, the only film up to that time that he didn't storyboard. He obviously hoped lightning would strike twice and decided not to sketch out his next film as well. "I did not storyboard *The Color Purple* at all because I wanted every day to be a new experience for me. Usually, I make my movies in my head, as you would design a house," said the director who once said that if he hadn't become a director, he would have been an architect. "And sometimes the best sequences were those that I did not have storyboards for because someone got sick or we had to change plans. I've enjoyed 'winging it' in my movies more than the planned scenes."

Despite its brutality and relative sexual frankness, *The Color Purple* oddly paralleled Spielberg's private life while he was making the film.

Referring to his on-again, off-again relationship with Amy Irving, he said, "Just as our breakup coincided with the unhappy experience of *1941* (and *Honeysuckle Rose*), this time everything coincided with the great experience of making *The Color Purple*.

"We figured it out later that Max was conceived on the day Menno Meyjes started writing the screenplay. Max was born on the same day we were shooting young Celie's birth scene in the movie.

"This movie is important to me. There were so many parallels with the movie and my life. I had been taking Lamaze classes while Amy was pregnant, and there I was, directing a fourteen-year-old girl in the childbirth scene, telling her what I had learned in my classes, telling her she was having twin peaks, about which she knew nothing, and the phone call came that Amy was in her fourth hour of labor."

The eerie coincidences continued as the filming of the birth scene and his wife's delivery progressed. "Just as we were pulling the rubber baby out from the bed, the phone call came and one of the assistant directors ran in and said, 'Your baby's on the way. Your *real* baby is on the way.' It was a wonderful moment in my life,"

It was a golden period in Spielberg's life. He and his prickly wife were still very much in love and devoted to one another. "She spent the entire time with me on *The Color Purple* in Monroe, North Carolina, and that's not a fun place to spend three months," he said.

The year 1985 was golden in another way. Actually, green is the operative color. That year, Spielberg came into his own as the producer of films directed by other people. And as a producer, he showed he had the same Midas touch which had made him the most successful director of all time. In 1984, he produced a monster hit about monsters, *Gremlins*. The next year, he scored an even bigger hit, producing *Back to the Future*, directed by his protege Bob Zemeckis. *Goonies*, an uninspired adventure about preteens and pirates, also fared well at the box office. Less stellar was the box-office performance of *Young Sherlock Holmes*, a wonderfully inventive and visually stunning film that nevertheless failed to grab audiences.

Back to the Future was the number-one box-office champ of 1985. It confirmed that producer Spielberg had a golden gut even when he wasn't directing. It also showed that he could be ruthless in the pursuit of getting things right.

Although his official title was executive producer, *Back to the Future* was his personal baby. Every studio in town had rejected the complex plot about time travel until Spielberg championed it. But almost as soon as filming began, Spielberg realized he had made a major mistake in casting the lead role of Marty McFly, the intrepid time traveler who wakes up to find himself marooned in 1955.

Spielberg had all along wanted Michael J. Fox for the role. In his early twenties, Fox had the boyish looks perfect for playing the role of a teen. Fox was also the star of a hit television sitcom, *Family Ties*, and it was hoped that his high level of recognition would bring in the all-important teen market. But Fox's popularity was a blessing and a curse. The series kept him tied up until the first of the year, and Spielberg wanted to start filming long before that in time for a summer release, so he and director Bob Zemeckis hired a talented unknown named Eric Stolz. Stolz was in fact a brilliant actor. The only problem was that he thought he was doing *Macbeth* when the producer and the director wanted something lighter. Stolz was just too intense. The dailies played like tragedy, not light comedy. After five weeks and $4 million,

Spielberg finally threw in the towel and summarily fired Stolz. He recalled with heartfelt guilt, "This was the hardest decision I've ever made. That was a real hard call. That made me miserable. And I'm still miserable, not about the decision, which was right, but what I should have done, which was to allow Bob Zemeckis to wait until the first of the year, when Michael was available. Michael was our first choice. He was not available due to *Family Ties*. I should have waited, and yet I wanted the film out for the summer. And for the record, I think Eric Stolz is a marvelous actor, in the same league with Sean Penn, Emilio Estevez and Matthew Modine."

Spielberg may have praised Stolz to assuage his guilt, but as usual, he turned out to be remarkably prescient. Stolz's film career is booming, while Fox's has stalled with one lame comedy after another.

His consistent success as a producer must have been especially gratifying after earlier missteps including *I Wanna Hold Your Hand* (1978) and *Used Cars* (1980).

But all his success as a movie producer in 1985 must have been diluted by the failure of his big-time return to the medium which had given him his start.

CHAPTER TWELVE

Not So Amazing Stories

STEVEN SPIELBERG HAD BEGUN HIS CAREER behind the camera as a teenager. When he returned to the medium sixteen years later, he was the king of features, and his return to the small screen was expected to be a triumph.

After all, how hard could television be to tame after he had wrestled such technical big budget films to the ground? Television was slumming, and Spielberg was expected to bring a little class to the much put-upon medium.

Spielberg was wooed back to television by an unprecedented offer. NBC was willing to give him $1 million per half-hour episode *and* an on-air commitment to run the show for two years. That was a $50 million gamble by the network. By contrast, the hit sitcom *Cheers* cost only $350,000 per episode at the time. Even if the series flopped, NBC would be forced to run every single episode, slowly twisting in the wind of low Nielsens for an agonizing two seasons. More understandably, the network gave him full creative control without any interference from the suits. It also promised not to monitor his dailies. In fact, the only bureaucratic entity the all-powerful filmmaker would have to answer to was the network's standards and practices department, i.e., the network censor. As if the king of PG entertainment needed a moral watchdog!

The network also committed to Spielberg's vision without seeing a pilot, another unprecedented concession, like buying a car before it even made it off the drawing board, much less the assembly line.

But Spielberg had a sterling track record: director of the number-one hit of all time. And in 1985, he had produced the number-one hit of the year, *Back to the Future*.

NBC felt he could do no wrong. Or as NBC's head of programming, Brandon Tartikoff, said slyly, "Steven Spielberg is an 800-pound gorilla," and we all know such a gorilla is allowed to sit anywhere he wants.

The director was not above pooh-poohing the medium that had given him his first big break. In a rather Olympian manner, he pronounced, "A feature film is a full exercise program, and *Amazing Stories* is like a quick hundred push-ups. It's just a great way to keep in shape." (Prophetically, Spielberg had once admitted he could not do a single chin-up.)

Universal's parent company, MCA, would produce the show. Delirious executives at the studio described the show as a "weekly series of the ordinary meets the extraordinary."

When the alliance between Spielberg and NBC was first announced in 1984, Tartikoff predicted, "I would expect it to be a show with a lot of fun, great adventure and imagination, with nice touches of comedy where called for. I don't expect it to be aimed at a juvenile audience," he said, with his eye planted firmly on the audience most coveted by advertisers, eighteen- to forty-nine-year-olds. "I think younger kids will enjoy the show, but I think it will be a general-audience-pleasing show, in the same way that a lot of Steven Spielberg's movies appeal to a broad spectrum of the movie audience. It will be sort of a throwback in some sense, to the great anthologies that were on television in the 1950s, like *Alfred Hitchcock Presents* and *The Twilight Zone*."

Even without the benefit of hindsight and the performance of other resurrected anthology shows, *Amazing Stories* in retrospect seemed like a crazy gamble for the network. As an anthology show, it would feature a different story and cast every week. The genre hadn't worked in years, not since the original *Twilight Zone* went off the air.

The reason continuing series do well is the very nature of their format. Each week the audience learns a bit more about the returning characters. Although sitcoms are routinely dismissed as lowbrow, after twenty-six episodes so many character traits have been revealed that the original stick figures have become multidimensional characters. An actor can get a big laugh just by repeating a line like "Dyn-o-mite" or "Oh, really?" because it has so many associations with past gags and incidents. The audience falls a little bit in love with the quirks and mannerisms of each cast member. After a hit show like *M*A*S*H** has been on the air for twelve seasons, the principals seem like members of the family.

No such love affair can blossom on an anthology show because each week an entire new cast of characters and stories are introduced. You have only twenty-three minutes to get to know total strangers.

But at its launch, no one seemed to worry about the self-limiting appeal of anthology shows.

Amazing Stories, Spielberg predicted, would be "a forum creatively for a lot of filmmakers to get together and take those little gems of ideas and thoughts that just aren't long enough for feature films. A hundred years ago, before movies and television were invented, they were called short stories."

Either the Spielberg name or the chance to realize some "little gems" of their own lured some major big-screen talent to the little screen. Clint Eastwood directed "Vanessa in the Garden" from a Spielberg script about a painter and his wife, with a supernatural twist. Irvin Kershner, the director of the second *Star Wars* film, made an ingenious segment, "Hell Toupe," about a hairpiece that transforms its wearers into holy terrors.

Only David Lean turned Spielberg down, jokingly agreeing to direct a half-hour segment if he were allowed six months to shoot his miniepic.

Spielberg directed four of the first twenty-two shows and wrote the stories for fifteen. He took valuable time out from his feature film schedule to direct an hour-long episode, "Round Trip," about a World War II bomber mission that goes terribly wrong. It starred an unknown actor by the name of Kevin Costner.

Another episode he directed, called "Ghost Train," was autobiographical, about a fantasy he had growing up in Haddonfield, New Jersey, when he heard a train coming through town every night. In the episode, which is most notable for being the only time he ever directed Amy Irving, the far-off train crashes through the house, which has been built on the site of long-vanished train tracks.

Spielberg had high hopes for the series and took full credit for its content. "TV stands for Tender Vittles. That's what we're givin' 'em, folks, Tender Vittles. I'm essentially able to say yea or nay to what is or isn't amazing to me. At the end of each show, people should look at each other if they loved it and honestly say, 'That was an amazing story!'"

People said a lot of things about the new show, but "amazing" wasn't one of them. The Nielsens went from unimpressive at the start to dismal by the end of the two-year ordeal. The critics searched for new adjectives to describe awful.

The *Washington Post*'s Tom Shales wrote, "I hear America asking, 'What was so amazing about that?'" after Spielberg's autobiographical episode about the train aired.

The critical drubbing Spielberg took for his excursion onto the small screen snowballed into a reassessment of his big screen efforts.

Pauline Kael asked rhetorically, "Why are movies so bad? One hates to say it comes down to the success of Steven Spielberg, but it's not so much what Spielberg has done but what he has encouraged. Everyone else has imitated his fantasies, and the result is an infantilization of the culture. Spielberg with his TV series now rips off his own things. I can't think of any other director who's started paying homage to himself so early."

Satirizing Tartikoff's 800-pound gorilla analogy, the *Los Angeles Reader* called the show an "800-pound turkey."

Susan Seidelman, the director of quirky, little comedies such as *Desperately Seeking Susan*, weighed in with, "Spielberg's success has definitely influenced the attitudes of movie people. They're just not interested in the movies anymore. They're more interested in the E.T. toys and bedspreads." When Seidelman was a student at New York University's film school in 1976, she said, "Everyone was imitating Godard and Bergman" but those glory days were gone "and it's all because of Spielberg. He's brilliant. I'm an admirer of what he does. But there are bad side effects. I get to read a lot of scripts and treatments, and now they're all about kiddies and spaceships."

Spielberg himself seemed to worry that he might have returned to the same creative well one too many times when he said during *Amazing Stories'* second season: "If you're here working every day, you start Xeroxing your own style. It gets incestuous."

For the first time in his career, negative personal stories began to surface about Spielberg, who up to that time had been portrayed in the press as some kind of "friendly elf," as one dis-gruntled ex-employee described the phenomenon. (*TV Guide* reported that "he was a vaguely unpleasant guy sometimes. It bugs associates to see his press clippings portray some sort of friendly elf.")

A former employee said, "On the job, he is extremely demanding. His attitude is, 'This is the best job in Hollywood and you'd better appreciate it.' People are scared of him and he assumes a huge place in people's minds. They see him like a god."

Another employee described him as aloof. "He doesn't say hello in the corridors. He doesn't observe the social graces except when he has to." Employees mordantly referred to Amblin, his production company, as the "Vatican."

TV Guide also claimed that when he soured on one employ-ee, he simply stopped speaking to the woman until she quit. The Spielberg snub wasn't reserved for minions. Bigger fish also have felt his wrath. He refused to say hello to two Universal executives because when they were at Columbia they passed on *E.T.*

Employees at Amblin were underpaid. One associate said, "He's afraid all his money is going to slip away." That wasn't quite fair. The director was notorious for insanely generous perks like an all-expense-paid vacation to Hawaii for an overworked personal assistant. He was so pleased with the job his interior decorator did on his office complex that he bought him a car.

One agent, who not surprisingly insisted on anonymity, portrayed the director as an omnivorous mogul who wanted every project in town. "This man is not the same as the soft and cuddly characters he creates. The amazing thing about Steven is that he would truly be happiest if he owned every project in town. This is nothing new about Steven. He's always been a very strong, very tough businessman. It's the rule of kings. 'I am the king, and I make the rules.'"

The usually sycophantic *Daily Variety* quoted industry insiders who claimed Spielberg was "an intensely aggressive and acquisitive businessman who goes after projects with a tenacity that is striking even by the hardball standards of Hollywood."

David Vogel, one of the producers of *Amazing Stories*, was the only person willing to go on the record and say something negative about his patron. "He eggs you on until it drives you crazy. When he left to direct *The Color Purple*, I thought, 'Oh, boy, he's off my back.' Then I'd get these calls from him about a script. He's always pushing to make it better."

More typically, only nice things were said about the most powerful man in Hollywood. Mike Medavoy, then chairman of Tri-Star, insisted that stories of Spielberg throwing his weight around were "completely undeserved. He's been meticulous about not doing it. This guy suffers a reputation that is unfortunate."

Celebrity attorney Bertram Fields also came to Spielberg's defense. "Anybody who has developed a position of effective power in this business and uses it to maximize his bargaining is going to get lots of complaining. Steven is very active in going after properties, but I haven't seen any behavior that I would call deceitful or unscrupulous."

Still, the persistent image of a self-obsessed executive emerged as his television career was submerging. "He never asks anybody about their personal lives," an employee said. "His only subject of conversation is the movies."

As one studio executive described both his interpersonal and business skills, "He directs better than he moguls."

That was an assessment Spielberg himself wouldn't necessarily disagree with. He said, "I don't like being a general. I like to think of myself still as a journeyman director." But he refused to accept claims that he was a tyrant, as one producer described him. On the other hand, he was no patsy either.

"I'm not a bully and I don't give orders," he insisted. "I'm very collaborative, but what I try to do is inspire in people who are collaborating that they've got to collaborate with me better than they have ever collaborated with anybody before. And so in that sense I'm demanding. I expect the best of anybody who works here."

CHAPTER THIRTEEN

Empire Building

Ⅰ
N 1987, STEVEN SPIELBERG MADE WHAT HE
called his "transitional film." *Empire of the Sun* would be the film
in which he made the transition from childhood to adult themes.

Ironically, the hero of the film was an eleven-year-old. But
it was about an eleven-year-old with problems that would have
overwhelmed any adult.

Spielberg's idol David Lean had once toyed with the idea of
directing *Empire of the Sun*, and thematically it was a project
Spielberg just couldn't resist.

"From the moment I read the novel, I secretly wanted to do
it myself. I had never read anything with an adult setting where a
child saw things through a man's eyes as opposed to a man discov-
ering things through the child in him. This was just the reverse of
what I felt was my credo. And then I discovered very quickly that
this movie and my turning forty happened at almost the same time
was no coincidence—that I had decided to do a movie with
grown-up themes and values, although spoken through a voice
that hadn't changed through puberty as yet.

"I was attracted to the idea that this was the death of innocence, not an attenuation of childhood, which by my own admis-

sion and everybody's impression of me is what my life has been. [*Empire of the Sun*] was the opposite of *Peter Pan*. This was a boy who had grown up too quickly, who was becoming a flower long before the bud had ever come out of the topsoil," he said.

Based on the autobiographical novel by science-fiction writer J. G. Ballard, *Empire of the Sun* told the story of Jim Graham, an upper-class preadolescent who lives a luxurious life in the British quarter of Shanghai on the eve of World War II.

When the Japanese invade Shanghai after Pearl Harbor, Jim's pampered life is turned upside down. He is separated from his parents and ends up alone in a ghastly concentration camp.

The theme of a child's separation from his parents was old Spielberg territory. As he did in *E.T.* and *Close Encounters*, Spielberg was engaging in a little self-psychoanalysis, still exorcising old demons of his own parents' divorce when he was fifteen.

The separation scene is more horrific than anything the director experienced in childhood, and the scene is arguably scarier than any of his more over-the-top chills in *Jaws*. The boy and his parents attempt to flee Shanghai in their Rolls Royce. Unfortunately, everyone else in the city has the same idea. After their car gets marooned in a sea of humanity, they get out and try to make their way on foot.

Big mistake. The crowd is like a tidal wave, pushing and pulling its human flotsam. As the crowd surges, the youngster is physically yanked away from his parents. His frantic and unsuccessful attempts to reunite with his hysterical parents are more terrifying than the appearance of the shark in *Jaws* and certainly more realistically nightmarish than any of *Indiana Jones'* creepy-crawling monsters.

That is just the beginning of poor Jim Graham's travails. His life in the camp is something out of *Oliver Twist*. Graham is transformed from a supercilious aristocrat to a crafty survivor who helps his older fellow prisoners withstand torture and starvation.

As usual, Spielberg proved himself a wiz as a director of children. Not since Henry Thomas's performance as Elliot in *E.T.* had a child actor, Britain's Christian Bale, turned in such a multi-faceted performance. Graham's transformation from snooty brat (at one point he brags that he's writing a book on contract bridge) to a *Lord of the Flies* urchin was the cynosure of the film.

Filming was almost as horrific as the subject matter. The production shot exteriors in Shanghai for three weeks, the first time the Chinese government allowed a major American film company to shoot in the People's Republic.

The thirteen-year-old Bale was appalled by the filth. He told me in 1987, shortly before the film's release, "There were four or five families living in these mucky shacks that looked like a garden toolshed. We tried to go shopping for gifts, and the stores were all empty."

Spielberg echoed his young charge's complaints. "*Empire of the Sun* was not fun to make. The subject matter, about a young boy in a POW camp, was so sad. It was like a descent into hell. And this boy was asked to do a lot of things. He was sworn at, he was abused by adults. It was hard for me to see. I suffered with the character. If there is such a thing as a method director, it was me then. But the filmmaking experience was the best I've had."

One of traumas the director put his star through had him crawling in the mud for days. When the script called for the starving POW to eat insects, he was required to eat bitter black seedlings take after take.

"They weren't as bad as eating insects, but they weren't tasty," Bale said.

For all the film's horror quotient, Spielberg had to suppress his natural tendency to inject humor into scary situations. It had worked well on *Jaws*—comic relief before the big bite—but on a fact-based film it would have been downright tacky and untrue to the spirit of the book.

After the critical crucifixion *The Color Purple* had undergone—not to mention the Oscar snub—Spielberg would have been forgiven if he had retreated to the greasy-kid-stuff style of filmmaking which had worked so well before he took on black lesbians and spousal abuse.

Instead, he decided to test the waters again, but without such a dramatic departure from his tried and true style as *The Color Purple*. Using an eleven-year-old character as his alter ego/star helped him make a more orderly transition from childish to adult themes.

"I'm trying to grow up in increments," he said a year after *Empire of the Sun* was released. "I don't want to come up to the surface so quickly that I'm going to have a terrible case of the bends. *Empire* still had a boy in it to help with that transition to a kind of genre I would like to play around with."

Empire of the Sun also allowed the director to explore his favorite era, the forties. When he was much less mature, he did a slapstick exploration of the period in *1941*. With only a bit more maturity, he returned to World War II with the missing bombers' subplot of *Close Encounters*. Regressing, he called on Nazis to be the cardboard villains of *Raiders*.

Empire of the Sun allowed him to explore his favorite era in a more sophisticated way. "I'm closer to the '40s than I am to the '80s," he said at the close of that decade. "I love that period. My father filled my head with war stories—he was a radioman on a B-25 fighting the Japanese in Burma. I have identified with that period of innocence and tremendous jeopardy all my life.

"It was the end of an era, the end of innocence, and I have been clinging to it for most of my adult life. I had been tenaciously clinging to my naivete, but I just reached a saturation point, and I thought *Empire* was a great way of performing an exorcism of that period."

The director was of course being premature. His real exorcism of that historical period would come five years later with *Schindler's List*.

Empire of the Sun was received more kindly by the critics than his previous effort. *The Color Purple* was almost treated as an affront. How dare the roller-coaster king try to dramatize the African-American experience! *Empire of the Sun* was still identifiably Spielbergian, yet it showed a growing awareness on the part of the director that there was more to film art than rolling boulders and sight-seeing spaceships.

The critics approved. The *Los Angeles Times* called *Empire of the Sun* his "most mature and searing work to date."

But the public apparently wanted the old magician back.

Empire of the Sun has the weird distinction of being one of Spielberg's best films—and his biggest flop.

It grossed only $66 million worldwide. Even the noxious *1941* brought in $90 million.

Empire of the Sun didn't make the studio any money, and you don't have to be a box-office analyst for *Variety* to figure out why. *Empire* had all the patented Spielberg elements: a child in peril, villain(s) of incomprehensible evil, separation from loved ones, and of course, a happy ending with family and friends reunited as the John Williams score swells over the closing credits. But *Empire* was only superficially a Spielberg-type film. The horror was perhaps too real. It's one thing to have the kids on screen—and in the audience—groan while the pint-sized hero eats monkey brains (*Temple of Doom*). It's quite another to have the youthful hero eat insects in the throes of starvation. Cartoonish Nazis (Indianas 1 and 2) supply digestible horror. Sadistic Japanese guards who inflict graphic beatings are not palatable as Saturday matinee fare. Plus the purely superstitious may think of the World War II curse that has afflicted Spielberg's filmography. When he took the war on for laughs, he bombed. When he examined the same war in a dramatic context, the failure was only slightly less profound, commercially at least.

Spielberg was philosophical about the film's disappointing performance at the box office. "At this point in my career I think I've earned the right to fail commercially. I knew going in that *Empire of the Sun* wasn't a very commercial project," he said.

That must have been a startling revelation to the film's producer, Warner Brothers, which he thanked after the fact. "*Empire of the Sun* ranks among the most satisfying experiences I've had directing. I will be forever in debt to Warner Bros. for risking all that money. It was a horrendous risk. But they pretty much let me make my large canvas, personal film.

"I knew it wasn't going to have a broad audience appeal. I knew I had to make this movie despite my producer hat, which kept nagging at me that this was not a movie to spend a lot of money on because you're not going to get it back. And yet sometime things need to be done regardless of commercial return," he said.

Spielberg, the crafty negotiator, was being a bit disingenuous here. His standard deal gives him a percentage of the gross from the first dollar taken in at theaters. That meant he would make a bundle regardless of whether *Empire* ever earned a nickel of profit.

The director's next film would reinstate him as the king of the box office, although that must have been sore consolation to Warner Brothers, since he made *Indiana Jones and the Last Crusade* for another studio.

CHAPTER FOURTEEN

Raiders of the Box Office Again

T HE ONLY REASON STEVEN SPIELBERG MADE the third installment of *Raiders*, *Indiana Jones and the Last Crusade*, was to honor his handshake deal with George Lucas. Financially it enriched him, but aesthetically it prevented him from directing the following year's Oscar champ, *Rainman*.

Rainman was a project he devoted five long months of his valuable time developing in preproduction. He abandoned the project with great reluctance. "I was very upset not to have been able to do *Rainman* mainly because I've wanted to work with Dustin Hoffman ever since I saw *The Graduate*. But I couldn't go to my best friend [George Lucas] and say, 'I know I'm a whore, but I found something I like better—hire George Miller' [*Mad Max*]."

Instead, he generously recommended his friend and protege, Barry Levinson, to replace him on *Rainman*. But Spielberg's generosity went beyond a friendly recommendation. He met with Levinson in a Westwood, California, restaurant and turned over his copious notes on the script from the five months he had spent developing it. "I sort of debriefed in front of Barry and gave him all of my notes and everything," he said.

Sadly, he recalled, "With *Rainman*, I spent almost half a year developing it with Dustin and Tom Cruise and [writer] Ron Bass. I kept trying to get the screenplay to be better and better while having a stop date of the 12th of January, at which time I had to start shooting *Indy III*. When I saw I was going to go past January 12th, and I would have to step down from *Indy III*, the promise I made to George was more important than making *Rainman*. So with great regret, because I really wanted to work with Dustin and Tom, I stepped down from the movie."

A year later during an interview to promote his film, *Always*, I asked him how *Rainman* would have been different had he directed it instead of Levinson. Referring to repeated snubs by the Academy of Motion Picture Arts and Sciences, he said without any bitterness, "Well, if I'd directed it it wouldn't have won all those Oscars."

Although he wouldn't complain about the Academy, he wasn't above speaking his mind about the flaws of the project he gave up. "I find *Rainman* to be emotionally very distancing. I think I certainly would have pulled tears out of a rather dry movie," he said.

The same year he gave up *Rainman* to make the third Indiana Jones flick, he passed—reluctantly—on another project that boosted the careers of several Hollywood principals. But this time, it was brotherly love, not scheduling problems, that made him walk away from a potential hit.

Big was the story of a thirteen-year-old boy who one morning wakes up to find himself a grown man. He's still a teenager, but he looks like an adult. The film would turn Tom Hanks, as the boy-man, into a superstar, and it would make its director, Penny Marshall, the most successful woman in Hollywood.

But it was another credit on the film that made Spielberg shy away from adding one more hit to his resume. His sister, Anne, had cowritten the script with Gary Ross. The same man who as a child had tormented Anne and his other sisters was now so solicitous about overshadowing his sibling that he voluntarily dropped out of the project.

"*Big* was something I flirted with for a couple of months with Harrison Ford to play the Tom Hanks role. But my sister wrote the script, and I felt that she'd been standing in my shadow long enough. Most of my life she's sort of been in the shade, and this was a great screenplay she and Gary Ross wrote—with no help from me. I began to consider the fact that if I directed it, people wouldn't give Annie any credit. Essentially, I would have stolen Annie's thunder, and I just didn't want to do that," he explained.

Such generosity more than makes up for having locked his sister in a closet and cut off her doll's head when they were kids.

As much as Spielberg wanted to honor his promise to Lucas, he was not about to throw himself into a project he found unsatisfactory just to make good on a handshake deal a decade earlier on a beach in Hawaii.

Despite a lot of heavy breathing by executives at Paramount, Spielberg kept putting off the third Indiana Jones movie. The director rejected four different screenplays proposed for the third installment. "I wasn't going to just go ahead and fulfill my obligation. I was going to make every effort to end the saga with a very unique and very thrilling finale. I wanted to take a risk, and I wanted to do a father-son story from the beginning," he said.

In fact, it was the addition of a dad for Indiana Jones that finally made Spielberg agree to direct. Collaborating with screenwriter Jeffrey Boam, who wrote several James Bond movies, Spielberg wondered, "Why not give Indy a dad?"

After two Indiana Jones escapist flicks, Spielberg was growing tired of the cliff-hanger, Saturday afternoon serial genre. He wanted something with more meat.

Unfortunately for their collaboration, George Lucas *loved* the serial format and wanted to make a film about the search for the Holy Grail. The two best friends eventually compromised. They would make a movie about Indiana's relationship with his father *and* the search for the Holy Grail.

Thus was born the third Raiders film, *Indiana Jones and the Last Crusade*. ("Holy Grail" was considered and dropped from the title because it sounded too much like a decades-old spoof by the British comedy troupe, called *Monty Python and the Holy Grail*. Spielberg and Lucas didn't want any inappropriate comparisons made between their seriocomic adventure and the over-the-top farce by the Python people.)

The returning star, Harrison Ford, was pleased with the addition of a father to flesh out his largely one-dimensional role as a whip-wielding archaeologist fond of colorful hats. As much as Spielberg, Ford was tired of the Jones genre until the director gave Indy a pop. "It outfoxed the sequel syndrome," Ford said with satisfaction. His director slyly added, "It was intentionally a father-and-son story I sneaked into an adventure plot."

Budgeted at a then whopping $36 million, the film began principal photography on May 16, 1988, in Almeria, Spain.

Spielberg had a ball working with two taciturn actors, Ford and Connery. "The biggest thrill was putting Harrison and Sean in a two-shot and calling, 'Action!' and trying not to ruin the take by laughing," he said.

In the two previous Indiana Jones adventures, the director had confronted his phobias over insects, heights, and bats. In the third film, he would deal with his fear and loathing of rats. For the project, 7,000 "custom-farmed" rodents were used for a particularly ghoulish scene that once again put Ford through his paces.

Every penny of the $36 million was on the screen, not in the principals' pockets. The production employed tanks, zeppelins, camels—and those 7,000 rats. Spielberg, Ford, and Lucas all took gross points instead of a salary, which paid off when the film became the biggest money-maker of all three Indiana Jones episodes, grossing a staggering half a billion dollars!

Despite his stern public persona, Connery was pretty laid back on the set. During a scene in the cramped passenger lounge of the zeppelin, the actor grew very hot in his heavy tweed suit. When he was seated behind a table in the lounge and his legs were out of camera range, he would remove his heavy pants. Between takes, he would stroll around the set in his underwear.

With the successful completion of *Indy III*, Spielberg had more than lived up to his handshake deal with Lucas. He had such a good time on the project, especially working with Connery, that he tentatively agreed to make a fourth Indiana Jones film. That's quite a departure for an artist who has refused to capitalize on all his other huge hits and crank out sequels.

Still, he hasn't signed on the dotted line yet. It all depends on what he considers the most important component of any project. "If someone can get the script right, I will direct the fourth Indiana Jones," he said.

With the box-office success of *Indiana Jones and the Last Crusade*, Spielberg was at the top of his form as a mass-market entertainer.

Some critics, however, felt he had gone back to the same well one too many times with the third installment of Raiders. The box-office formula which he and his best friend had concocted was derisively referred to as "lucasberger."

Not surprisingly, Spielberg defended his popcorn tastes: "Is this Indiana Jones adventure worth the amount of emotional energy the audience has to give to the film? It's a group experience for large numbers of people sitting in movie theatres, not for two or three people sitting in front of the television at home. You need to feel the audience clapping and yelling and screaming in order to get the total effect of the Indiana Jones saga."

If this meant he was serving up lucasberger, so be it. The public couldn't get enough of it even while the critics were complaining about all those empty calories.

Unfortunately, his personal life was not prospering apace with his professional triumphs. The same year that *Indy III* grossed half a billion dollars, his four-year marriage to Amy Irving was falling apart. Even casual observers could tell that something was definitely wrong. At a charity tribute to the director, Spielberg enthusiastically spoke about his desire "to direct my wife in a movie." At that, Irving turned away "coolly," in the words of an eyewitness.

Occasionally, Irving sounded more amenable to the idea of working with Spielberg. "I'm not insecure about it. We've been together twelve years and I've gotten along fine without him in my career. If I were to work with him now, I'm not worried about being accused of his taking over my career at this point. I come from a family that worked together. I watched my father direct my mother [Priscilla Pointer] all my life. So it's a natural progression for me," she said.

What she didn't say was that despite their professional collaboration, her parents eventually split.

Despite her misgivings, Spielberg did direct his wife once, but the project was one of his least successful, the premiere episode of his disastrous television series, *Amazing Stories*.

A year before the divorce, the couple was apparently deep in denial. Through their attorneys, they sent cease and desists orders to magazines and newspapers that reported they were about to divorce. A year later, the same publications announced the end of their four-year union.

The one thing their friends all agreed on was that his second wife was not the cause of the split from his first. It was logistics, not infidelity, that caused the breakup.

Some magazines reported that ever since she starred in *Indiana Jones and the Temple of Doom*, Capshaw had been trying to snare Spielberg. A London magazine quoted her as calling her wooing of Spielberg a "hunt."

He denied the charges. In fact, he admitted that during filming, he had come on to her, and she had rebuffed him.

Despite Spielberg's gallant denials, Capshaw herself admitted that there was some hanky-panky going on between them while he was still married to Irving.

She told gossip columnist Liz Smith in 1994 that she never lost hope that she would bag her man. She almost threw in the towel when Irving and Spielberg's son Max was born in 1985. "I thought, 'That's it,'" Capshaw said.

But Spielberg invited her to meet him on the sly in London in 1984 while they were promoting the European release of *Indiana Jones and the Temple of Doom*. "Steven thought nobody would find out," Capshaw admitted with more amusement than guilt. "Naive. Everybody found out. Amy found out through the *National Enquirer*."

Capshaw wasn't exactly discreet, and the *Times of London* even accused her of "taking every opportunity to be photographed" with the director. And when there were no inquiring paparazzi around, she was even more indiscreet.

She told the London paper, "I didn't even hide when room service brought something into his room."

A mutual friend thought it was understandable that the director was so smitten. "It's easy to see how he fell in love. She is the warmest, sweetest woman."

While in London, the romantic pursuit continued in a rather adolescent fashion. During a joint appearance on a British talk show to promote *Indy II*, Spielberg claimed that he passed mash notes to Capshaw during the commercial breaks. "I remember that," he said with a laugh. "I did appreciate her, but she wouldn't have me then, so it never worked out. She sort of rejected me back in '84 so I gave up on her for years." Within a year of his fling with Capshaw, Spielberg became a father as Irving gave birth to their son Max. That was followed by his marriage to Irving. Capshaw had by then seen the writing on the wall, dropping out of Spielberg's sight until 1989 when his marriage to Irving was clearly on the rocks.

So what broke up the marriage? Amy dismissed competition as the source of the split. Maybe she realized she would never be able to meet, much less surpass, her husband's success. It was the demands of two separate careers that caused the rift. As Irving tersely put it, "*You* try having a relationship with someone who's on a set in China for four months. It's close to impossible."

Irving was fiercely protective of her independence. About a year before they divorced, I asked her if being Mrs. Steven Spielberg had helped or hurt her career. She bristled and said, "I've been an actress a lot longer than I've been Mrs. Steven Spielberg. I still have to read for certain things. I had to audition for one film because the writer didn't know if I could do it."

I also asked why she had never starred in one of her husband's blockbusters, which would have been a good career move. "We've talked about it for the far-off future," she said of a future that was never to be. "When we come home, we park our careers at the door, and we're just husband and wife and Max's mom. Our careers are already complicated enough."

Irving took Max that year to London to be on the set of *Empire of the Sun*. It was a difficult time. The actress felt unemployed and adrift. "I miss acting," she told me. "It's very frustrating for me to be on the set of a movie I'm not in. But right now my 'project' is to be a wife and mother."

Spielberg had tried to hold the marriage together by following his wife all the way to Israel in 1986 when she made the execrable *Rumpelstiltskin*, an embarrassing vanity production directed by her brother and co-starring her mother and stepfather.

That was quite a sacrifice for the world's most successful and busiest director to make—becoming in effect Mr. Mom in order to spend time with his wife.

Ironically, Irving participated in one of her husband's big screen projects, but she didn't *appear* in it. Although Kathleen Turner supplied the speaking voice of Jessica Rabbit in the Spielberg produced *Who Framed Roger Rabbit*, it was Mrs. Spielberg who did Jessica's singing.

Irving's involvement was serendipitous. In fact, she was a pinch hitter on the film. She explained, "They needed someone to sing a temporary track so the animators would have something to draw from. It was a complete surprise to me that they were gonna use it in the movie! I saw what Jessica looked like—and my voice changed; it wasn't how I sing normally."

Despite her ice princess image, Irving had her defenders. And it says something about the veracity of the defense that one of her biggest boosters was also one of her husband's best friends, Richard Dreyfuss.

"She's protective of her family and friends," Dreyfuss insisted. "I don't think she lets a lot of people get to know her. But if people perceive her as cold, it's not true. She's got a real soft heart. And she can hurt. She's very vulnerable. There's a side to Amy that is so giving and caring."

On the other hand, Dreyfuss would not prove himself a good analyst of the marriage's prospects. The same year the couple divorced, Dreyfuss said not very presciently, "They've been together a million years. I think they're getting *better*. If she leaves the room, he's asking, 'Where's my wife?' They're very attached."

A cynical observer suggested that if Spielberg was indeed wondering where his wife was, it was so he could slip his girlfriend Kate Capshaw into the room during Irving's absence.

Just as she had avoided getting sucked into her husband's films, Irving had no intention of letting her son Max join the family business any time soon. Although her mother and stepfather co-starred with her in *Rumpelstiltskin*, and her brother directed the embarrassment, when he asked Max to play the baby, she turned her brother down flat.

"I turned down the role for Max. I don't want him to be in the movies. When he's old enough he can make that choice, but when he doesn't even have a say in the matter, I don't think that's fair."

I asked Irving how old Max would have to be before he could "have a say in the matter." She replied with a firm laugh, "Twenty-one."

On the surface, their life together was perfect. They shared a refurbished home in Brentwood; a glass walled co-op in the ultraluxurious Trump Tower; Amy's small adobe house in Santa Fe; a Pennsylvania Dutch-style barn they moved from Pennsylvania to East Hampton, Long Island; and a sumptuous compound of homes in Pacific Palisades, California, overlooking the ocean.

The official announcement of their split was noteworthy in its amicability. Their joint statement said, "Our mutual decision, however difficult, has been made in a spirit of caring. And our friendship remains both personal and professional."

Indeed, a week after the announcement, the two were seen dining together at a Los Angeles restaurant.

Irving basically summed up why they split when she said, "I started my career as the daughter of theater director Jules Irving. I don't want to finish it as the wife of Spielberg or the mother of Max."

The marriage and the prior relationship in the seventies had been troubled from the start. At least the breakup was civilized. Irving got a reported $100 million, or half the money her husband had earned during their four-year-marriage.

Irving had always protected her financial independence. Even when they were married, she kept their finances separate. "I wouldn't call it a fuck-you fund," she said a year before the split, "but we don't have the same checking account. *I have a lot that's mine.*"

Fortunately for the director, his wife was not a gold digger. She rejected advice from attorneys that she sue for even more money, palimony, based on the time they had lived together before their marriage.

The one person who didn't suffer from the breakup was their son, Max. Remembering the feeling of abandonment when his father left the family, Spielberg remained a fiercely involved dad, saying, "I have joint physical custody. Amy has Max one week, and I have Max the next since we live very close to one another. I'm a full-time, hands-on parent. What they call in California an 'involved parent.' The week Max is with me, I stay home and don't work. When he's not here, I work overtime to make up for the week I'm not working. I'm mad about Max. I drive him to school, feed him, tell him stories. When he was very small I used to give him his bottle and change his nappy. I was present at his birth—I even cut the umbilical cord. By the time Max was one, I no longer had any choice. He took first place and nothing else would do."

Irving's life post-Spielberg has been a downward spiral professionally if not personally. In 1990, she had a son by Brazilian director Bruno Baretto, whom she met on the set of *A Show of Force*. That film, which Baretto directed her in, went nowhere as did her other screen efforts following the divorce.

Irving was too classy to use the term "blacklisted," but she couldn't help noticing that directors and producers who were only too happy to consider Mrs. Steven Spielberg weren't falling over themselves to audition Bruno Baretto's girlfriend.

It was a double whammy: being married to Steven Spielberg and then *not* being married to the most powerful man in Hollywood.

"I was out there trying. I couldn't get meetings. I couldn't beg through the door," she said of life post-Steven.

"I think it hurt being Steven Spielberg's wife, and then it hurt being the ex-Mrs. Steven Spielberg. It was awkward for a while. I don't know why. I only know that I felt nonexistent. During my marriage to Steven, I felt like a politician's wife. There were certain things expected of me that definitely weren't me. One of my problems is that I'm very honest and direct. You pay a price for that. But then I behaved myself and I paid a price too."

But the good times still outweighed the bad times. Years after they split, she remembered the good old days as the girlfriend, then wife, of the biggest name in the movie business.

She said wistfully, "When we were together, I used to have terrific dreams."

By 1994, her dreams must have seemed like nightmares, at least as far as her career was concerned. Her latest, *Kleptomania*, couldn't even get a distributor. It was still on the shelf, which must be particularly galling, since she felt the film was a personal showcase.

"I think *Kleptomania* is the best work I've ever done. I put my heart and soul in that film, and it breaks my heart that it may never get released," she said.

Some speculated that her fading career had more to do with her reputation as being difficult and less to do with being the ex-Mrs. Steven Spielberg, a charge she summarily dismissed. "I'm not a princess. I've had a lot of shit to swallow and stuff to work out. I have scars nobody knows about. People shouldn't waste time thinking about whatever happened to Amy. I'm living in a very beautiful, intimate way. Maybe I'm less ambitious, but my life is so full. So excuse me for having an incredibly wonderful life."

In 1994, the *Los Angeles Times* almost gleefully reported, "While her ex-husband glories in unprecedented success, the 40-year-old actress finds herself working for relatively little money at a small regional theater." It wasn't quite as bad as the *Times* made out. The "regional theater" was the prestigious Long Wharf in New Haven, Connecticut, and the play, *Broken Glass*, happened to be the latest by America's preeminent playwright, Arthur Miller. As for working for very little money, that was hardly a concern since she had pocketed $100 million in the divorce settlement.

Ironically, Spielberg's film company, Amblin, was set to produce her boyfriend's next film, *Casanova*, with Antonio Banderas in the title role. Irving wouldn't have a role in the film, however, admitting she was "too old."

A semiotician would have enjoyed the iconography at the American Film Institute's Life Achievement Award ceremony honoring Spielberg in May of 1995. Seated next to the director on the dais was his second wife, buxom and blonde and gorgeous. Her ear-to-ear grin suggested she was thoroughly enjoying her reign as consort of the King of Hollywood.

Every so often, the camera would almost mischievously focus on a tiny, shriveled-looking woman who appeared exceedingly glum. Her hair was frizzy and pulled back in an unflattering chignon. Her dress looked as though it had come from grandma's closet. It took a while to figure out who this sad-sack figure was and why the camera was focusing on an unknown while Jack Nicholson and Clint Eastwood were within camera range. It was, of course, the first Mrs. Spielberg.

It wasn't until a year after the divorce that Capshaw made the director's reacquaintance. Then she moved fast. She knew right away that this was Mr. Right, but not because of his position as the most successful filmmaker of all time. It was her nose that told her to follow her heart.

"I think it was just the way he smelled," she said in all seriousness. "He smelled like my family. It was a smell of familiarity. I'm speaking not just metaphorically but olfactorily. They say once a woman takes a whiff of her infant you can blindfold her and march twenty babies in front of her and she'll pick hers, and that's how it felt to me. I felt like I was blindfolded and took a smell and said, 'This is the guy.'"

A year after she took her first whiff, they were married on October 12, 1991, at his home on Long Island. On Friday night, they had a casual dinner at Nic and Tony's in East Hampton.

There was a civil service the next morning at Guild Hall. Saturday afternoon they played a Kennedy-esque touch football game. That night there was a formal black-tie wedding, a traditional Orthodox ceremony in a large tent, presided over by a rabbi flown in from California.

The reception was star-studded. The reclusive Barbra Streisand attended, as did Sally Field, Robin Williams, Dustin Hoffman, and Richard Dreyfuss, who pronounced the ceremony "very sweet." Spielberg's longtime mentor and father figure, Steve Ross, chairman of Warner Brothers, spoke after the service. Robin Williams did shtick under the big tent.

It was Spielberg's second marriage, his wife's third.

As with Irving, his first child with Capshaw, a daughter

named Sasha, was born before they got married. After the marriage, they had a son, Sawyer, named after Huck Finn's pal.

Earlier, Capshaw had adopted an African-American foster child, Theo, when she was single. She also had a daughter, Jessica, now nineteen, from a previous marriage.

Spielberg described this blended brood. "It's an interesting group. I'd make them into a sitcom, but I don't do very well on TV. I don't want to screw around with my family and fail," he said, recalling his disastrous excursion into television with *Amazing Stories*.

Unlike his icy first wife, Capshaw was a nurturing, mothering type. Before becoming an actress, she had enjoyed an entire life and different career. She earned two degrees, a bachelor's in education and a master's in learning disabilities from the University of Missouri, and taught educationally handicapped children in Missouri schools for two years before chucking it all for a modeling and acting career in Manhattan.

"I was working one-on-one with the learning disabled, and I didn't like it," she recalled, adding guiltily, "Yet by comparison, acting is a very vain, selfish profession. I found it hard, at the end of a B.A., M.A. and two years of teaching to say, 'I want to go to New York and be an actress.' It wasn't like I was going to New York to save the world."

Long before Spielberg made her crawl on her hands and knees through an ocean of bugs, she had married a school principal, her college sweetheart, and had a daughter by him.

From the beginning of their relationship, Capshaw was a much better psychological match than Spielberg's first wife.

He once described himself as "the guy at the party in the corner eating the dip." Capshaw was no social butterfly herself. "There's a whole Hollywood scene that I don't even know about. It's the scene that has to do with big parties and drugs. I'm not a part of that. But I do love going to the movies, and so when they have a screening of something I want to see, I'll be there. Then, when they take my picture and it's in the *Hollywood Reporter*, it looks as if I'm making the Hollywood scene when I'm really just going to see the movies."

A Methodist, Capshaw converted to Judaism before the marriage, she said, "because I like the religion's emphasis on family, and I wanted my child to be born a Jew. When I converted, Steven was delighted, but then all the people in his family who were supposed to fall to their knees in exultation didn't say a word, because they so wanted me to know that it didn't matter to them."

And in contrast to Irving, Capshaw was willing to subvert her career in the service of her husband's.

She recalled watching *Temple of Doom* one night on television and turning to her husband to ask, "What happened to my career after that movie?" Spielberg replied, rather chauvinistically, "You weren't supposed to have a career. You were supposed to be with me."

Instead of hitting him, Capshaw agreed: "It's true. I think you have to have a great deal of ambition—these careers of our A-list ladies don't happen by accident. And if they do, they don't sustain. And I didn't do the things you have to do. My focus was on Steven and a large family."

She says she has no intention of ever starring in one of her husband's films, and not for the aesthetic reservations his first wife had about his style of filmmaking. Capshaw says simply, "I'd rather be in life with him than make a movie."

The only area of incompatibility, it seemed, was his obsession with films.

"My problem," she once said, "is that I'm not a movie buff. So I had difficulty understanding Steven. He talks in movie language, you see. He'd say, 'Remember that scene in *It Happened One Night*—the one where Claudette Colbert did such-and-such?' And I'd say, 'Steven, I never saw that movie.' And he'd groan and reply, 'Kate, how can I possibly communicate with you?'

"Really, I must get hold of some of those old movies and study them. Otherwise, I'm never going to know what people like Steven are talking about," she said.

Despite his wife's low movie IQ, friends claimed the workaholic director became more serene and happier after having two children with Capshaw. His former producer, Kathleen Kennedy, feels his second marriage brought a new balance to his life. "He has a personal confidence now and isn't trying to prove anything to himself anymore."

Spielberg would not disagree with his colleague's assessment. Of fatherhood, he says, "The best thing that ever happened to me, really, is having kids. I only make a movie every eighteen months as a director, and between movies I'm in my kids' face. I'm in my house every night by 5:15, and I'm not in the office until 9:30 a.m. I get on the floor and play with everybody. I can act sillier than my seven-year-old. I'm the guy who tries to keep the kids downstairs when my wife is trying to get them to bed."

Ironically, before the director fell in love with Capshaw, and while he was still going through a painful divorce from his first wife, he made one of his most lushly romantic films. The fact that it would fail at the box office hints that Spielberg's heart may not have been in the right place to take on such romantic subject matter.

CHAPTER FIFTEEN

Never

"THERE ARE CERTAIN PICTURES THAT ARE blatantly exploitative, that are terribly cast and executed, like poorly made sequels or bizarre remakes."

Steven Spielberg wasn't thinking about his own decision to remake the 1944 film, *A Guy Named Joe*, but his remake, renamed *Always*, was strangely cast and unevenly executed.

When he was fourteen, he saw the original film starring Spencer Tracy as a World War II fighter pilot who dies and comes back as the guardian angel of his best friend, a fellow pilot. Tracy also helps his buddy romance Tracy's ex-girlfriend.

Spielberg was so entranced with the story he countermanded his own belief that remakes rarely work. "This is the only remake I would really ever consider directing myself," he said before *Always* went into production. "It's a story that touched my soul when I was fourteen years old and saw it on television. It was the second movie that ever made me cry that didn't have a deer in it. And it's a reassuring story. It's about life and saying it while you're here and doing it while you can."

Still, he resisted the whole concept of remakes. "I wouldn't have done a remake if I had been able to do a movie that was about the same thing as *A Guy Named Joe*, but I couldn't find a script as good as the original."

Almost a decade earlier, the director had commissioned a screenplay based on *A Guy Named Joe*, but he felt he wasn't mature enough to make it at the time.

It wasn't just immaturity that kept the film in preproduction hell. The industry's biggest workaholic attributed the delay to laziness. He hadn't gotten around to making the film, he insisted, "because I'm lazy. I couldn't get the script right. I couldn't get the tone right. I guess I just didn't know what kind of movie I wanted to make. Between 1980 and 1985, eight drafts of the script were written. Then four more after that."

Eventually, Spielberg decided to update the story to the present day and turn the fighter pilots into fire fighters in the Pacific Northwest.

Richard Dreyfuss and Spielberg had discussed the idea of remaking the film while shooting *Jaws*. "After I told him that some day I wanted to do a remake of *A Guy Named Joe*, he kept nagging me to play the Spencer Tracy role. He told me, 'If you cast anyone else in the role I'll kill you!'"

Friendship only goes so far, and Spielberg resisted Dreyfuss's entreaties and sought out more traditional leading men. "At the time, Richard had this little round face and wasn't right for the role. He grew into the role over the last fifteen years!"

Both Robert Redford and Paul Newman were interested in the role Dreyfuss coveted. Spielberg wanted to cast one in the Tracy role and the other as the best friend. Superstar egos got in the way.

As Spielberg recalled, "They both quite liked the notion of the story, but both of them wanted to play Pete, the Spencer Tracy character, so I couldn't make that work."

Spielberg had never made a full-blown love story and he was intrigued by the challenge. However, he hedged his bets by sticking close to a theme that had worked well for him before, the supernatural. He'd take a risk making a love story, but he'd insure box office by throwing in a high concept about coming back to life.

His casting decisions were not so well thought out. Giving in to Dreyfuss's pleas, he cast the nerdy actor in the romantic lead. The director defended his decision, saying, "I think the best love stories are about people we perceive to be just like us. And I've always looked at Richard Dreyfuss as Everyman."

In his defense, Spielberg may have been influenced by Dreyfuss's romantic role the year before in the cop movie, *Stakeout*, when *Newsweek* hailed him as a new kind of romantic hero.

The female lead was harder to cast. After a long search, Spielberg happened to be watching a film about a feisty female television news producer, *Broadcast News*. Although he had never seen the actress before, ten minutes into the film he knew he had found his leading lady. Holly Hunter would re-create the role originated by Irene Dunne.

"Holly Hunter is Everygirl, feisty, smart and extremely opinionated. I've always been attracted to forthright women who aren't afraid to lay it on the line, even if sometimes that line goes right across our chests."

The script for *Always* had an exalted pedigree. One of Britain's greatest playwrights, Tom Stoppard, wrote several drafts, although he didn't receive a credit. Spielberg and the playwright had become close friends after collaborating on the script for *Empire of the Sun*.

It's a mutual admiration society that continues to this day. Stoppard, in fact, has a contract with Amblin, Spielberg's production company, to read books and screenplays and offer his opinion.

"It's a good partnership because what I think I've done is to introduce Tom to telling the story with pictures and Tom introduced me to telling the story with some dialogue. He showed me an interesting way of talking, not to the point, but around the point. You don't just come out and say what you mean. Let the audience figure it out for themselves. Give them all the clues and then confirm, after they figure it out, that they were right."

Always may be most memorable because it gave fans one last on-screen look at Audrey Hepburn before her untimely death just a few years later.

Spielberg originally had wanted Sean Connery to play the role of God since their working relationship on *Indiana Jones and the Last Crusade* had been so fruitful. But Connery had other film commitments, so in a burst of inspiration Spielberg decided to recast God as a woman!

In one scene, Hepburn appears in a burned-out forest. The script called for her to be dressed all in white. In order not to smudge her costume, Hepburn literally had to be carried on a stretcher to the middle of the forest by six burly members of the crew.

Spielberg recalled, "She was embarrassed to be carried around like a queen and kept explaining to anybody who would listen that her unusual mode of transportation was just to keep her clean."

Spielberg loved his cast. At the conclusion of filming, he gave each of his stars an unusual present, a Mazda Miata.

Spielberg explained his unusual generosity: "I loved working with those people so much. Usually you just have a cake at a wrap party and say goodbye. I wanted to give them something to remember the film by."

The Miatas were indeed memorable. The cars had just been introduced into the United States at the time, and they were so immensely popular they were almost impossible to come by. As *Always'* co-star John Goodman, a recipient of the director's largesse said, "When you're Steven Spielberg, it's not hard to get anything you want."

The gigantic Goodman struck an amusing figure driving around town in the tiny Mazda, but he liked the car and didn't mind the cramping.

Always was a modest commercial success, although the critics barbecued it. The film cost $30 million, a bargain considering the expensive aerial footage of forest fires and crashing planes. It grossed $77 million.

But you get the impression Spielberg would have made the film even if he had a crystal ball that could predict which of his films would hit and which would miss.

"I don't look at a screenplay and say I can't make this because it won't make a lot of money. It's all a throw of the dice. So, I just make a movie and don't worry about its commercial potential because you never know at that stage whether it will make money or not. *Empire of the Sun* and *The Color Purple* didn't look like money-makers on paper, but *The Color Purple* turned out to be a huge hit. It's all a crapshoot." You will notice he didn't comment on *Empire*'s paltry box-office take. *Empire* was the downside of the crapshoot.

Most importantly, regardless of its box-office take, *Always* was a film Spielberg was completely satisfied with. Or as he more strikingly described it, "*Always* is a film I can stand naked on top of!"

Spielberg may have felt so *gemutlich* about the blah *Always* because its story line vaguely paralleled his own personal life at the time. *Always* deals with the end of one suffocating relationship and the beginning of a healthy, enriching one. In 1989, Spielberg's romantic life was in transition as he ended his tortured relationship with Amy Irving and renewed his on-again, off-again affair with Kate Capshaw. The glow his new liaison gave off must have been reflected in his rhapsodic crowing over a turkey like *Always*.

CHAPTER SIXTEEN

Hooked

IN 1990, STEVEN SPIELBERG FELT ADRIFT. HIS career was in a holding pattern. No one was ready to declare him washed up, but he felt artistically stalled.

One studio executive, who spoke off the record (natch), said, "Spielberg chose his last few projects unwisely." The executive mentioned *The Color Purple*, *Empire of the Sun*, and *Always*.

That was too harsh an assessment. Only *Empire of the Sun* was a certifiable flop, but it had earned Spielberg some of the best reviews of his career. With his track record, he could afford the occasional *succès d'estime*.

Spielberg's track record as a movie producer, however, was spottier. While he had helmed hits like *Gremlins* and *Who Framed Roger Rabbit*, he had also made duds like *Innerspace*, *Young Sherlock Holmes*, and the unintelligible *Joe Versus the Volcano*, which had the distinction of being the only film in which Tom Hanks and Meg Ryan ever turned in a bad performance.

With films like *Empire of the Sun* and especially *The Color Purple*, Spielberg was trying to grow up, to escape the world of cuddly aliens, serial cliff-hangers and special effects extravaganzas. But whenever he tried more mature subject matter, either the public or the critics deserted him.

In the early eighties, Spielberg had drifted away from his agent, Jeff Berg, chairman of ICM. Why give somebody ten percent of a billion dollars when you can negotiate your own sterling deal? But in 1990, Spielberg, the most powerful director in Hollywood, signed with the most powerful agent in Hollywood, Mike Ovitz, then the chairman of Creative Artists Agency and now president of Disney. A studio executive speculated on why Spielberg was willing to surrender 10 percent of his earnings to Ovitz.

"If anybody can finally get Spielberg off producing his umpteenth knockoff of *Jaws* and *E.T.* and directing grown-up movies, it's Ovitz at CAA."

Spielberg reportedly was peeved that he was not being offered the best scripts. One script that got away was *Dead Poet's Society*, a film that he would have dearly loved to direct. His own handlers had passed on *Silence of the Lambs* without even mentioning it to him, because its subject matter—cannibalism and serial murder—was not Spielberg territory. "Even my staff tends to pigeonhole me," he lamented.

No one in development lost his or her job at Amblin' after failing to run *Silence of the Lambs* past the boss. This kind of forgiveness isn't necessarily typical of many filmmakers. When executives at Mel Gibson's production company turned down the script of *Ghost* without even mentioning the project to their boss, Gibson fired his entire staff. Spielberg tends to be more passive-aggressive with employees who fail to please. As one ex-staffer said, "Steven never fires anybody. He just stops talking to you until you feel so left out you quit."

Spielberg personally rejected another project, *Full Disclosure*, in galleys even though it was by the author of his biggest hit, *Jurassic Park*. Although nowhere near as graphic as *Silence of the Lambs*, *Full Disclosure* gave him the creeps. (It's hard to imagine the director who shied away from showing Whoopi Goldberg's vagina in *The Color Purple* directing Demi Moore to say a line like, "I want you to put your cock in my mouth.")

His alliance with CAA would give him first crack at the agency's 300-plus client list of writers and access to the agency's roster of A-list actors.

Mike Ovitz had perfected the art of the package, putting together a raft of agency clients in one project, from director to writer to stars. CAA was a one-stop operation. Step right up and get your superstars, director and script here.

Spielberg's first CAA-fueled project represented Ovitz's packaging at its apotheosis.

The film was *Hook*, and it was a veritable cornucopia of CAA stars: Dustin Hoffman, Robin Williams, Julia Roberts, and writer Jim V. Hart.

The only fly in the ointment of this superstar mix was that a decidedly B-list director, Nick Castle, was already attached to the project. But as soon as the king of Hollywood expressed interest, the studio paid Castle $850,000, net profit participation, and a story credit to go away. Sony's subsidiary, Tri-Star, had bankrolled the film, and its then chairman, Mike Medavoy, took the blame for firing Castle. In fact, Medavoy claimed that Spielberg balked at causing a colleague to be muscled off a project. Spielberg's long-time producing partner, Frank Marshall, said that Spielberg was unaware that another director was attached to *Hook*, and when he found out about the firing, "he was horrified."

For years, it was rumored that Steven Spielberg, the director who refused to grow up, would make a film about the famous boy who refused to do the same thing, Peter Pan. In the early eighties, the totally unsubstantiated story that Spielberg would direct man-child Michael Jackson in an updated version of the J. M. Barrie tale was reported as fact, even though Spielberg consistently denied any intention of tackling the story.

What hooked Spielberg on *Hook* was its twist on the J. M. Barrie theme. The updated script examined what happens when Peter Pan finally grows up. The writer, Jim V. Hart, said the idea for *Hook* came to him when his six-year-old son asked, "Dad, did Peter Pan ever grow up?' An hour later I had my story. I knew Spielberg too had been obsessed with Peter Pan. He had never been able to crack it, and when he found what I had done, it answered his questions too. I guess a lot of us had grown up."

In the film, Peter Banning (né Pan) is indeed all grown up. He's an attorney who leads corporate takeovers. The quintessential shark of the eighties' Decade of Greed.

Hook was the quintessential Spielberg movie. All his adult life, critics had been urging the director of children's films to turn his prodigious talents to more adult themes. *Hook* would allow the director to play both sides of the field, to explore his childlike wonderment and counterpoint it with witty adult satire.

Five years before he made *Hook*, Spielberg confessed to *Time* magazine, "I have always felt like Peter Pan. I still feel like him. It has been very hard for me to grow up."

Although Spielberg had once said, "My main drive is not to use people who were on the cover of *Rolling Stone*," he contradicted himself later saying, "I have a stomachache because I haven't worked with Dustin [Hoffman]. I have a pain in my right side because I haven't worked with De Niro. I would love to do something with Meryl Streep and Tom Cruise."

But that was before he linked up with the star-studded CAA, which gave him the services of three stars who had graced the cover of the hip music magazine: Dustin Hoffman, Robin Williams, and Julia Roberts.

Besides hooking him up with *Rolling Stone*-quality talent, CAA also worked out one of the richest deals in history for Spielberg and his cover-boy cast. Spielberg, Williams, and Hoffman divided among themselves 40 percent of the film's gross from all markets, including theatrical, video, television, and precedentially, merchandising. Usually, filmmakers get only 10 percent of the take from toys.

Hoffman played the title role, Roberts was a seven-inch-high Tinker Bell, and Williams played the boy who wouldn't grow up—grown up.

Williams had his pick of scripts since he had starred in one blockbuster after another. He picked *Hook* because the original text haunted him. "The story is really an exorcism. If you read the book, Peter is a lethal boy. He's also very egocentric. There's a real dark side to him that was expunged in the cutesy Disney cartoon version." (In fact, Disney originally had planned to produce *Hook* but backed out when the budget ballooned to $60 million.)

Williams was intrigued by the ghoulish side of the character he signed on to play. "In the book, Peter kills fourteen pirates. This is not a child you go up to, pinch his cheeks and say, 'Oh, how cute!' Remember, he scared the shit out of Captain Hook. He doesn't give a shit about anybody but himself. This is not a simple little child. Macaulay Culkin could not play this kid," Williams told me.

The supporting cast was eclectic to say the least. Bob Hoskins, a personal favorite of Spielberg's since they had worked together on *Who Framed Roger Rabbit*, was cast as Captain Hook's valet or batman, Smee. Two-time Oscar winner Maggie Smith played Peter's original love, Wendie, now a creaky dowager. Glenn Close was invisible in pirate drag. Rocker David Crosby also played a cutthroat, joined by fellow musician Phil Collins as a London bobby. Missing from the cast were the "Redskins" and "Tiger Lily," who were personally cut from the original script by Spielberg. In an era of heightened sensitivity, treating Native Americans like cigar store Indians was taboo.

Spielberg may have wished he had stuck to his intention of never working with a star who had been on the cover of *Rolling Stone*.

There were superstar collisions of ego from day one. As he had on *Rainman*, Hoffman brought his own personal script doctor to punch up his scenes. His choice of personal scribe was a strange one, Malia Scotch Marmo, whose biggest credit was the flop *Once Around*.

Hoffman also fancied himself a fencing expert and reportedly directed most of his dueling scenes himself. "We would go to the dailies and hear Dustin clearly shouting the directions," one crew member recalled.

Williams was just the opposite of the demanding superstar. The comic actor was a mass of insecurities, terrified of Hoffman's superior talent.

"For the first week I was scared shitless Dustin would act me off the screen. I thought, 'Why can't I play Hook?' But Dustin turned out to be helpful and not competitive at all."

In fact, the two men became fast friends. In the makeup trailer, they would do impromptu riffs off one another that witnesses said was Vegas-quality material.

Hook was shot on the backlot of Sony, formerly the home of MGM. The production took up nine stages, including the *Wizard of Oz* stage, Esther Williams's swimming tank, and the soundstage where the Bounty crew staged their mutiny.

The budget was $60 million, even though the stars didn't take a salary up front. The lavish sets suggested where the money had gone. They were created by John Napier, the Tony-winning designer of *Cats*, *Les Miserables*, *Nicholas Nickleby*, and *Starlight Express*.

The pirate ship was an eighty-foot black and gold galleon. It was built on a soundstage and then launched by flooding the entire set. The ship was so tall that the cinematographer, Dean Cundey, had to move out into the street and shoot through the doors to get the whole ship in one frame. The giant tree house where the Lost Boys hung out took up two entire soundstages.

The *Hook* set became a private Disneyland for superstars working on other projects at Sony. Warren Beatty, Annette Benning, and director Bugsy Siegel dropped by from *Bugsy*. The VIP guest list also included Michael Jackson, Michael Ovitz, Bruce Willis and Demi Moore, Tom Cruise, the Queen of Jordan, and the chairman of Sony, who flew in from Japan. The set was closed to lesser mortals.

One of the fringe benefits of making the film was that the director and Williams became best friends. They still play video games together, and when separated by a continent, they continue the game over the phone via modem. Some superstars have personal trainers; others like Dustin Hoffman have personal screenwriters. The king of Hollywood has his own personal comedian, who also happens to be one of the biggest stars in the business.

Ah, clout.

The director didn't enjoy such a happy collaboration with his female star. During an interview on television's top-rated news show, *60 Minutes*, a reporter asked him if he would ever work with Roberts again. After a painfully long pause, he said tersely, "No."

It was the rejection heard around the world.

Roberts definitely heard it. She happened to be watching television when she surfed over to *60 Minutes*, and there was the man she considered a good friend implying she was a pain to work with.

In an interview in *Premiere* magazine, Roberts was described as "on the verge of tears" when she recounted Spielberg's public rejection of her. "People disappoint me," she said. "It's too bad. Steven and I had an enjoyable time. The last day on the set, a friend shot a video of me and Steven saying, 'You are just the greatest Tinker Bell . . . I love you. And you were fabulous. You dealt with all that crazy technical blue-screen isolation, blah blah blah.' I didn't leave *Hook* on bad terms with Steven. We hugged and kissed and did the whole good-bye thing in what I felt was a genuine way. It was so nice.

"Then to unknowingly turn on my television and watch him on *60 Minutes* . . . that's surprising. He obviously missed some aspect of me as a person. You can only find disappointment in an expectant mind, and I don't really expect anything from Steven."

There was one widely reported incident that suggested just how prickly the atmosphere was on the set. Standing in front of the cameras one day, Roberts grew tired of waiting for filming to begin. Finally she said, "I'm ready now." Spielberg replied, "We're ready when *I* say we're ready, Julia."

More problems arose when Roberts shut down production for one whole week while she checked into Cedars-Sinai Hospital in Los Angeles. The official report said she was suffering from a severe fever. Persistent rumors, which she later denied, insisted the troubled actress was being treated for heroin addiction.

It was during *Hook* that Roberts made headlines for another reason: the abrupt cancellation of her much ballyhooed wedding to actor Kiefer Sutherland. Roberts further delayed shooting by running off to Ireland for a week with her new boyfriend, actor Jason Patric, after practically leaving Sutherland standing at the altar.

Roberts's absenteeism led to reports that Michelle Pfeiffer, among others, had been interviewed by the director to replace the errant Roberts. To spike such rumors, Spielberg generously appeared with Roberts at a press conference outside the studio gates and insisted for the record that Julia's job was secure.

It's interesting this man says he loves women, and indeed has a largely female staff at his production company, yet the only people he ever seems to have trouble with are his female stars. Karen Allen bad-mouthed him and found herself blacklisted from the rest of the Indiana Jones films. Teri Garr accused him of treating her like a puppet. And Dee Wallace Stone found her career on a downward spiral after clashing with Spielberg over the advertising campaign for *E.T.*

Spielberg had an even worse time with lesser cast members on the set of *Hook*. He's a devoted father and playmate to his brood of five kids at home, but too many child actors can drive him up the wall. On the set, the usually genial director found himself turning into the grumpy title character of *Hook*.

"I had never worked with that many kids . . . and I never will again," he said with a shudder. "You'll know when I'm trying to self-destruct if you read I am making a movie about a school teacher teaching a class of thirty-five kids," he told me at the Century Plaza Hotel in Los Angeles.

"I am really good one on one with kids, and of course I adore my own children. But when they're all together on a set, it's kind of like you're a classroom teacher. You are the principal and you become the ugly authority figure.

"I'm afraid I became Captain Hook to some of these kids. I had. We had to make a movie, and most of the kids weren't actors. They were just kids off the street."

The discipline problem at one point became so annoying Spielberg confessed that he threw a good old-fashioned superstar tantrum. He warned one pint-sized extra, "If you don't keep quiet, you will be replaced." The child immediately shaped up so he wouldn't be shipped out.

Spielberg was no doubt more diplomatic with the children of his stars, who all had cameos in the film. Perhaps as a sign of who had the greater clout, Hoffman's son made the final cut (he was the child staring out a window) while Williams's kid ended up on the cutting-room floor.

The studio suits were ecstatic when they saw the final cut. Forgotten was the $60 million price tag and the stars' take of 40 percent of the gross. Preview audiences gave the film a rare 95 percent approval rating, saying they would recommend the film to their friends, the kind of glowing endorsement studio executives fantasize about.

Tri-Star chief Medavoy said with typical executive hyperbole, "If you look at Steven's entire body of work, and you read the *Hook* script and see the movie, it's the culmination of all those years rolled into one. It looks like the pinnacle of his achievement. This is his real shot at the Oscar!"

Those overwrought sentiments were not shared by the critics, who called the film "bloated" and "overproduced." Before seeing the film, the *New York Times* prematurely announced that "in *Hook* he finally confronted the grown up side of himself, by examining the life of Peter Banning, *ne* Pan, a hard-driving takeover lawyer who struggles with the conflicts between creativity and ambition, between fatherhood and the pursuit of power, speaking to a side of himself the director has long tried to obscure."

But when the *Times* finally saw the film, it agreed with the rest of the critics who felt this was the same old Spielberg with better sets and costumes than usual.

Newsweek compared *Hook* to a "huge party cake of a movie, with too much frosting." British film critic Alexander Walker quipped, "The child in me, I'm afraid, just threw up." But another film critic, George Perry, hailed it as "quite simply the best kids' film in many years."

The audience didn't agree, and Spielberg et al. ended up with 40 percent of the film's worldwide gross of $288 million. And that tally didn't even include the money brought in by all those Peter Pan and Tinker Bell toys and lunch boxes, of which they also earned 40 percent.

The sets from *Hook* were disassembled carefully and stored amid rumors that Sony planned to use the movie as the centerpiece for a backlot theme park. Just more money for Spielberg, Incorporated.

Hook didn't impress film critics but the public loved it. His next film would please both constituencies.

CHAPTER SEVENTEEN

A Culmination

MICHAEL CRICHTON, A HARVARD-EDUCAT-ed physician and best-selling novelist, came up with an ingenious idea for a book. What if scientists unearthed a piece of amber in which was imbedded a mosquito from the days when dinosaurs roamed the earth? And what if the mosquito had feasted on one of those dinosaurs? And what if the DNA from the dinosaur's blood in the mosquito's gut provided a blueprint for creating a real-life dinosaur? And what if some entrepreneur came up with the idea of creating an amusement park populated with a whole menagerie of reconstructed tyrannosaurus rexes and velociraptors?

The answer to those hypotheticals would lead to a best-selling novel, *Jurassic Park*, and the most successful movie in the history of the industry.

Spielberg envisioned the project as a sequel of sorts to his previous number-one film. "With *Jurassic*, I was really just trying to make a good sequel to *Jaws*. On land. It's shameless," he said.

As he had with *Jaws*, Spielberg immediately began to tear the novel apart and reassemble it to fit his cinematic vision. The billionaire entrepreneur who builds the amusement park was a greedy, amoral sludge in the novel. Spielberg cast the avuncular

Sir Richard Attenborough in the role and made him more of a father figure cum Santa Claus (a role Sir Richard would play a year later) and less an Ivan Boesky with Walt Disney delusions of grandeur.

The exteriors for *Jurassic Park* were shot on the Hawaiian island of Kauai, standing in for the novel's Costa Rica, site of the reptilian amusement park.

Despite the mind-boggling logistics involved, *Jurassic Park* actually came in under budget and a few days ahead of schedule.

Spielberg joked that good old-fashioned guilt made him cost-conscious. "In the old days, studio heads would go over to a director and say, 'You're behind schedule. If you don't catch up, I will personally kill you with my bare hands.'

"Today, the same studio head will come over and say, 'If you don't pick up the schedule, I'm going to lose my job and my children will leave me.' It's a whole new technique, but both are effective."

It was new technology, not guilt-tripping studio executives, however, that prompted the director to scrap two expensive processes in favor of cheaper computerized animation.

Spielberg originally had planned that most of the dinosaurs would be life-sized robots. Only the largest reptiles were to be miniatures, animated by a nerve-wracking process called "go-motion," in which each film frame is shot separately, then the miniatures are moved a fraction of an inch per frame to create the illusion of fluid motion when the frames are run together at the speed of twenty-four frames per second.

Then the director saw *Terminator 2*, which achieved many of its lifelike effects through CGI, a new technology that stood for Computer-Generated Imagery. What specifically changed Spielberg's mind about CGI was when his visual-effects supervisor Dennis Murren created a single test shot of 200 dinosaurs running through the tall grass like so may stampeding deer. When he saw the scene on the page, Spielberg had cut it from the production, suspecting it would be an impossible nightmare of logistics: 200 large reptiles running around in one frame. But Murren's test shot, which was completely created on a hard disk, made Spielberg a convert to CGI. Universal refused to comment officially, but a studio source estimated that this particular conversion saved the studio a whopping $10 million that would have been spent on the herky-jerky movements of life-sized robots and stop-action puppets.

Not all the dinosaurs, which Spielberg paternalistically insisted the crew refer to as "creatures" not monsters, were created inside CPUs. Although it was technically a "miniature," i.e. not life-size, the tyrannosaurus was plenty big. Eighteen feet tall and 9,000 pounds. It was the largest animatronic (remote-controlled) robot ever created for a film and took two years to construct. For one scene in which a tyrannosaurus smashes into a tree and obliterates it, a computer-generated dinosaur was used, saving the expense of destroying the robot along with the tree. For another scene both a robot and a CGI were used to show one creature (a robot) nudging a jeep while another tyrannosaurus (computer generated) pops into the frame. The more expensive robot was used to nudge the jeep because only the head and shoulders were seen in the shot, while the other, computerized tyrannosaurus showed its entire body.

Keeping to schedule and budget was all the more amazing since Spielberg had to contend with an act of nature that no one could have foreseen.

While filming on Kauai in 1992, Hurricane Iniki struck the island. Spielberg, the director, turned into Spielberg, the television news reporter. He bravely reported live by telephone from Hawaii for a local Los Angeles news station.

Doing an Indiana Jones turn, he bravely stepped outside during the full force of the hurricane to get a better view for his television reportage. The rest of the cast and crew huddled inside the hotel while Indiana Steve described gale force winds and toppling palms.

At a sneak preview of the film, as the lights went down, a child in the audience yelled out, "This better be good."

If box office is any indication, it was *very* good. Released in the summer of 1993, *Jurassic Park* soon became the number-one film of all time, knocking out the previous champ, although the director of that film, *E.T.*, couldn't be too upset, since he had made both films.

At last count, *Jurassic Park* had grossed $850 million. Toys and other trinkets have brought in even more, an estimated $1 billion.

Spielberg, per usual, got 10 percent of the toys. His take from the box office was a reported $250 million—the most, *Forbes* magazine breathlessly reported, ever made by a single individual from a movie or any other form of entertainment.

The magazine estimated his hard assets at $460 million in 1994. Throw in his 100 percent ownership of his production company Amblin Entertainment, and *Forbes* acclaimed him the first billionaire director.

In an interview with the magazine, Spielberg claimed, "I'm a gambler. I haven't taken a salary for almost a decade now. I love gambling to see what's going to make it and what's not."

The magazine was not seduced by the hype. Spielberg was as big a gambler as Mother Theresa.

The difference between Spielberg and a *real* gambler is that Spielberg can't lose. Every time a Spielberg film came out, it wasn't a question of whether he would make any money, but how much.

Forbes provided a thumbnail sketch of the typical Spielberg movie deal: The studio financed all the costs, including production, advertising, and distribution. If Spielberg only produced the film, he got 5 percent of the gross from the first dollar that made its way to the ticket booth. If Spielberg directed the film, he got an additional 15 percent of the gross. So even if a film flopped, Spielberg made money. For example, although *Empire of the Sun* didn't turn a profit after costs were factored in, it did bring in $66 million, of which Spielberg as producer and director earned a whopping 25 percent. For a flop!

Forbes estimated that after the studio paid all the overhead, the typical split between the director and the company was fifty-fifty.

Every studio in town was more than eager to give in to such an extortionate deal. Mike Ovitz, who rarely talks to the press, was willing to come out of his cocoon and tell *Forbes*, "It's easier to ask for a partnership when you have the extraordinary track record he has."

Tom Pollock, the chairman of Universal, said simply, "He has the clout to make any deal he wants."

With its aesthetic eye firmly directed toward the bottom line, *Forbes* described "creativity" in dollars and cents. "If creativity is defined as a feel for mass tastes, Spielberg may be the most creative person in the entertainment history." After all, he had directed six of the top fifteen money-makers of all time.

Jurassic Park broke other records for Spielberg. In the period 1993–94, Spielberg earned $335 million, an all-time record. The previous record holder was Michael Jackson for 1988–89, with a mere $200 million. When Spielberg ascended to the top spot, he knocked former protege Oprah Winfrey off her perch. Oprah, during the same time period, had made only $105 million.

Although in the past he had called sequels "cheap carny tricks" and only made the Indiana Jones series as a personal favor to a good friend, *Jurassic Park*'s payday made him more amenable to duplicating himself. Sure enough, a sequel to dinosaurs on the lam was announced for 1997.

This must have all been heady stuff for a college dropout with a reading disorder who had made all of $100 from his first professional film at sixteen. But there was this little irritant gnawing at him. He hinted at this when he commented on the work of a good friend, Martin Scorsese:

"I don't have to make *Mean Streets* to prove I'm a great director. I think my friends' definition of 'importance' is that nobody goes to see your movies, but the critics like them."

For his next film, Spielberg finally would nail the green-eyed monster and bury it forever under an avalanche of Oscars and effusive reviews.

Way back in 1983, the same year the novel *Schindler's List* was published in America, the critic Charles Derry wrote of Spielberg: "His vision is that of the child-artist, the innocent and profound imagination that can summon up primeval dread from the deep as well as transcendent wonder from the sky. If Spielberg's films may sometimes be attacked for a certain lack of social issues or 'adult concerns,' they may be defended on the grounds that his films—unlike perhaps so many of the special effects action films of the '70s and '80s—never seem to pander to their audience, but derive, rather, from a sensibility which is sincerely felt."

For years, fans of the director's technical prowess wished he would lend his consummate talent to something more worthy of his great gifts than careening boulders and twinkling mother ships.

With *Schindler's List*, he would more than satisfy all those wishes.

In *The Movie Brats*, authors Michael Pye and Lynda Myles discussed the theme of Spielberg's works long before *Schindler's List* came out. But their analysis would turn out to be prophetic when it came to understanding the protagonist of the book and the film.

Spielberg's themes, the authors wrote, deal with "how the ordinary person transcends the limitations he expects to find and becomes a hero, a martyr, an adventurer. It is at once a glorification of suburbia and a pointer to escape routes from that class. It expects identification from the audience. That may be why certain Spielberg films have so extraordinarily wide an appeal. They show the way out of most people's live."

With *Schindler's List*, Spielberg was through glorifying suburbia, and his film was escapist only in the literal sense of escaping the greatest horror of the twentieth century, the Holocaust.

And for his hero, he chose someone who was arguably subordinary, an amiable loser who for a short period of time transcended his limitations to achieve greatness.

Schindler's List was based on a prize-winning novel by Australia's Thomas Keneally. It was a fact-based account of a Nazi Party member, Oskar Schindler, who secretly saved more than a thousand Jews from the gas chambers.

Oskar Schindler came to Cracow, Poland, in 1939 in the wake of the invading German army. He had big dreams of making it rich. To that end, he bought an enamelware factory that had been "Aryanized," i.e. expropriated from its Jewish owner.

Schindler was no saint, although he ultimately would perform good deeds that went beyond saintly. He was a bon vivant who kept a wife in Germany and a girlfriend in Cracow, while conducting an affair with his Polish secretary.

The book and film title refers to the list Schindler compiled to save lives. Claiming he needed Jews who were about to be deported to Auschwitz to work in his factory, Schindler put everybody on his list, including children and even babies. To smooth over his larceny, he plied Nazi bureaucrats with black-market brandy, cigars, food, and other luxuries. He risked his life and wiped out his personal fortune to save the 1,100 Jews on his eponymous list.

Universal's Sid Sheinberg, who had bought the rights to the book in 1982, showed it to his protege, telling him, "This is the film you have to make."

Spielberg agreed, but it would take him more than ten years to make the "film he had to make."

"I wasn't ready in '82 to make Schindler's List. In 1982, when I acquired the rights, I wasn't mature enough. I wasn't emotionally resolved with my life. I hadn't had children. I really hadn't seen God until my first child was born. A lot of things happened that were big deals in my personal life that I didn't give interviews about. But they changed me as a person and as a filmmaker. And they led me to say, 'I want to do it now. I need to make it right now.'"

Though this emotional immaturity slowed *Schindler's* progression to the screen, getting the script right was also a ten-year ordeal. Keneally, the author of the book, turned in a first draft, but it was the length of a mini-series! Kurt Luedtke, the Oscar-winning writer of *Out of Africa*, labored over the project for three years and finally gave up in frustration. Sydney Pollack and Martin Scorsese expressed interest in directing the film. And it was Scorsese who found the writer, Steven Zallian, who finally could wrestle the book into script form.

Spielberg was fascinated by the intrinsic drama of Schindler's story. But he had bigger reasons for tackling the project.

"I wanted something that would confirm my Judaism to my family and myself, and to a history that was being forgotten. When my son was born, it greatly affected me. I decided I wanted my kids raised Jewish, as I was. I have wonderful memories of my Judaism when I was child—not a teenager, but a child," he said, perhaps recalling the high school bullies who bloodied his nose and shoved his face into the water fountain. "I wanted my children to be proud of the fact that they were members of the oldest tribe in history."

As he has said in interviews, Spielberg's childhood memories of Judaism were more cultural than religious. Although he was Bar Mitzvahed, his family, he has said, was not observant. One of his happiest childhood recollections was guiltily boiling forbidden lobsters with his mother. He seems to have had only two memories of what it meant to be Jewish when he was a child. He remembered Hasidic elders in *shul* passing him ritual Matzoh, and his mother lighting candles on the Sabbath. It's not surprising that Spielberg should remember the ritual rather than the theology of his life. Many an adult ex-Christian atheist has fond childhood memories of Nativity scenes, Midnight Mass, and stockings stuffed with goodies on Christmas morning. The fact that Spielberg wasn't raised in a strictly religious household doesn't diminish his enthusiastic embrace of Judaism as a middle-aged man. When Barbra Streisand was directing *Yentl*, she underwent a similar religious rediscovery.

Newsweek magazine noted that in a twenty-year career, Spielberg had never confronted his Jewish roots on film before. "Until *Schindler's List*, Spielberg's Judaism never touched his work . . . The fantasies he concocted were the ultimate triumph of assimilation. He colonized the world with his imagination."

Besides finally exploring his roots, he was fascinated by the character of Oskar Schindler. "He changed from a Great Gatsby to a great rescuer and it fascinated me. He was like an agent, like a Michael Ovitz, on top of the mountain pulling strings in every fiefdom down below. One of my role models for Schindler was Steve Ross," the chairman of Time-Warner, who died in 1993. Like Sheinberg and Wasserman at Universal, Warner Brothers' chief was a father figure and a good friend to the director. In fact, to help Liam Neeson, who played Schindler, understand the role, Spielberg gave him home movies of Ross so he could duplicate his mannerisms, including Ross' expansive use of body language.

Schindler's List would be a major departure for Spielberg, and not just because he retired his bag of cinematic tricks to make the low-tech film. "I came to realize the reason I came to make the movie is that I have never in my life told the truth in a movie. My effort as a moviemaker has been to create something that couldn't possibly happen."

It's not surprising that *Schindler's List* intrigued Spielberg. The real life story of Oskar Schindler had more derring-do than anything concocted for Indiana Jones or the kids who bicycled E.T. to freedom. When a few of Schindler's factory workers were deported to Auschwitz, Schindler took a train to camp and demanded his "employees" be freed because they were "essential personnel" needed for the war effort. Making enamel pots and pans?

The concentration camp commandant, with the *douceur* of a hefty bribe of diamonds, returned the prisoners, including small children, to Schindler.

Schindler's List was a film Steven Spielberg *had* to make.

When he received the Irving Thalberg Memorial Award at the Oscars ceremony in 1987, his acceptance speech excoriated filmmakers for paying more attention to the image on the screen than on the words coming out of the actors' mouths.

Before any critic in the audience could shout out, "The pot calls the kettle black," Spielberg anticipated such criticism and admitted he perhaps was the biggest sinner in this area.

The director need not have apologized too profusely for preferring the visual over the verbal. Film, after all, is a visual medium. Scholars write monographs on the films of John Ford, who "painted" epic Western vistas, not the films of Noel Coward, who stuck a camera in a drawing room and let it run. More likely, Spielberg's self-deprecating acceptance speech was a way to show a little humility at such an ego-gratifying event like receiving the Thalberg award.

In 1987, the director was still dismissed as a maker of roller-coaster rides. He was the king of techno-films, from *Jaws* to his last, pre-Schindler high-tech orgy, *Jurassic Park*.

It wasn't surprising that Spielberg had sought refuge in the world of special effects. Whenever he tried to make a sensitive, relatively small, people-oriented film, he either was ignored by the public or the Oscars.

Despite the critical drubbing of his character-driven film *The Color Purple* and the box-office failure of *Empire of the Sun*, the director decided to put aside his bag of special effects tricks and elaborate camera shots to make the story of Oskar Schindler.

"I didn't want a style similar to anything I'd done before. First of all I threw half my toolbox away. I canceled the crane. I tore out the dolly track. I simply tried to pull the events closer to the audience by reducing the artifice. Most of my films have been the stuff of imagination. For the first time, I felt free to abandon 'form' to tell the story of a life."

To increase the sense of immediacy, he also employed something he had never used before, a hand-held camera.

To make *Schindler's List*, Spielberg had to suppress a talent and proclivity that had made him the most successful film director in history:

"My problem is I have too much of a command of visual language. I know how to put a Cecil B. DeMille image on screen. I can do a Michael Curtiz [*Casablanca*]. If my mojo's working I can put one tenth of a David Lean image on screen. But I've never really been able to put *my* image on screen, with the exception of *E.T.* perhaps. And certainly not until *Schindler* was I really able to not reference other filmmakers. I'm always referencing everybody. I didn't do any of that on this movie."

Schindler's List was a dicey proposition, even with Spielberg behind it. And even though Sheinberg had been urging him to make the film for ten years, the studio hedged its bets by keeping the budget relatively low. Before Spielberg showed interest in the subject, the Holocaust was considered too harrowing and uncommercial for any studio to risk making. Even Spielberg was only able to squeeze a relatively paltry $23 million out of Universal, making *Schindler's List* his cheapest film since 1974's *The Sugarland Express*.

When the production was announced, more than one entertainment journalist cynically speculated that Spielberg had embarked on such an uncommercial project so he could at long last win an Oscar. Spielberg dismissed such cynicism out of hand. "There's nothing self-serving about what motivated me to bring *Schindler's List* to the screen. I don't give any credibility to other people's cynicism," he said.

The actual shooting of *Schindler's* in Poland just outside the concentration camp at Auschwitz was hellish for many reasons.

Not just the subject matter, which was emotionally enervating enough, but the logistics and the demands of the workaholic director's schedule also made it a bone-wearying time.

While he was shooting scenes of depravity in Poland, on the weekends he flew to Paris to edit *Jurassic Park*. While Nazis were rampaging in a re-created concentration camp on the weekdays, weekends he had to contend with only slightly less destructive reptiles. Soon, the editing of the dinosaur epic spilled over into the weekday. The film had to be ready for a big summer rollout.

Spielberg received the footage of *Jurassic Park* via a satellite transmission which was beamed into a parabolic dish in the front yard of his rented house in Cracow, Poland. After putting in a twelve-hour day amid the horrors of the Holocaust, he would return home to Capshaw and the kids, who had accompanied him to Poland. Always a hands-on father, even in the middle of this back-breaking schedule, Spielberg religiously took time out to have dinner and read bedtime stories before putting the kids to bed. Then it was back to the movieola to edit the fanciful tale of creatures millions of years old brought back to life through the magic of DNA splicing—and a lot of special effects.

The filming of *Schindler's List* was an emotional nightmare, a roller-coaster of ecstasy and grief. With all the verisimilitude that Hollywood is able to create with expert craftsmanship and cosmetics, Spielberg was personally reliving the Holocaust, or as his relatives long ago called it, "The Great Murder."

When he first came to Auschwitz, he was surprised by his reaction to the setting of mass murder. Instead of crying, which he expected would be his reaction, "I was deeply pissed off. I felt so helpless that there was nothing I could do about it. And yet I thought, 'well, there is something I can do about it. I can make *Schindler's List*. It's not going to bring anybody back alive, but it maybe will remind people that another Holocaust is a possibility.'"

The film crew was not welcomed with open arms. While the Polish government was delighted to have a big American film company bringing in hard currency, the director of the museum inside the former camp blocked Spielberg's access to the site.

Jerzy Wroblewski, the director of the state museum at Auschwitz, didn't object to the subject matter, even though it portrayed a Nazi in a heroic light. It was the nonideological disruption that any film crew causes. Wroblewski made international headlines when he said, "We were against it from the start. Thousands of extras bring devastation and destruction."

Wroblewski had already dealt with several other Holocaust-themed productions, including the miniseries *The Winds of War* and the feature film *Sophie's Choice*.

"We have experience of previous films," Wroblewski said. "Extras drink on location and urinate in the barracks. I know the scenario. This film could be shot at any small railway station."

To avoid further controversy, Spielberg simply—or maybe not so simply—re-created a portion of Auschwitz just outside the gates of the real camp.

Schindler's List was an obvious attempt to rediscover his religious roots, but it was also his horrified comment on what was happening today. In particular, the "ethnic cleansing" in Bosnia angered him, and he saw it as the Holocaust redux. "It was a combination of things: my interest in the Holocaust, and my horror at the symptoms of the Shoah again happening in Bosnia. And again happening with Saddam Hussein's attempt to eradicate the Kurdish race. We were racing over these moments in world history that were exactly like what happened in '43. *Schindler's List* is about human suffering. About the Jews, yes, but it's also about AIDS, the Armenians, the Bosnians. It's part of all of us."

It took three days to shoot one of the more horrific scenes in the film. Stripped nude, extras were required to jog in a circle for the scene in which the Nazis decided which concentration camp inmates were fit enough to work and which were to be consigned to the gas chambers.

After the first day of shooting the scene, Spielberg tried to come up with excuses not to come back to the set the following day.

"I don't look at ugly things very often," he said later. "I'm a real strong avoider. Most of my movies aren't real life. There were moments in *The Color Purple* and *Empire of the Sun* that had real life in them, but they're not start to finish real life. And this time (on the *Schindler* set), I knew I had to look. Then when I started looking, I couldn't stop."

The consummate professional, he of course turned up on day two, but he was unable to look through the camera while the scene was being shot. Even the technician whose job it was to keep the camera in focus didn't look through the lens.

Spielberg had dealt with carnivorous dinosaurs and omnivorous sharks, but those monsters were nothing compared to the real-life monsters who populated the Holocaust. After a while, studying the historical nightmare under the microscope of a camera began to take its toll on his emotional health.

"Every day shooting *Schindler's List* was like waking up and going to hell. Twice in the production I called Robin Williams just to say, 'Robin, I haven't laughed in seven weeks. Help me here.' And Robin would do twenty minutes on the telephone."

Amazingly, despite this emotional pain, Spielberg felt strangely refreshed by his suffering. "This has been the best experience I've had making a movie. I feel more connected with the material than I've ever felt before."

Perhaps this connectedness allowed him to give up a certain kind of control. For certain crowd scenes in *Schindler's List*, he would simply tell hundreds of extras to mill about in the street and improvise their actions. Then he would send the stars into the middle of this morass and shoot them improvising lines and behavior. This from a man who used to in the words of Teri Garr treat his actors like "puppets."

Spielberg may have told his extras to, in effect, do their own thing because of a creepy realization he had in the middle of giving these bit players more explicit directions. Because he did not speak the language of these extras, who were mostly recruited from nearby Polish towns, he at first directed them with gestures. Suddenly, he felt like the notorious Dr. Mengele, who similarly directed arriving inmates at Auschwitz to the right or left, one way meaning life, the other immediate gassing. Spielberg said of the awful realization, "I felt like a Nazi."

The actors did not have the luxury of goofing around between takes. On other sets with less serious subject matters, practical jokes and fraternity-level pranks are perpetuated by the most serious actors. Filming right outside the actual location of the death of three million Jews, none of the cast or crew felt like indulging in panty raids or whoopee cushions.

Ben Kingsley, who played Schindler's alter ego and camp inmate Itzhak Stern, said simply, "The ghosts were on the set every day in their millions." Spielberg underlined the mood: "There was no break in the tension. Nobody felt there was any room for levity. I didn't expect so much sadness every day."

Not all scenes were so emotionally draining. *Schindler's List* is at its heart a story of optimism, fueled by the belief that even the most unlikely of people can rise to the occasion. One scene particularly lightened the director's emotional burden. Toward the end of the film, *Schindlerjuden* extract gold from their teeth to make a ring for their benefactor. The real survivors were so grateful, in fact, that they supported Schindler financially after the war until his death in 1955. They used the clever formula of "one day's pay per year" to keep afloat Schindler, who engaged in one business disaster after another, including raising nutria (a minklike animal) to make apparel.

Grateful Holocaust survivors gave Spielberg a replica of the ring they had made for Schindler. Inscribed on the inside was, "You save one life, you save the world." Spielberg made copies of the ring and gave them to Sid Sheinberg and Lew Wasserman at Universal.

Schindler's List was not Spielberg's first collision with Nazism, but in the first and third installment of the Indiana Jones saga, the Nazis were cardboard villains. With *Schindler's List*, the realism of atrocities became too much, and the director found himself feeling hostility toward the German actors whenever they got into Nazi uniforms.

He recalled his hostility finally evaporating when the Germans "all showed up for a *seder* and put on yarmulkes, read from the Haggadas, the *seder* text, and the Israeli actors moved right next to them and began explaining it to them. Race and culture were just left behind."

In counterpoint to that scene of reconciliation, there was an ugly incident off the set in a hotel bar in the city. A German businessman approached one of the actors, an Israeli, who was having a drink with Ben Kingsley, who co-starred in the film as Schindler's assistant and conscience. The executive asked the

Israeli if he were a Jew, and when the actor said he was, the executive drew his finger across his neck and pulled an imaginary noose above his head, saying, "Hitler should have finished the job." The Israeli actor had to stop Kingsley from slugging the man.

Before *Schindler's List* was released to universal acclaim and the lion's share of Oscars, Spielberg worried about the reaction to a film that made a hero out of a Nazi.

He predicted inaccurately, "It will probably get the same resentment *Das Boot* got when it came out. People said, 'How can you root for these Nazis?' Well, they weren't Nazis, they were just sailors.

"If anybody holds a press conference condemning the project, we'll hold a press conference of our own and trot out some of the survivors who were saved by Schindler or their children." In fact, Spielberg preempted the need for a press conference by featuring the survivors in the color epilogue to the film.

Oskar Schindler, who died in 1974, had asked in his will to be buried in Jerusalem. The epilogue takes place at his grave in the Catholic cemetery on Mount Zion in the Israeli capital. In the epilogue, 128 *Schindlerjuden*, Jews whom the Nazi saved from extermination, were flown in from around the world to pay homage at his gravesite. Schindler's wife Emilie also attended the memorial ceremony.

Richard and Lola Krumholtz were two *Schindlerjuden* who were invited by Spielberg to appear in the film's epilogue. During a break in shooting, the husband and wife, who now reside in Los Angeles, described two instances in which Schindler was directly responsible for saving their lives. During the day the Krumholtzes had worked twelve-hour shifts in Schindler's enamelware factory for most of the war. At night, they returned to their cramped apartment in the Cracow ghetto. One day Schindler showed up on the factory floor and told the Krumholtzes that under no circumstances were they to return to their apartment. He offered no explanation, but they heeded his advice and slept overnight on the factory floor. The following day they found out the reason for Schindler's strange order. During the night, all their neighbors had been rounded up and put on cattle cars bound for the death camps.

On another occasion, Schindler took their identity papers and imprinted an official looking stamp on them. The Krumholtzes believe the bogus stamp saved them from deportation. Before the Academy Awards ceremony, Lola told the *Los Angeles Times* that *Schindler's List* deserved the Oscar for best picture. Her husband went his wife one better.

"This picture should be nominated in the documentary category," Richard Krumholtz said. "That's how real it seemed to me."

Such realism was Spielberg's goal. "A film like this could be studied through a microscope, and it's going to be scrutinized by everybody from Talmudic scholars to Ted Koppel. The film has to be accurate," he said. "It cannot in the least come across as entertainment. And it's very hard when you're making a movie not to violate one or all of those self-imposed rules. That's why the film has been in development since the early '80s."

The wait was worth it.

The *New Yorker* hailed it as the "finest fiction film ever made about the century's greatest evil."

The *New Republic*'s acerbic Stanley Kauffman, who makes Pauline Kael look like Glinda the Good Witch, admitted he had seen the film several times. The first time "I had thought it superbly made, but [the second time it] seemed even more astonishingly made."

Almost as an antidote to this ecstasy, the *New Republic* three weeks later called in its Washington correspondent, Leon Wieseltier, to take a contrary view. Wieseltier must have seen a different film than the rest of us did because he condemned *Schindler's List* for being "glib." Glib! He also nitpicked that the Jews in the Cracow ghetto spoke Hebrew with Israeli accents. (Does Mr. Wieseltier really know what a Polish Jew, circa 1943, sounded like?)

New York magazine's David Denby said after a screening, "I didn't think I could be affected this way anymore."

A handful of editorial pages complained that Spielberg had used all his trademark talents to make *Schindler's List* entertaining, in effect turning the Holocaust into one big roller-coaster of thrills and chills (and three million deaths). But the *Washington*

Post's Julie Salamon felt the film finally showed the real talent underneath the master entertainer: "*Schindler's List* only emphasizes what has always been Mr. Spielberg's real genius: His poetic visual imagination, his intelligence and the sense of humanity that so profoundly informed his earlier films."

After a private screening of the film, Sid Sheinberg wept and said, "It was a landmark. It will be remembered when *Jurassic Park* is long forgotten." Spielberg couldn't bear to watch the film with his mother, who sobbed throughout a screening.

Schindler's List ended up grossing $96 million. Not a large sum by Spielberg and *Jurassic Park* standards, but it was an amazing figure considering the basic uncommerciality of the subject matter.

Spielberg didn't take a dime for making *Schindler's List* (except for the Director's Guild minimum which is mandated by union rules).

His friendship with the late chairman of Time-Warner, Steve Ross, had given him a new outlook on wealth and what you could do with it beside spend or save it.

"After I met Steve, I went from being a miser to a philanthropist because I knew him, because that's what he showed me to do. I was just never spending my money. I gave nothing to causes that were important to me. And when I met Steve, I just observed the pleasure that he drew from his own private philanthropy. And it was total pleasure. And it was private, anonymous giving. So most everything I do is anonymous. It's one of the things Steve Ross opened my heart to," he said fondly.

He broke his rule of anonymity when he set up two very public foundations with his take of the proceeds from *Schindler's List*. Part of his profits from *Schindler's List* went to a foundation named in honor of Oskar Schindler, the Righteous Persons Foundation, which will be devoted to the study of gentiles who helped rescue Jews during the Holocaust. Spielberg stole Margery Tabankin away from the Barbra Streisand Foundation to serve as his foundation's executive director.

The other was also a new organization. On September 30, 1994, Spielberg announced the founding of the Survivors of the Shoah Visual History Foundation to keep alive the memory of the six million Jews and others who died in the Holocaust. (Shoah is the Hebrew name for the Holocaust.) The foundation will record the memories of camp survivors.

Its daunting task: to record 50,000 first-hand accounts of the Holocaust. There wasn't a minute to lose. Survivors are a vanishing breed, and Spielberg, the archivist, wanted to preserve their experiences before it was too late.

"The majority of Holocaust survivors are in their seventies and eighties," Spielberg said when he announced the creation of the foundation. "The window for capturing their testimonies is closing fast. This archive will preserve history as told by the people who lived it and lived through it. It is essential that we see their faces, hear their voices and understand that the horrendous events of the Holocaust happened to people and were committed by people. Racial, ethnic and cultural intolerance, sadly, are current events. This project stands as a monument to remembering the past, and to always examining our present."

Two of *Schindler's List*'s producers, Gerald Molen and Branko Lustig, himself a survivor of the death camps, will serve as executive producers of the project along with Karen Kushell, who is head of special projects at Spielberg's production company, Amblin.

Senior producer of the foundation, James Moll, said, "Our primary goal is to interview people not yet interviewed."

"There has never been a multi-media system of this size," Moll also said, adding that twenty-five to thirty employees were already compiling research and postproduction plans. The project uses digital technology to record the testimony. A newly invented database will allow users of the material to access instantly any piece of information on the video. Interviews will include experiences of the survivors before, during, and after World War II.

"Steven is the visionary behind this. He's the driving force," June Beallor, another senior producer for the foundation, said. Moll added, "His heart is really in this project."

Spielberg will split his profits from *Schindler's List* with the foundation and the Righteous Persons Foundation, also formed by the filmmaker to fund other Holocaust and Jewish charities. The Shoah Foundation asks Holocaust survivors to contact it at (800)

661-2092 or write Survivors of the Shoah Visual History Foundation, Box 8940, Universal City, CA 91608.

The Shoah Foundation will be the first major archival database to use multiple media. Spielberg said the software will be simple enough so that a seventh-grade student will be able to access information, including first person accounts of life in the death camps.

Calling the project a "race against time," Spielberg said, "My whole dream is to take as many testimonies as is humanly possible and make their stories available for no fee for those who want it."

Spielberg's initial contribution totaled $16 million. Also contributing funds are the Lew Wasserman Foundation, MCA, Time-Warner, and NBC, all partners with Spielberg in various commercial projects. With understatement Spielberg said, "I don't think we'll have a problem raising money."

By June 1994, the project had recorded 100 interviews with survivors. The foundation is sending filmmakers, rabbis, psychotherapists, scholars, and adult children of Holocaust survivors around the world to interview survivors. The interviewing process is expected to cost from $50 million to $60 million over a period of several years.

The director estimates that there are 300,000 Holocaust survivors. He hopes to record testimony from 150,000 of them by the year 2000.

Spielberg admitted that some potential interview subjects did not greet his emissaries with open arms. "You should know," he said in an interview with the *Los Angeles Times*, "that some people would not talk to us. There are a lot of Jewish survivors that would like this to die with them because the memories are too horrible to confront."

Eventually, the foundation will record testimony from non-Jewish survivors, who include Gypsies, Jehovah's Witnesses, gays, and other minorities deemed by the Nazis as "sub-humans." The director defended focusing on Jewish survivors first "because the Holocaust was really about what happened to European Jewry—the destruction of Jewish culture on that continent."

The recorded testimony includes more than just the despair of the Holocaust. Interviews, planned for two to three hours each, will not only describe the horrors of the camps but also, in typical Spielberg fashion, the stories of the survivors who rebuilt their lives after World War II.

"The technology is just unbelievable. We're creating a global network," producer June Beallor explained.

The computerized archives will be a godsend for researchers—and easy to use. By typing key words into the computer, scholars will be able to call up interviews by last name, hometown, topic, camp name, or other subject. The database also should help survivors locate fellow inmates with whom they have lost contact over the years.

Beallor hopes easy access will attract people who normally shy away from literally dusty research. Beallor says, "One of the problems of oral histories is the volumes and volumes of written material that are so thick that few people will actually look for them. This gives you instant accessibility. If you're interested in what happened to a particular town—who went to Auschwitz and who lived—you can call up certain key words and find out. If you want to find out about where people slept, what they ate, the kinds of latrines they used, you type in a certain word—like 'latrine'— and it takes you to exact points in interviews where people talked about it."

Recording the testimony has taken its toll on the project's principals. Beallor was particularly touched by the testimony of one survivor who was forced by the Nazis to hang his own father.

The son of another survivor thanked Beallor for finally getting his father to talk about his camp experiences. After recording his account, the man gave a copy of the videotape to his son. Only then, half a century after the event, were father and son able to discuss the older man's nightmare.

The idea of an audiovisual memoir of the Holocaust came to Spielberg during the filming of *Schindler's List*. Survivors showed up on the set in Poland and began telling him their stories. "I kept saying to them, 'Thank you for telling me, but I wish you could say this to a camera because this is important testimony.' I asked them if they'd be willing to do this, and they all said yes.

"I felt that a much more important contribution to remembering the Shoah would be an aural-visual history."

His interest in the Holocaust dates back to his childhood, when his classical pianist mother would welcome fellow musicians who had survived the Holocaust into the Spielberg home. "There were people playing cellos and violas with Auschwitz-Birkenau tattoos on their arms," Spielberg recalled.

But what really prompted Spielberg to spend millions on the project was the debt he felt he owed posterity. He wanted to help young people "wake up to the fact that we are all part of every episode that has happened."

Many of the volunteers operating the foundation's hotline are survivors themselves. Milie Stern, who works out of a trailer used on the production of *Jurassic Park*, is a volunteer interviewer who as a child hid from the Nazis in the Netherlands during World War II. Many of her callers, she says, "are reluctant at first. They haven't talked before. It's very painful. I make sure to identify myself. I tell them I'm a survivor. It helps them."

Another survivor-volunteer, Daisy Miller, says, "I generally ask people to give me a picture of what life was like before the war, their family life. Then they start talking about their wartime experience. Once the floodgates open, memories return."

Zofia Evenoz survived the war in a Polish ghetto, where she was raped by a Nazi soldier in 1941. In her taped testimony for Spielberg's foundation, she confesses that she was never able to speak of the incident before. "I had a nervous breakdown years later. If I had been able to retell my experiences sooner it might have been better."

Renee Firestone, a survivor-interviewer, recalled her experience at Auschwitz in 1944: "My sister and I were pointed to the right, while my mother was taken the other way. We then tried to find out where my mother had been taken. The commandant simply pointed to a chimney. 'Do you see this? There go your parents. When you go to this chimney, you will be reunited with them.'"

Mel Mermelstein was the only member of his family to survive the camps. "I just remember seeing my father shortly before he died. He was so ill, so weak, such a small man then. I had always seen him, like any son, as big. His last words were that if I ever did get out I was to tell the world."

With the help of Steven Spielberg's Shoah Foundation, Mermelstein has fulfilled his father's dying wish.

If the director ever decides to dramatize the Holocaust on film again, he will have an invaluable source for his imagination.

USA Weekend magazine asked Spielberg during an interview about the Shoah Foundation if, after making a film about one of the darkest chapters in human history, he would ever be able to return to making sunny, optimistic movies. Laughing, Spielberg replied, "Sure I can, because I have a sunny, optimistic nature. But I don't think the two are mutually exclusive."

<hr/>

Until *Schindler's List* swept the Oscars in 1994, the Academy Awards had always been more of a curse than a blessing in Spielberg's career. Every time one of his films made half a billion dollars or whatever, there was usually the sour note of the Academy voters saying in effect, "So you can make money. Why don't you make art now?"

The first time Spielberg had the legitimate right to feel snubbed by Academy voters was in 1973. His very first feature film, *The Sugarland Express*, was good enough to win the best screenplay award at the Cannes Film Festival, which usually honors more sophisticated films than the Oscars, especially at that time. Spielberg, with his "story by" credit for the script after Barwood and Robbins were hired to rewrite it, wouldn't have received an Oscar nomination even if the screenplay had been so honored. But it would have been a gratifying vote of support for him. The director may have comforted himself with the realization that the original screenplay competition in 1973 was stiff indeed and included three other films that eventually would be considered all-time classics: *American Graffiti*, the bittersweet piece of nostalgia that put Spielberg's best bud, George Lucas, on the map; Ingmar Bergman's difficult but ultimately rewarding *Cries and Whispers*; and *The Sting*, the intricately plotted caper film, produced by his mentors Zanuck and Brown, which won the best screenplay Oscar that year.

Spielberg's next film, *Jaws*, which quickly became the number-one box-office hit of all time, was honored with a best picture nod. *Jaws'* nomination reflected a short-lived phenomenon in Oscar history when hugely commercial but artistically lowbrow films often received a best picture nomination, almost as a way of the Academy thanking the studio for keeping the industry afloat. How else do you explain such inexplicable best picture nominees as *Airport*, *The Towering Inferno*, and *Love Story*? (Even *Cleopatra* made the best picture list, although it's hard to figure what kind of message the Academy was trying to send the industry: make films that will almost bankrupt your studio?) Spielberg could at least derive some comfort from the fact that *Jaws* was beaten by another soon-to-be-classic, *One Flew Over the Cuckoo's Nest*.

Close Encounters of the Third Kind was a more critically respected film than *Jaws*, earning Spielberg his first best director nomination. The film itself was shut out of the best picture category, however, as the Academy apparently felt that one sci-fi nominee per year was sufficient. (*Star Wars*, not *Close Encounters*, was nominated that year, as was its director, George Lucas.) But a film light years away in style and content took the best director and film prize, Woody Allen and his *Annie Hall*.

Spielberg's next hit (not his next film, *1941*) earned him another best director nomination, and this time there was no similar entry to knock *Raiders of the Lost Ark* out of the best picture category. Competition was fierce that year, and Spielberg would have been genuinely sincere had he spouted that old bromide, "It's an honor just to be nominated." His competitors were the great Louis Malle for the cult classic *Atlantic City*; the sentimental favorite, Henry Fonda's last film, *On Golden Pond*, directed by Mark Rydell; Warren Beatty for *Reds*; and the year's big winner, *Chariots of Fire*, by a little known British director, Hugh Hudson.

The director reached the pinnacle, albeit a temporary one, of his career with his next film, *E.T.*, which not only made you weep over the fate of a rubber hand puppet, but also soon earned more money than any other film up to that time. The Academy recognized the achievement with best film, director, and script nominations, but the only Oscars it won were sound effects editing and visual effects. Partisans of Spielberg were starting to get paranoid over these repeated snubs of their boy. But in defense of the Academy, the competition that year (1982) was fierce and filled with socially important message films that also made a raft of money (although not *E.T.*-level amounts). *Gandhi* (the eventual winner), *Missing*, *The Verdict*, and even *Tootsie* dealt with deep dish themes like passive resistance, alcoholism, gender identity, and political torture. *E.T.*'s theme of childhood alienation wasn't socially as significant as the Mahatma freeing an entire subcontinent from British tyranny.

Three years later, the debate over Spielberg's love-hate affair with the Academy was by now getting downright nasty. Granted, *E.T.* was about a polyurethane geek from outer space, but *The Color Purple* was a different animal. Based on a Pulitzer Prize-winning book, the movie dealt with socially relevant issues like spousal abuse, the emancipation of women, and heroic black women. And it contained fine performances by untried actors, Whoopi Goldberg and Oprah Winfrey, both of whom the Academy did deign to honor with nominations. The person who directed these Oscar-caliber performances, however, was once again ignored. And adding insult to injury, the Academy nominated directors who had made good but not truly great films (Sydney Pollack, *Out of Africa*; John Huston, *Prizzi's Honor*; Akira Kurosawa, *Ran*; Hector Babenco, *Kiss of the Spider Woman*; and Peter Weir, *Witness*).

Moreover the old theory that the Academy resented Spielberg's box-office success didn't even apply. Both *Witness* and *Out of Africa*, the best picture winner, made more money than *The Color Purple*.

Unlike *The Color Purple*'s reception by the Academy, Spielberg could at least console himself with the fact that his next film, *Empire of the Sun*, was treated equally by the Academy and the public. Both ignored it—although the public ignored the box-office dud even more than Oscar voters, who nominated it in the lesser categories, cinematography, art direction, costume design, sound, editing, and original score.

The conventional wisdom in 1987 was that another film, a critical and box-office smash, *Hope and Glory*, stole *Empire of the*

Sun's thunder because both films viewed World War II through the eyes of a young boy. Ironically, *Hope and Glory*'s vision was definitely rose-tinted, whereas Spielberg, often criticized for sanitizing his films, presented a truly horrific vision of wartime atrocities.

By the time *Jurassic Park* was released, the Academy had dumped its quaint custom of nominating huge commercial hits simply because they were huge commercial hits. (Call it the *Towering Inferno* syndrome.) No one, not even his biggest fan, his mother, cried foul when *Jurassic Park* was nominated in only technical categories. E.T. and T-rex were both reptilian, but only E.T. made you cry, while the screams elicited by rampaging Mr. T's were not the kind of response that usually attracted serious Oscar consideration.

Spielberg didn't have much time to obsess over the Academy's indifference to *Jurassic Park*. That same year, Oscar voters made amends for years of snubs and damnation with faint praise by heaping just about every statuette they could find on *Schindler's List*.

Although for years Spielberg had denied Oscar-envy, when the awards finally came his way, he was elated. "Anyone who has ever been nominated for an Oscar, who denies it ever being a goal at the time, is loopy," he said in a fit of honesty after years of much public denial.

In his acceptance speech, he thanked "the six million who can't be watching this among the one billion watching this telecast tonight. In so many American schools, the Holocaust really is a footnote in the history books."

With the commercial and critical success of *Schindler's List*, not to mention its Oscar haul, the Holocaust would never again be an afterthought or a dry paragraph in an obscure history book.

The day after the Oscars, Spielberg said, "If this is a dream, don't wake me up."

After the emotionally draining work of filming a re-creation of the Holocaust, Steven Spielberg pronounced himself exhausted. He claimed he would take an eighteen-month vacation away from the camera.

In the summer of 1993, he told *Daily Variety* columnist Army Archerd, "I have absolutely no plans to start a new movie. I spent many sleepless nights in toxic shock, going between the two movies," *Schindler's List* and *Jurassic Park*.

And when he did go back to work, it wouldn't be the usual roller-coaster ride. Or so he said:

"Whatever I do after *Schindler's List* has to be something that moves me deeply."

His resolution to play hooky didn't last long. Within months he was back at work. The project he chose to devote his energies to, however, didn't jive with his plans to do a deeply moving work.

But it was work. And the workaholic director had to keep busy, even if it meant going from the holocaust to a kids tale about a friendly poltergeist.

CHAPTER EIGHTEEN

Next

W HEN YOU'RE NOT DREAMING UP YOUR
next billion-dollar business venture or Oscar-winning film, how do
you relax?

Steven Spielberg, his wife, and their five children move
from homes in the Hamptons to Malibu to Trump Tower in New
York.

But their primary residence is a sun-drenched, Mediterra-
nean-style compound in Pacific Palisades, a suburb of Los Angeles
near the Pacific Ocean that attracts other box-office royalty like
Arnold Schwarzenegger, and until he decamped to Miami,
Sylvester Stallone.

The main house of the sprawling compound is huge, white,
and airy. The garden is a forest of expensive palm trees. There are
several large outbuildings housing a screening room, office, and
guest houses. The spread is something of a landmark for nostalgia
buffs. David O. Selznick lived there while producing *Gone With
the Wind*. Other owners include Douglas Fairbanks Jr. and Cary
Grant with his then wife, heiress Barbara Hutton. Spielberg renovated much of the aging structure. In the living room, there's a
small Modigliani on the wall opposite a huge, luminous Monet.

Much of the furniture is Arts and Crafts style by Gustav Stickley. On a table under the Monet are three scripts under glass: originals of *Citizen Kane*, *Casablanca*, and Orson Welles' radio broadcast for *The War of the Worlds*. Spielberg's favorite painter, Norman Rockwell, is represented everywhere.

Spielberg renovated his spread in 1989, but five years later he felt he and his expanding brood had outgrown it. So he commissioned architect Harry Newman, who had done the previous renovation, and designer Frank Pennino to add a guest house where "our friends can feel at home with us but at the same time have complete autonomy." The director also ordered up a study separate from the main house as a "place where I can read scripts, do storyboards and kick off my shoes."

Spielberg was a big fan of designer Pennino, whom he had tapped to decorate his Amblin offices at Universal. Spielberg liked Newman because the two had developed a short hand on architecture. "He captures my fantasies in a way that doesn't involve a lot of communication," the director said. "Harry will take the practical and make it comfortable."

The interiors of the new structures, like the original, were decorated in the Arts and Crafts style, to reflect Spielberg and his wife's love of old, lived-in things. Some of the furniture is museum-quality (circa 1904), originally owned by the designer who created them, Gustav Stickley. But Spielberg and his wife are not collectors for collecting's sake. When other Stickley pieces were unavailable to complement the originals, they had reproductions made.

The floors of the two additions were certainly old, made of recycled 100-year-old pine that had been ebonized to a glossy shine. Spielberg got that decorating tip when he saw the same kind of flooring at friend Calvin Klein's East Hampton home.

"We shamelessly told Frank we wanted black floors in the guesthouse. It was the first thing we asked for," the director said.

The study is one large space with low partition walls rather than separate rooms. Spielberg wanted all the light to be natural, so the architect designed a motorized skylight that takes up the entire ceiling.

State-of-the-art electronic equipment is carefully hidden from view in oak cabinets that allow the old-fashioned look of the house to remain intact. The study has an old-fashioned drafting table where Spielberg does his famous storyboards.

Spielberg added two Norman Rockwell paintings to the study, but he realized his children would probably visit Daddy at work and he didn't want them to damage his artworks. So the paintings were shielded by Plexiglas, "just in case," he said with a laugh.

Whether he was dreaming up his next blockbuster or contemplating his next videogame move against Robin Williams via modem, Spielberg could survey his surroundings with perfect contentment.

"We couldn't ask for anything more," he said.

But you don't become the most successful director in history by taking eighteen-month-long sabbaticals. Despite his resolution to kick back and play with the kids, Spielberg couldn't stay away from the glorious grind of filmmaking.

Unfortunately, there was no project worthy of his new seriousness to occupy him. But he had to work.

A few months after backing up a U-Haul to the Dorothy Chandler Pavilion to carry home his Oscar trove, Spielberg was back at Amblin on Universal's backlot , the happy worker bee.

The only big screen project in the works was a kiddie movie based on a beloved comic book figure, Casper the Friendly Ghost.

Although his official title was executive producer, Spielberg was hands on all the way.

He actively participated in story conferences, during which a round table of gag writers contributed jokes like some shticky assembly line. It was the same gang process that had created the execrable *The Flintstones* the previous year and resulted in thirty-two writers claiming dubious credit for writing the saga of Bedrock.

One of the older writers at the Casper round table, Lenny Ripps, said, "*Schindler's List* would have been a lot funnier if we'd done it this way."

Buh duh bup.

Spielberg wasn't very good at coming up with shtick, but he had a million ideas. The same man who had crafted the heart-wrenching images of the Holocaust could be just as resourceful when it came to bringing a ghost to life. At one story conference, it was planned to have a ghost possess an unwitting host by having the specter enter through the victim's ear while he was sleeping. Spielberg had a better idea. It would be funnier, the director suggested, if the ghost entered through the mouth while the victim inhaled, snoring.

The Spielberg touch remained golden. When *Casper* opened in the early summer of 1995, it was lambasted by the critics as greasy kid stuff of the worst kind. But it was also the number-one film its opening weekend, grossing a record-setting $22 million in three days and blasting Bruce Willis's third *Die Hard* detonation out of first place.

But thinking up shtick for a spectral figure wasn't enough to occupy Spielberg's febrile mind for long. On October 12, 1994, in a gilded conference room at the Peninsula Beverly Hills Hotel, right next door to Mike Ovitz's CAA, Steven Spielberg, ousted Disney president Jeff Katzenberg, and billionaire record mogul David Geffen announced the formation of what Katzenberg modestly called the "Dream Team."

Incorporated with a $2 billion influx of cash, the official name of the company was DreamWorks SKG, the initials standing for the three founders, Spielberg, Katzenberg, and Geffen.

There were many reasons for the inauguration of this much heralded event, but as with most phenomena in Hollywood, the motivating force was ego.

Jeffrey Katzenberg was out of a job, and he wanted a new, even splashier one than head of film production at Disney. In August of 1994, Katzenberg had been unceremoniously dumped at Disney by his ungrateful boss, Disney chairman Michael Eisner, with whom he had worked for almost two decades, first at Paramount and then at the Magic Kingdom.

Katzenberg headed the mythically successful animation department at Disney and the mythically inept live-action film division as well. Under Katzenberg's anal control, the animators had cranked out one huge hit after another, climaxing with the billion-dollar-grossing epic about a bunch of talking animals in Africa, *The Lion King*. The film had been the highest grossing picture of the year and Disney's biggest money-maker ever. Having grossed $700 million at theaters, *The Lion King* took in an additional $450 million within two weeks of its release on video.

Katzenberg's track record with real-life actors and human stories was not so eminent. He was responsible for one flop after another, including such disappearing acts as *Cabin Boy* and *Honey, I Blew Up the Baby*.

Although Eisner and Katzenberg together had propelled Disney from an industry joke in 1984 (remember *The Black Hole?*) to the most successful studio in Hollywood ten years later, the two men had always had a troubled relationship that some compared to a tyrannical father and a rebellious son.

While some industry observers accepted the Pop Freud interpretation, others posited a simpler explanation, one closer to the bottom line. Wells, an MBA, had an extensive business background. Katzenberg had always been involved on the creative end, picking film projects not portfolios.

One industry heavyweight, however, begged to differ with that conclusion. In a rare interview in *Los Angeles* magazine, David Geffen attributed the phenomenal growth of Disney over the last decade to Katzenberg, not Eisner. "Eisner is responsible for EuroDisney and Hollywood Records," Geffen said of the conglomerates' two most embarrassing failures. "Katzenberg is responsible for everything else."

When the number-two man at Disney, Frank Wells, died in a plane crash, Katzenberg, showing little sentiment—or tact—immediately started lobbying for the job by studiously drawing up a three-page list of reasons why he deserved the number-two job now vacant. On August 24, Eisner summoned his underling to his office. Before Katzenberg could even pull out his list, Eisner told him flatly he wasn't moving up to number two.

Katzenberg had said, in effect, "Please, dad, please, can I have the car?" Eisner told him to take the bus.

Humiliated, Katzenberg had no other option than to leave the studio he had enriched to the tune of billions of dollars thanks to hand-drawn characters on acrylic.

Katzenberg didn't sulk. He wasn't the most kinetic executive in Hollywood for nothing. Within six days, he had signed up two of the biggest names in Hollywood for his new effort. *Time* magazine, commenting on Katzenberg's mojo, did a variation on the Spanish proverb, saying, "Revenge is a dish best eaten in public."

The deal began when word of Eisner's ingratitude spread. Spielberg called to console his close friend Katzenberg. The director was in Jamaica, vacationing at the home of his protege, Robert Zemeckis. Spielberg had given Zemeckis his first break by producing his script for *I Wanna Hold Your Hand*, then gave him an even bigger break by letting him direct *Back to the Future*.

While Spielberg was trying to think up nice things to say to soften the blow of Katzenberg's dismissal, Zemeckis in the background shouted out a concrete suggestion: "Why don't you guys do something together?"

At first Katzenberg thought it was a joke. "We were teasing, I guess," he later said. "But there was a moment when it went from a playful and fanciful idea to a great idea."

Spielberg was intrigued by the pairing from the outset. For years he had rented space on the backlots of Warners and Universal. As he grew older, he became tired of renting. He wanted to buy.

"I grew up and began to foster children and have a large family," Spielberg said of his growing realization that he needed roots. "I have five children. I felt I was ready to be the father of my own business. Or at least the co-father. It benefits me because the idea of building something from the ground up, where I could actually be a co-owner, where I don't rent, I don't lease, I don't option but actually own—that appeals to me."

The duo's biggest personnel coup was securing the services of the richest man in Hollywood, record mogul David Geffen, who had discovered such platinum groups as the Eagles, Guns N' Roses, and Nirvana. He also had a nifty sideline, producing blockbuster movies like *Risky Business* and *Interview With the Vampire*.

With typical insouciance, Geffen explained his participation in the dream team as simply a way to do something different with his money. "Steven and I have tremendous amounts of money. You can't spend or even use most of it; it's just on some financial statement, and other people are playing with it. So I'm not in this because I need or want to make another billion; that would have no value. It's all in the doing, all in the journey," he said.

Spielberg had agreed to participate partly out of loyalty to an old friend, Katzenberg, whom he felt had been mistreated by Eisner. But Spielberg was even more loyal to older friends. Planning to fold his company Amblin into DreamWorks, he first sought his old mentor Sid Sheinberg's blessing. Actually, it was more like permission. The director didn't mince words when he told Sheinberg, "Sid, if you don't want me to do this I won't. You don't even have to explain yourself. You can just say, 'No.' I'll call Jeffrey and David."

What a guy!

Actually, Sheinberg's blessing may have been a blessing for the executive himself. Since his boss Matsushita sold MCA-Universal to liquor magnate Edgar Bronfman Jr., Sheinberg may soon find himself out of job. If that happens, no doubt, his old protege will be there waiting at the studio gate with a fat contract and an executive suite at DreamWorks.

Of the troika, Katzenberg took the biggest gamble. Each man agreed to put up $33 million—lunch money for the billionaire director and record mogul. But Katzenberg, a former studio employee and wage slave, had to mortgage everything he owned to cough up his share of the investment.

"I have not just figuratively bet the ranch. I have literally bet the ranch," Katzenberg said with mangled syntax. "My entire net worth is riding on the success of this company."

Everyone with a checkbook rushed to join the Dream Team. Chemical Bank gave them a $1 billion line of credit. The Korean electronics giant Samsung tried to get in on the deal, but Spielberg nixed the conglomerate's participation when the chairman of the company seemed more interested in semiconductors than celluloid. The biggest contributor was Paul Allen, cofounder of Microsoft, who kicked in half a billion dollars in return for a mere 20 percent stake in the company.

Allen's erstwhile partner, Bill Gates, belatedly signed on to create interactive computer videos with the Dream Team. The man who had conquered his phobias toward snakes and insects was at first fearful of meeting with the enfant terrible of software.

"We were a little reluctant to meet him and get into business with him because his reputation preceded him. People warned me about the jaws of the shark. But when he walked in the room, I saw someone my mother would like. He's a *haimisher* guy. What he said sometimes flew over my head, but his enthusiasm was pretty kinetic," Spielberg recalled.

The director was even more bullish on his biggest investor, Paul Allen. "I hugely related to him the second I met him. And he knows how to take a vacation. I'd just taken a year off, so the first thing we began talking about when we met was boating."

If Spielberg and Geffen needed a challenge, they got one by forming such an iffy proposition. No new studio had succeeded since Mary Pickford, Douglas Fairbanks, Charlie Chaplin, and D. W. Griffith had formed United Artists. And that was back in 1919.

Since then, the history of Hollywood was littered with the wreckage of wannabe ministudios like First Artists (Barbra Streisand, Paul Newman, and Sidney Poitier's baby), Orion, the Ladd Company and another state-of-the-art dream factory with high hopes, Francis Coppola's Zoetrope. Even Spielberg's biggest fan, Sid Sheinberg, offered some sobering statistics about DreamWorks' viability: "I share the view of the world that they'll have great children. I also know that the reality is that 50 percent of all marriages in America end in divorce. So, we'll all wait and see."

Sheinberg wasn't the only one to sound a cautionary note among all the unchecked predictions of success.

Newsweek implied that Spielberg and his partners had performed a confidence trick of sorts on their fellow investors. For a total investment of only $100 million, Spielberg, Geffen, and Katzenberg own two-thirds of DreamWorks. Paul Allen, Microsoft, and others put up $900 million for a mere one-third ownership. At that ratio of one-third equals $900 million, Spielberg and his partners' two-thirds ownership is actually worth $1.8 billion, or $1.7 million more than they invested. Without making a single film or cutting a single record, the three principals made a paper profit of $567 million each.

The prognosis for the other investors doesn't look good. Geffen's office predicted that DreamWorks would return 20 percent per annum to stockholders. To meet those figures, DreamWorks would have to grow in value to $50 billion in ten years. That's an unlikely scenario since a major studio like Paramount, with a huge film library and Madison Square Garden among its holdings, is worth a relatively paltry $10 billion. Even Disney is valued at $29 billion, and it owns half of Florida.

But hopes run so high for the company that if there were an initial public stock offering, the other investors probably could sell their stocks at a tidy profit. However, Geffen's office says firmly there will be no such offering. Why bother when suitors like Microsoft and ABC are begging to be let in on the deal?

Insiders say DreamWorks would be a sure bet if it had *Jurassic Park II* or *The Lion King Returns* in the pipeline, but sequel rights to those two hits belong to other studios. Still, optimists feel that Spielberg and Katzenberg can duplicate their previous successes with a whole new franchise of hit television series and films designed to be followed by many Roman numerals.

Spielberg and Katzenberg may be a perfect fit, with each man shoring up the other's weaknesses. For Disney, Katzenberg has spun out one animated hit after another, beginning with *The Little Mermaid* and climaxing with the big *Lion King*. Spielberg's track record in animation, especially on the big screen, has been mixed. Hoping to capitalize on the dinomania generated by *Jurassic Park*, the director produced *Dinosaurs!*, an animated feature that laid an egg as big as a stegosaurus'. Two other features, *An Animated Tail* and its sequel, *Fievel Goes West*, both about a cuddly rat, also flopped. His efforts with animation on television have been slightly better. Despite the collaboration of the live-action cartoon maker Tim Burton (*Batman*), the *Family Dog* cartoon, told from the point of view of the household pet, flopped on network television. However, Spielberg has had two huge hits in syndication, *Tiny Toons* and the delightfully subversive *Animaniacs*.

Katzenberg can benefit from Spielberg's live-action prowess, since under the executive's stewardship Disney had made one embarrassing, low-budget, low-grossing film after another. And alienated half the creative talent in Hollywood with his Scrooge-like bean counting.

Each of the founders of DreamWorks has his area of strength. No one can beat Geffen when it comes to spotting promising musical talent. But Geffen is also a successful film producer, and it remains to be seen whether his powerful ego and Spielberg's can coexist when they make films together.

The feature film division of DreamWorks has $800 million in start-up money, which isn't as much as it sounds since the workaholic director plans to produce twenty-four full-length films in the next five years. Katzenberg's animation division, in contrast, has a relatively paltry $200 million to make his cartoons. The first animated feature, scheduled for Christmas 1998, is *The Prince of Egypt*, a cartoon retelling of the Biblical story of Moses. Following that will be *El Dorado: Cortez and the City of Gold*.

Both subject matters, the Bible and a fact-based historical yarn, represent risky departures from the kind of animated films Katzenberg made for Disney. The hits there tended to be based on classic fairy tales (*Beauty and the Beast*) or politically correct ecological fables like *The Lion King*.

Although he let his employee go, Michael Eisner may be sweating it out now that Katzenberg has teamed with two powerhouses. Officially, Eisner showed the glacial calm that has made him one of the most feared executives in Hollywood when he wished his new competitors well (but not too well): "Competition ignites and stimulates excellence. And for that I wish them well. I think they'll do well. And I think they'll force us to do even better than we've done in the past," Eisner said in a statement.

As soon as Katzenberg left Disney and announced his new plans, rumors spread that he would engage his former employer in a bidding war for the talent who have made Disney's animated hits. Eisner took a raft of Paramount executives with him when he left for Disney ten years ago. Could his second in command now do the same?

One studio executive says that scenario is unlikely since Disney has most of its animators under long-term—and not so generous—contract. Another reason the animators will stay put is safety versus the iffy proposition of joining a new studio that may not be around as long as the Magic Kingdom.

Arnold Rifkin, head of the film division of the William Morris Agency, doesn't think DreamWorks will be a flash in the pan, however. "All they have to do is show up in the morning," he says of the SKG troika. "They're not reinventing anything they've not done before."

Katzenberg also will head DreamWorks' television division, which already has a production agreement with ABC. Here, he actually has a better track record than Spielberg, the creator of *Amazing Stories* and the currently low-rated embarrassments, *seaQuest DSV* and *Earth 2*. Disney has produced such Nielsen hits as *The Cosby Show* and the current number-one hit, *ER*. If Katzenberg can produce just one or two similar blockbusters under the DreamWorks banner, the studio will be out of the red before Spielberg has the time to shout action on his first big-budget feature.

The director is hoping DreamWorks will allow him to realize a secret fantasy. "A dream I have is to produce ABC's Saturday-morning schedule, because I think I can lift it up," he said.

DreamWorks sounds as though it will be a dream place to work. The company has some profit-sharing ideas that smack of socialism. "It will share equity with all its employees, all the way down to the secretarial pool. Writers and animators will get gross points in the movies they help create. With a lion-size hit like *The Lion King*, gross points in a billion dollar movie will be a precedent-setting windfall for Hollywood's most underappreciated artists, writers," *Time* magazine reported.

Actor Tom Hanks knows all three men and feels each has a different way of operating that will allow for a delicate collaboration rather than collision of superstar egos.

Hanks says, "David does business in an ephemeral, gossamer way. Jeffrey is Mr. Bottom Line, Mr. Brass Tacks. He operates every meeting with a strict agenda. Steven has almost a cartoonist's point of view. He can draw anything on paper and make it come to life."

Hanks imagines how the three men might operate in tandem: "David would say [to a potential employee], 'We think you're great, and if you want to work with us, fabulous; if not, we still think you're great.' Jeffrey would say, 'You're great, and here are seventeen reasons why you need to be with us.' And Steven would say, 'I love that thing you did in that movie five years ago where you had the platypus dancing on the edge of the table, and if you could do that, you can do anything.' That's the way the meeting would go. And it would be over in twenty-two minutes."

While the three men are clearly first among equals, they seem to be willing to give in when one of them *really* wants something. Geffen and Katzenberg hoped to put off building a physical home for their new studio, but Spielberg wanted his own backlot, and he's getting it. Spielberg personally designed the layout for his dream studio. It looks like a college campus rather than the usual assemblage of warehouselike soundstages. Cost—$200 million—or as Sid Sheinberg, who may join them at the new pile, might say, "It's the box office on *E.T.* in Venezuela."

George Lucas will get a chance to pay Spielberg back for foregoing *Rainman* to direct *Indiana Jones and the Last Crusade*. Unconfirmed reports say that Lucas will allow DreamWorks to distribute *Star Wars 4*, set for a 1998 release. Sweetening the deal for Lucas, no doubt, is another unconfirmed report that Spielberg will direct the film, which would be his only sequel other than the Indiana Jones trilogy.

Way back in 1981, Spielberg said, "I'd love to do the fourth *Star Wars*." That may have been the director merely thinking out loud during an expansive moment. When asked recently about the possibility of his boss directing *Star Wars 4*, Amblin spokesman Marvin Levy said gruffly, "Never heard of it. That's ridiculous."

It will be interesting to see who has the greatest effect on the others' work habits. Geffen is so laid back he makes a throw rug look kinetic by comparison. "I'm the laziest of the three of us," he says with studied languor. Spielberg is a workaholic, but he resembles a welfare recipient compared to the greatest Jewish exponent of the Protestant Ethic, Katzenberg, who once told his Disney thralls, "If you don't come to work on Saturday, don't bother to show up on Sunday."

Spielberg's wife, Kate Capshaw, already is worried about her husband being infected by the Jewish-Protestant Ethic bug. "I love Jeffrey," she told her husband, "but I never want you to *become* Jeffrey. I don't want you to become involved in that lather of workaholism."

There's no danger Katzenberg would ever deliver an ultimatum about Saturday work obligations to Spielberg.

"I perfectly understand the ground rules," Katzenberg says. "8:30 to 5:30, Monday to Friday, is mine. Everything else is Kate's."

In a cover story, *Time* magazine predicted that Geffen could be the first to defect from the troika of overworked overachievers. "I made a staggering amount of money, and I enjoy being an investor. Before this came up, I was thinking very seriously of spending my time doing that." If the day-to-day grind of running a major miniconglomerate grows too burdensome, Geffen could drop out and clip coupons.

While Spielberg was playing mogul with pals Katzenberg and Geffen, his wife was getting bored at home.

The same year he announced his new film-TV-record company, Mrs. Spielberg came out of retirement.

When she did, it was with a bang as workaholic as anything her husband had ever done.

She starred in four films back to back: as Warren Beatty's girlfriend in *Love Affair*, as Sean Connery's lawyer wife in *Just Cause*, as the hippie mom in *An American Quilt*, and as James Woods's wife in Showtime's *Next Door*. Capshaw apparently was so hot to work, she even agreed to star in a cable movie, something a star of her stature and with her connections rarely does.

Capshaw admitted that her husband was less than ecstatic about her revived career. "This is the first time I've put the working hat on," she said. "I've been the domestic manager. It's fun, but I think Steven has mixed feelings about it."

In the spring of 1995, Capshaw was about to go on location for yet another film when Spielberg put his foot down—gently.

"Steven's first words were, 'Where does it film?' You know if something's good, everyone feels happy to be supportive. We go and set up a gypsy camp on a film—we've done it before.

"He said, 'Let's keep looking, hon—maybe we'll find something to do together.'"

They're still looking.

Regarding her husband's aspirations for her, she said with a laugh, "It's really a case of 'Yeah, I have a job for you. How about rustling up some dinner?'"

After the earthquake, the Spielbergs like many other terrified Angelenos noisily announced they were moving out of state, probably to New York, where there may be more muggers but at least the ground doesn't move underfoot while you're being rolled.

Those plans were put on the back burner when the reality of uprooting their children and finding new schools for them sank in.

"The big move won't happen for about a year and a half," Capshaw said in March 1995. "We have to find schools for the kids . . . . Our apartment isn't nearly ready."

Then there was their amply comfortable home overlooking the Pacific Ocean, which beats a view of Brooklyn Bridge or Fire Island any day.

Selected Films of Steven Spielberg

Amblin' (1969)

This is the one that started it all. Spielberg specifically made this twenty-two-minute silent film about a boy and girl hitchhiking from the Mojave Desert to the Pacific Ocean to attract the attention of studio executives. It did so in spades. The day after Sid Sheinberg, then head of Universal Television, saw *Amblin'* at a private screening, he offered the twenty-one-year-old college student a seven-year contract. Spielberg later would dismiss *Amblin'* as "crass commercialism" with about as much depth as a "Pepsi commercial," but he was being too hard on himself. (Later, the highbrow film critics would take over that job.) Despite its creator's misgivings, *Amblin'* went on to win top prize at the Atlanta Film Festival and another award at the Venice Film Festival. Trivia note: In 1970, this modest student film was seen by millions when the studio released it on a double bill with the year's biggest hit, *Love Story*. Another trivia note: Spielberg doesn't forget old comrades. Allen Daviau, the cameraman on *Amblin'*, later would be tapped for similar duties on the big one, *E.T.*

Duel (first aired November 13, 1971, on ABC)

This made-for-television movie was almost as silent as *Amblin'*, with less than fifty lines of dialogue in its eighty-five minutes.

Travelling salesman Dennis Weaver hits the road and finds himself relentlessly pursued by a huge truck whose driver, never seen, seems intent on running Weaver off the road. Spielberg called *Duel* an "exercise in paranoia," although the truck, like his later shark, poltergeists, and Nazi commandants, are terrifyingly real. The "realness" of Spielberg's alleged paranoid fantasies brings to mind Henry Kissinger's famous aphorism: "Even paranoid people have enemies." *Duel* was released overseas in movie theaters in 1973. Ten years later, in the wake of *E.T.*'s success, Universal released *Duel* in American movie theaters.

The Sugarland Express (1973)

Ex-con Goldie Hawn springs her husband from prison so they can retrieve their kids, who have been placed in an orphanage because mom and dad are cons. En route to the foster home, they are pulled over by a policeman, whom they take hostage. The ensuing pursuit by a parade of police cars displayed for the first time Spielberg's mastery of the logistics of filming car crashes and crowd scenes. Ironically, his first feature film, although it received rave reviews, barely broke even, giving no hint of his future as a box-office champ.

Jaws (1975)

This megahit typifies the definition of a high-concept movie, one that can be described in a simple declarative sentence—in this case: shark terrorizes resort community. The world's largest great white, unseen like *Duel*'s truck driver for much of the movie, plays havoc with the tourist industry of an island off Martha's Vineyard. Roy Scheider is the local police chief, Richard Dreyfuss the nerdy ichthyologist, and Robert Shaw is the great white shark hunter, who all team up to hold a giant fish fry. The production careened over budget and over schedule, but no one complained when it quickly became the biggest money-maker of all time (until Spielberg's *E.T.* knocked it out of first place). Trivia note: Spielberg wanted Charlton Heston for Scheider's role. (The screen's Moses wasn't interested.) However, the director turned down established stars Jeff Bridges and Timothy Bottoms in favor of an unknown, Dreyfuss.

Close Encounters of the Third Kind (1977)

Spielberg shifts gears dramatically here, with the unseen horror gradually revealed as a benevolent presence: a twinkling, xylophone-playing spaceship. Trivia note: Carlo Rambaldi, the master puppet-maker who later would breathe life into E.T., also designed the mother ship. Richard Dreyfuss returns as Everyman, a telephone lineman who is mysteriously beckoned aboard the spacecraft. Spielberg's running preoccupation with children separated from parents, a throwback to his parents' divorce, is dramatized here when the aliens literally suck a four-year-old out the door of his mother's home. The theme of separation, already explored in *The Sugarland Express*, would pop up again in films as diverse as *Hook*, *E.T.*, and *Empire of the Sun*.

1941 (1979)

After two monster hits back to back, it seemed Steven Spielberg could do no wrong. Then he made *1941*. The director claimed he laughed himself "sick" when he first read the script, cowritten by Robert Zemeckis, who later would make a little confection called *Forrest Gump*. Plain sick, however, is the way the critics and the audience reacted to this overblown farce about an imagined Japanese attack on Los Angeles in the paranoid days following Pearl Harbor. Spielberg at least learned a valuable lesson. Never again would he attempt a flat-out comedy, preferring instead tongue-in-cheek humor sparingly rationed out in action adventure films.

Raiders of the Lost Ark (1981)

After the disastrous box-office performance of *1941*, industry experts were ready to count Spielberg out, calling him the Orson Welles of action films. Chastened by *1941*'s failure, Spielberg allowed himself to be mentored by *Star Wars*' auteur, George Lucas. Lucas kept a tight fiscal rein on Spielberg as he directed (under budget and ahead of schedule) this affectionate homage to Saturday matinee serials. A whip-wielding archeologist who leaves academe to track down the Biblical Ark of the Covenant, Harrison

Ford encounters along the way Nazis, snakes, and a heroine (Karen Allen) who is arguably scarier. The producer and the director would collaborate on two sequels, creating a big thrills, no-brainer style that some critics derisively nicknamed "lucasberger." Trivia note: Spielberg originally hired Tom Selleck for the Harrison Ford role, but CBS, which aired his hit series, *Magnum, P.I.*, wouldn't give Selleck time off. Today, Ford remains one of the most respected—and bankable—stars in Hollywood. Selleck last appeared in a cable movie for TNT.

E.T.—The Extra-Terrestrial (1982)

Once again, Spielberg remained unique among filmmakers by depicting space aliens as nice, not nasty. The eponymous hero was nothing more than a pile of polyurethane and radio-controlled moving parts, but Spielberg coaxed such a performance out of his star that serious film critics lobbied for an Oscar for the reptilian figure. Despite its sci-fi theme, *E.T.* is a deeply autobiographical film. Nerdy, friendless Elliot, anguished by his parents' divorce, is the young Steven Spielberg, a fish out of water (or in Spielberg's case, a Jew in Wasp hell). If only Elliot had a friend of his own who understood him. His wish is granted when a very special friend literally drops from the skies. E.T.'s suffering, death, and resurrection has led some film scholars to decode him as a Christ figure, but Spielberg didn't have such theological pretensions: he was creating a happy ending for his unhappy childhood. Trivia note: At $10 million, with 10 percent of the budget spent on the puppet alone, *E.T.* was the box-office record holder until some ravenous velociraptors gobbled up its record.

The Color Purple (1985)

After a brief pit stop back in Jonesville (1984's execrable *Indiana Jones and the Temple of Doom*), Spielberg was ready to tackle the Big Picture and the Big Themes: racism, incest, spousal abuse, black lesbians. As one industry pundit said, "After *Raiders* and *E.T.*, Steven Spielberg could have made a film about black lesbians, and the studios would have let him." He did and they did. Spielberg fell in love with the book by Alice Walker, but he felt that a woman or a black should direct this story of an abused southern woman who liberates herself from male oppression and finds freedom in the arms of another black woman. African-American music mogul Quincy Jones, who owned the rights to the book, finally convinced the nice Jewish boy from Scottsdale that he could make a film about the African-American experience by saying, "You didn't have to come from Mars to do *E.T.*, did you?" That of course begs the question, since there were no underemployed directors from the Red Planet waiting in the wings to make *E.T.* Spielberg, long accused of treating his actors like, well, spaceships, managed to wring Oscar-nominated performances from two newcomers, stand-up comic Whoopi Goldberg and a short, obese woman who had just started hosting a national talk show named Oprah Winfrey. Critics cavilled that the black experience had been "lucasbergered." Black men complained that the director had perpetuated stereotypes with Goldberg's incestuous father and physically abusive husband. Even the Oscars seemed to take Spielberg to task when the Academy gave the film nominations in just about every category (eleven in all) except best director. (The film didn't win a single Academy Award.) Everybody seemed to hate *The Color Purple* except the public, which turned it into a $143 million hit.

Empire of the Sun (1987)

Despite the shellacking *The Color Purple* took from the critics, Spielberg, to his credit, didn't retreat to his tried and true escapist style for his next film. Instead, he chose a project whose subject matter was almost as difficult and painful as *The Color Purple*'s.

Empire of the Sun was based on a real-life account of a British boy who was imprisoned by the Japanese during World War II. The film contains many of Spielberg's earlier thematic preoccupations, including separation from parents and the dissolution of the family unit, but *Empire of the Sun* was a major stylistic departure from his previous roller-coaster rides. Scenes in the film include the spoiled upper-class eleven-year-old growing up quickly and painfully. In the prison camp, the starving child is reduced to eating insects and stealing shoes from corpses. Routine beatings by the sadistic camp guards make this film in many ways scarier than

Jaws or *Poltergeist*, since the terror is based on fact, not fantasy or supernatural intervention. The screenplay had an impeccable pedigree. Based on the autobiographical novel by science fiction writer J. G. Ballard, the script was penned by one of Britain's greatest living dramatists, Tom Stoppard. He and the director had such a mutually enjoyable collaboration that Spielberg put the playwright under long-term contract to read and critique scripts for possible production by Amblin.

Empire of the Sun is one of Spielberg's most accomplished and involving films, but again both the public and the critics failed to applaud his attempts to stretch beyond the mass-entertainment mode. The film was one of his biggest flops, and the critics were equally unkind. As Spielberg said of the reaction in the press, "I got a bollocking from the critics who didn't like the idea that I was suddenly trying to stretch my character."

Always (1989)

Spielberg returned to the seemingly safer world of fantasy for this remake of the 1943 cult classic, *A Guy Named Joe*, about a fighter pilot who comes back from the dead to counsel his best friend, who has fallen in love with the pilot's girlfriend. Richard Dreyfuss was fatally miscast in the leading man role of the dead pilot. Brad Johnson was physically more appropriate as the studly best friend, but his male-model good looks couldn't hide a hopelessly inept performance by a neophyte actor. And the typically brilliant Holly Hunter failed to compensate for an underwritten script and role. (Strangely, Spielberg threw out the first draft by the great Tom Stoppard and shot a version by former television hack Jerry Belson [*The End*].)

Spielberg obviously had a lot of fun shooting forest fires and airplane stunts, but the core of the movie was a romantic comedy, and the light touch required for this genre was apparently beyond the director's heavy-handed grasp.

Always enjoys the dubious distinction of being his most boring film, if not his worst. (That honor, of course, goes to *1941*.) Trivia note: Spielberg had asked Sean Connery to do a cameo as God, but prior film commitments prevented his participation. The late Audrey Hepburn was tapped for the role instead.

Hook (1991)

For years it had been a cliche: Steven Spielberg was a real life Peter Pan, the boy who refused to grow up. After he tackled such adult subject matter as lesbianism and child abuse, the Peter Pan analogy was growing rather thin. Not surprisingly, the director was intrigued when he found a script that dramatized what happened to Peter Pan *after* he grew up.

Robin Williams plays the adult Peter Pan, who has become an only slightly less scary version of Ivan Boesky and Michael Milken, a Wall Street arbitrageur who gobbles up and spits out companies for breakfast. Captain Hook (Dustin Hoffman), still smarting from the loss of his right hand after a run-in with the young Peter, shows up and kidnaps Williams's kids. Peter must rediscover his inner child to rescue his children, which occasions a return to Neverland, which cost $70 million to build on the same soundstages used for *The Wizard of Oz*. Julia Roberts does an embarrassing turn as a miniature Tinkerbelle. Heavy-handed and witless, *Hook*, however, boasted brilliant production design and state-of-the-art special effects, which turned it into one of the director's most commercially successful films.

Jurassic Park (1993)

Scientists find zillion-year-old dinosaur blood in the belly of a mosquito preserved over the eons in amber. The blood supplies DNA from which dinosaurs are cloned and exhibited in a Central American amusement park, a reptilian Disneyland. Industrial spies screw up the security system that keeps the park's wildlife safely penned in, and dinosaurs run amok. As terrifying as the similar-themed *Jaws*, Jurassic Park benefits from nearly two decades worth of computer advances since the release of the 1975 shark epic. Spielberg lightened the dark tone of the bestseller by Michael Crichton, which reflected his own temperament and also left open the possibility of a sequel. (In the novel, the dinosaur "problem" is solved by atom-bombing the island which houses the amusement park.) Computer-generated and animated dinosaurs make *Jurassic Park's* preposterous premise believable and eminently watchable. The public couldn't take its eyes off the film and quickly turned it into the No. 1 hit of all time, knocking another film about a reptilian creature out of first place.

Schindler's List (1993)

With his masterpiece about the Holocaust, Spielberg once and for all refuted charges that he was merely a glorious hack. The commercial success of *Schindler's List* also proved that the third time was the charm after two quixotic attempts to tackle World War II (*Empire of the Sun* and *1941*). *Schindler's List* also represented the director's third cinematic depiction of Nazis, although this time the cartoon villains of the Indiana Jones films were replaced by a real life psychopath, Ralph Fiennes's searing camp commandant Amon Goeth. Liam Neeson's Oskar Schindler is hypnotic as an amiable Nazi who inexplicably rose above his moral mediocrity to become a heroic rescuer of more than a thousand Jews destined for the gas chambers. Spielberg tackled this difficult project for many reasons: to exorcise the demons of his youth, which included alienation as a Jew in Wasp suburbia and physical attacks by other kids because of his religion; to film a riveting if unlikely real life story; and not the least of which, to preserve and honor the memory of the dead as survivors and eyewitnesses died off.

The need to keep the memory of the Holocaust alive was urgent, as evidenced by the number of quack savants who claimed it never took place. One horrifying result of the film itself: reports that neo-Nazis in Germany were flocking to the movie because they enjoyed "scenes of the Jews being killed." Both phenomena underlined the wisdom of philosopher George Santayana who said those who cannot remember the past are condemned to repeat it. *Schindler's List* is both a classic of the cinema and a vigilant warning. And it unequivocally places Spielberg in the pantheon of his idols, John Ford, Howard Hawks, and David Lean.

Whither Steven Spielberg?

It's hard to handicap Steven Spielberg's next move. In the past, when the critics or public loathed a film which represented a departure from his mass entertainments, he didn't always turn tail and retreat to tried-and-true popcorn filmmaking. Similarly, after a monster (literally) success like *Jurassic Park*, he didn't duplicate himself in his next outing.

After the encomia heaped on *Schindler's List*, Spielberg could just as likely direct another character-driven masterpiece or crank out some paranoid fantasy about things that go bump in the dark of the theater.

If he chooses a pop flick, you can be sure it will be storyboarded and planned to the last nanosecond. Predicting the subject matter of an artistic endeavor is a dicier proposition. If he goes the latter route, it probably will be be based on an established classic, like *The Color Purple* or *Schindler's List*. (With his instinctive nose for sniffing out both class and crass, Spielberg buys the film rights to novels while still in galley form.)

The director has said he would like to make a musical some day. He would have been an interesting fit for the film adaptation of *Evita*, but it's hard to imagine him putting up with the amateurish acting efforts of the woman cast in the title role, Madonna. Spielberg's second favorite studio, Warner Brothers, owns the film rights to *Phantom of the Opera*, and the complicated logistics of filming that baroque extravaganza also would be a perfect match for Spielberg's field-general style of directing action movies. (What he couldn't do with that crashing chandelier after all his practice on rolling boulders!)

During the nightmare of running herd on *Hook*'s cast of kiddies, Spielberg found himself turning into the Joan Crawford of movie directors. He has publicly promised himself he will never helm such a group effort again. However, fatherhood has been his most satisfying accomplishment. There are five kids in the immediate Spielberg-Capshaw tribe. And childhood themes have been a preoccupation of at least six of his previous fifteen films. While he is unlikely to direct a cast of thousands of kids, he would not be averse to focusing on just one child and his or her predicament. If so, count on the project to tackle the interrelated themes of alienation, divorce, and separation from parents, all pages from Spielberg's unwritten autobiography.

Spielberg directing the fourth *Star Wars* film sounds like a project concocted in publicists' heaven and every studio executive's dream. Amblin's reps deny any such project is in the works there.

But it's a fun fantasy. Almost twenty years have passed since Luke Skywalker's first outing, and the computer revolution since then would make *Star Wars 4* a marvel of near virtual reality thrills. The synergy of Spielberg and Lucas once again collaborating could give *Jurassic Park* a run for its box-office money.

One industry source says, "Steven showed what he could do with *Schindler's List*. It would be a shame if he abdicated his talent and went for a crass cash-in like *Star Wars 4* or *Jurassic Park 2*. He's marvelous with character-driven material. I'd hate to see him wasting his time on aliens from outer space or giant lizards in Central America."

Whatever his next move turns out to be, serious or slam bang, it's certain to be riveting and thought provoking.

And of course, thoroughly entertaining.

INDEX